Angel Flight of '82

'82

DEAN DOUDNA

ISBN 978-1-0980-2580-9 (paperback)
ISBN 978-1-0980-2581-6 (digital)

Christian Faith Publishing, Inc.
832 Park Avenue
Meadville, PA 16335
www.christianfaithpublishing.com

Printed in the United States of America

CHAPTER 1

Landing at Wonju (KNW)

23 December 1982, Republic of South Korea (ROK). 0900 Hours.

When we left Camp Humphreys (KSG), snow was not forecasted for the morning flight period, but there was snow forecasted for the afternoon flight period. The afternoon forecast period was foreboding for the flight, but if all went as planned, I felt we could squeak this mission in just under minimums for the morning flight period. The weather guys have a tough job. It seems to me that their occupation is likened to crystal ball guessing rather than science. I remember teasing one of the USAF airmen embedded with our unit for weather forecasting one morning before another mission that I was tasked to fly. I saw the forecaster outside the weather hooch as my crew and I were approaching, and I asked him surely he had not abandoned all that high-tech weather forecasting equipment to come outside and view the weather? He smiled as he reported that I would be surprised just how often a weatherman did just that. We went inside, and he labored over the weather forecast. My copilot, an LT, and I watched him check the blocks on our -1. Flyable weather we agreed but only if we got out and back before the real snow hit. As it turned out, on this mission day, we quickly discovered that the forecaster's poorly combined modern forecasting techniques and outside eyeballing as the forecast for the afternoon's snow onset were a total miss. Bad news for helicopter operations in the ROK.

The forecast highly motivated me to adjust the mission to arrive in front of the afternoon snow forecast. Our arrival to Wonju hours before the afternoon flight period required an adjustment to my mission, so I asked our operations officer to contact our passengers (PAX) and adjust their schedule. I was flying general officers this morning, and that is never an easy adjustment to make. General officers come with their own set of difficulties, and our operations officer said that, given the imposing weather, he was sure that they would agree. Canceling the mission was something they did not want to consider. We had flyable weather for the morning period. Why not try? Somehow, our operations officer secured a mission adjustment, and we were allowed to depart earlier.

The LT, Ryan, and I had arrived at the aircraft, completed the preflight, and started the helicopter. We were running through the before takeoff checks when we saw a jeep pull up near the helicopter with our PAXs. According to the mission sheet, we were to fly to Osan and pick up the PAXs at Osan before departing for Wonju. I knew we had successfully changed the mission departure time but was surprised when I saw the PAXs.

I mused, "Hey, LT, this is how quickly missions change." I could see that there was an American major general, a two-star, and a Korean admiral. I was unsure of how many stars the Korean admiral had as I was unfamiliar with their ranks. I'm guessing that he was a two-star also. From my mission sheet, I knew for sure, however, that he was an admiral. With each mission, a mission sheet is created and given to the PIC for his planning purposes. These guys were just PAXs to me, essential PAXs for the mission, but PAXs nonetheless. There was no time now. They were here; no need to fly to Osan. We had to adjust quickly. I mentally adjusted our route of flight. Our crew chief (CE), Ryan, jumped out and saluted and welcomed them aboard. Accompanying the flag officers was a major. According to my mission sheet, he was the aviation liaison. As he approached the aircraft, I noticed he had a star on his wings. That will rate him as a senior aviator.

The flag officers got into the seats along the transmission bulkhead as directed by my crew-chief. The major jumped into one of the two jump seats behind the pilot's station. Doing so, he chose the one on the far right and grabbed the only headset we had for the party. He saw the WO1 bar on my shoulder and said, "Good morning, Chief. No time for formalities let's get off the ground as soon as possible and get to Wonju." Before I could turn and address him, he had already removed his headset and began talking loudly over the noise of the engine and rotating rotors to the flag officers.

I turned to the LT, and said, "You heard the man. Let's get out of here."

The flight north was busy. Since we did not need to pick up the PAXs at Osan, we bypassed railroad transition and picked up the Seoul-Pusan Highway. The weather was 700-2, so I elected not to go cross country. I would have preferred to go cross country, but given the weather, I elected to fly the highway. A safer choice as the weather was marginal. It did not take long to complete our northward trek up the Seoul Pusan, and right on cue, we made a right turn and followed the Wonju Highway eastbound. The LT was following instructions well. Even though the weather was less than desirable, she didn't seem to be the least bit intimidated by it. Eastbound now and I am noticing where the snow had accumulated on the ground from previous showers. It shouldn't have been, but it was a surprise. It was difficult to see the Wonju valley to the north because of the weather. 700-2 may be flyable, but it is still two miles visibility, and the seven-hundred-foot ceiling totally masked the mountains. I asked the LT to slow down so that I could double-check our position on the map. She happily did so, and I was happy that we had not passed our pending left turn into the Wonju Valley. It was still five minutes or so up and to our left. Eerily the valley cut into the mountains and began to expose itself. I directed the LT to leave the Wonju Highway and start a left turn through the cut.

"Okay, LT, this is the final leg into Wonju. Just follow the river north, and Wonju will be on our right side," I said as I was straining to see. The weather was holding at 700-2, but the existing and real snow on the ground made the identification of anything more complicated. I was astonished at how the snow that had fallen over time had changed the landscape. Like a ghostly figure in a storm, the airdrome began to birth itself from the landscape and materialize. I directed the LT's attention to it. Since I had placed her in the right seat, she had the best vantage point to see the airdrome. I could clearly see the airdrome from my seat. I could clearly see the airdrome, and I was surprised that the LT could not yet make it out.

0900 hours, and we were on short final to our landing at Wonju. Surprise, surprise…we were about to land in snow conditions. There was not supposed to be any snow during the morning flight period. I did not see this coming and was genuinely surprised by the circumstances. Thus far this winter, there had only been snow flurries, more like rain really, and only occasionally at Camp Humphreys. Wonju was quite a bit north. I should not have been surprised, but I was surprised. I explained to the LT that I needed to take the controls and make the landing. She was totally okay with giving the flight controls over to me. She had never done a snow landing either, so I took the flight controls from the LT and negotiated my first snow landing. On approach, I was low and slow, suspecting that the ground cover would turn into a snow-whiteout landing. In retrospect, I began to go over the forecaster's comments in my head. So much for the snow not arriving 'til the afternoon! Of course, it had been snowing up here. The forecast did not talk about the snow that was already on the ground from previous snow showers. The forecaster only spoke of what would fall out of the sky during my mission profile. I should not have been surprised by the snow cover at all. There was plenty of snow on the ground from previous days of snowfall. Experience is a great teacher. This experience taught me to take my head out of my backside and consider that there may be snow already present at locations other than Camp Humphreys…duh. During the landing, I silently asked God for some assistance. I had not done a snow landing from the left seat before. Come to think of it, I had not done a snow landing from the right seat either. The arrival went off reasonably well. Gravity was a great helper. Something about the whole mission began to bother me. I felt that I needed to make a decision right then and there to change the mission…again…and get a bag of gas and return to Camp Humphreys. Fatefully, I did not follow that intuition. My mission and its VIPs did not support those thoughts. I still did not have the flight experience to recognize just how bad things were to come. An experienced helicopter pilot understands environmental changes and adjusts the mission to his best advantage so that he may survive to fly and fight another day. Since I did not have enough front seat experience yet to recognize the dangers that lie ahead, ignorance was bliss, as they say, and we foolishly continued with the mission. During my first snow landing, I quickly discovered to stay ahead of the snow cloud caused by my rotor wash until arriving in parking. Fortunately, parking was just at the end of the active and to the right. Keeping up my momentum to stay ahead of the snow cloud, I quickly maneuvered the aircraft to parking. I settled into the snow to quickly. As I said earlier, gravity was a great helper. The landing was a bit rougher than I had hoped for, but we were skids down and safe. The LT and I quickly transitioned to the engine shutdown phase.

With the helicopter's engine shut down and the rotors slowing to a stop, one could easily see that there was a light snow falling upon two feet of snow that had fallen over the winter season thus far. It was very, very cold, so the snow that was falling, as well as the snow that was on the ground, was not particularly wet. Because of the extreme cold, the snow was light and airy instead, so the snow was not sloshy, and because it was so light and airy, it was not easily compacted—something new I discovered while landing and hovering into parking. As soon as the rotor blades disturbed the air, the snow began to move around, swirl, and cause whiteout conditions. I started to get an ache in my stomach. I knew it was a warning of things to come, and I did nothing.

I turned around to talk with my PAXs as soon as the engine was secured, leaving my crew and me behind. They jumped out of the helicopter, ducked down, missing the still rotating main rotor blades, and departed on their own to their meeting. All I could see were three guys walking as quickly as snow would allow up to a slight incline to be picked up by a waiting jeep assigned to escort them. Approximately ten minutes before landing, following standard protocol, I put fuel on request with Wonju operations and likewise told them that I had two codes onboard. Of course, operations personnel would have known that by examining my flight plan, but I knew that I would have suffered the brunt of the VIPs' irritation if operations did not scrutinize my flight plan on their own and prepare for VIP pickup, so I was glad to see that the radio call made before the landing facilitated an escort for these guys.

I may have been a card-carrying, diploma-hanging army aviator, but to those guys, I was just a taxi driver. While wrestling that perception and blow to my ego, I asked the CE if they said anything before they left. He reported that the major, who spoke for the major general and Korean admiral, said that they were running late and would get back to us soonest. Another blow to my ego. Even with the mission change, I had arrived a full forty-five minutes before the planned arrival time. The last thing I needed was to be the cause of two flag officers missing some sort of hubbub meeting. They were not late on the count of me. In fact, they should have been early. I pondered what the CE had reported and just kept to myself. We were forty-five minutes early. The Red Baron operations officer may have adjusted the departure time out of Humphreys for the weather, but I had to wonder how that adjustment fit here in Wonju. Should we have been early? Is it too far-fetched to think that the early departure from Camp Humphreys was not relayed to Wonju adjusting their mission here? Still early by my rendering. With the PAXs gone, I was robbed of an opportunity to defend a late perception. We had not arrived late, I kept telling myself, but none of that mattered now. Lost in my thoughts, my CE, SP4 Ryan Duncan, was trying to get my attention. "Sir, I have completed the walk-around and found all the big pieces present and accounted for, found no leaks, and tied down the main rotor."

So that my copilot could log some right seat time, I elected to take the left seat during the flight from Camp Humphreys to Wonju. I looked up from my left seat and, sure enough, saw that the rotor blade was straight out in front and tilted slightly upward, meaning that the other rotor blade was tied to the tail boom securing the rotor system. Walk-arounds are typically conducted by the pilots after shutdown. The best crews work together. Securing the helicopter should always be a team effort, but I was zoned into the logbook closeout and the mission adjustment all while my copilot was waiting on an assignment from me. Waiting for a task. Not much of a surprise at this point as she was as green as they come. This was her first mission in the country. With today's weather conditions, I could have used an experienced copilot.

"Thanks for that, Ryan," I said. "Jump inside, warm up a bit, and don't forget to close the door. I'll be a few minutes working the logbook, and then we can head up the hill after the fuel truck arrives. Hey, Ryan, is this the same helicopter I flew with Mr. Wills for that hook mission servicing Poncho at Salem Top?" I asked.

"No, sir, this is Roberts aircraft. He is on mid-tour leave, and I am looking out for it while he is back in the world. There is a lot wrong with it that I would not have tolerated if it was mine," he began to say before the fuel truck pulled along our right side to refuel us. As advertised the fuel truck was Johnny on the spot. Ryan bounded out of the aircraft for the refueling duties while I finished the logbook. Ryan was right, there were a lot of deficiencies that could have easily and quickly been addressed. But today I was not a maintenance guy. I was a PIC on a mission. Today I needed to remain in PIC mode, not maintenance mode. In no time, we were refueled, and the three of us headed up the hill to Wonju airfield operations. No jeep escort for the taxi drivers...

CHAPTER 2

Wonju Airfield Operations

23 December 1982, ROK. 0940 Hours.

I found operations inviting if only to get out of the cold, and wow, was I glad to get in out of this weather? The snow may have been airy and powdery, but my combat boots felt like they were soaked and frozen. They were not soaked of course, but it sure felt that way as the cold was difficult to combat. I did my best to be manly and not complain, but the ever-present cold seemed to radiate up my legs into my very core. Neither Ryan nor the LT complained but I knew if I was feeling the ache of this cold, they must be too. This was my first winter experience in Korea. I have seen many movies of soldiers suffering from Korean winters. I was not here thirty years ago. I have not undergone what they underwent thirty years ago. I am here now however so I may have some understanding how the ROKs cold weather must have affected them.

I made my way over to the operations desk where I found Ryan. He had located the coffee pot and was smiling from ear to ear. "Sir, Ma'am, there are cups in that cabinet and the coffee pot is hot and inviting," he was delighted to report. Hard to resist that sort of endorsement, so I followed the LT to the coffee pot. The pour of the coffee with its steam and aroma already made me feel warmer. I just stood there welcoming the warming steam of the full-body black Army Joe (aka coffee.)

When my operations officer passed me the mission sheet last night, it had required me to plan for four hours of ground time at Wonju while our PAXs conducted their hubbub meeting. I was aware that my PAXs were at Wonju to coordinate for an upcoming Team Spirit maneuver. My job in their mission? Transport them. Mutual Defense, or show of force, whatever the current political jargon, Team Spirit remains a combined exercise conducted with US-ROK forces. Rather than a peace treaty, an Armistice Agreement was signed at the end of the Korean War in the '50s which technically means there remains a state of war between the North and South Korean countries. In the event of another conflict, getting the current soldier headcount multiplied and deployed from the US to the Korean peninsula to address the threat is a significant deal, and those sorts of details are discovered during Team Spirit maneuvers. Pretty intense show of force for sure and cooperation between the US and the ROK has to be spot on. The whole operation rattles the North typically. Typically conducted during the spring months Team Spirit may be better practiced in full-on winter, but hey, I am just a taxi driver today not a military strategist. I thought about letting some of those known facts spill out while getting to know the crew over the hot Joe, but the LT was a graduate of West Point and frankly I did not want to have what I remembered from my meager High School education corrected, so I just keep quiet.

The Wonju operations building was unremarkable. It was old poorly lit and, except for the Joe, uninviting. There were just a few lightbulbs hanging throughout the room with strings from the bulb switch that turned them off and on. The absence of natural light from the small windows was ever-present. Even with the natural light struggling to make it in from the windows, the lights still needed to be switched on. The dimness seemed to make the room even colder. This was a Korean operations center, and the few Korean soldiers in the operations center did not seem to notice how poorly lit the place was nor how uninviting the operations center was. I had witnessed this minimalist persona numerous times within the Korean culture. I had to wonder if theirs was the right approach as compared to ours. I wanted to turn every light on as well as add more circuits. I tried unsuccessfully to generate heat by moving around and stomping my feet to warm my body, still cold to its core. I would have felt better if there was some light music to lighten the dreary mood cast by the entire scene before me. All that ran through my mind as I sat on homemade benches along the walls listening to a single military FM radio that was continually breaking squelch. The very same radio used for airdrome communication that I had called when I called while on short final to Wonju for the VIP escort.

What an annoying noise the FM creates in squelch. I never understood what the need for squelch was. I did know however that when the radio was out of tune with the desired frequency, or when the mike was keyed, the emitted squelch likened to an annoying chalk and blackboard moment that you just want to stop. Without seeming to hear the squelch at all, they just droned on with each other in their native language. We Americans called it "honguel." I only spoke a few Korean words, and they would talk honguel so quickly that I rarely heard the few words that I did know how to speak. While I sat and enjoyed my Joe and listening to them talk, I further examined the construction of the operations center and became interested in the wall construction.

I believe that it was shiplap on the wall. Substantial engineering, I thought. At first glance, it looked like the same wall construction of a rental that my wife and I rented while previously stationed at Fort Hood, Texas. After I strained to get a closer look at the shiplap on the wall, I discovered that the wood was not shiplap at all, but instead was ammo crates that had been disassembled and placed on the wall just like shiplap. I smiled as I realized that they had repurposed ammo crates for shiplap. Wonder what their operating budget is? Walking over to the wall, I began to examine the remnants of labeling that remained on many of the pieces of wood. I read, "2.75 INCH HE COMP B4 WARHEAD M151."

Stepping back a bit farther, I could see that that same inscription was all over the place. Some upside-down, others right side up. Guessing they had unpacked a bunch of 2.75 rockets to create the shiplap necessary to cover the inside of the operations building. Very clever. Minimalist persona at its best. But that was one of the enduring things that I found so beautiful about the Korean people. I find them to be very hard-working people who overcome what life throws at them. As a people in general, their proverbial bootstraps has seen many pulls. I greatly admired their tenacity, and I found many things in my own life to parallel the need to grab bootstraps and give a hearty tug.

I decided against having another cup of Joe. There still remains plenty of flying ahead of me, and over the years, I have trained and calibrated my bladder to a two-hour rule. The fuel load of the UH-1 generally lasts two hours. We call that a bag of gas and I have learned to calibrate my bladder to the same two-hour requirements of the aircraft, so no more Joe for me. The LT's., question interrupts my thoughts when she asks, "Isn't the snow beautiful?" It was, indeed, beautiful. When given further thought to our current conditions, no need for me to dwell on its beauty since it has the propensity to kill us. "Until we have to go out and fly into it," I reply. "LT I am going to direct our CE to take off the engines barrier filters. Since the weather guys missed the conditions here at Wonju during this morning weather briefing, I don't know how much worst it can get. I don't want to take a chance and fly into unknown conditions with the barrier filters on." You could see the LT pondering that. She simply said, "okay." I would have expected more pushback or at least feedback from my copilot. Taking off the barrier filters is pretty extreme.

"Hey Ryan, you ready to join me at the aircraft? "I want to take the barrier filters off the aircraft in case we get into icing on the return flight back to the Hump." For his three years in service, SP4 Ryan Duncan was a very astute CE. I have a kinship for enlisted crewmembers. A quick look at my WO1 bar would have told the casual observer that I was a newly minted aviator from the Fort Rucker Flight School. Correct, I was freshly minted, but I grew up on a flight line, however. I had graduated flight school only 10 months previous to this flight, so his answer did not surprise me when Ryan declared, "Mr. Doudna, you cannot do that and fly the aircraft. Removing the barrier filters will ground the aircraft." I was not the run of the mill Warrant Officer Junior Grade (WOJG) W1 fresh out of flight school and fully expected Ryan's feedback. Good for Ryan for having a backbone. This, however, was not the time for a debate. In my Army Leadership Training, I learned over the years that you do not need to run over people just because you are in a position of authority. I respected Ryan and simply wanted to grow him. I did not have the engine inlet barrier filter section of the Operators Manual (-10) memorized, but flight school made us all very familiar with the -10, so it was pretty easy for me to loosely paraphrase the -10 when I reminded Ryan that the aircraft we were flying had a non-purging particle separator and that it was highly recommended to remove the left and right barrier filters if the crew suspected icing conditions along the route of flight. The top barrier filter, however, had to remain in place. I went on to tell him that he would find that as a CAUTION somewhere in chapter 8 of the -10. Upon hearing this, he was stoically silent. He could have been a great poker player as it was hard to read his reaction. You could tell he was awash with thought and he finally broke the silence when he said, "headed out to the bird. I am going to review that in the -10." I was pleased that it was a professional exchange rather than me flexing my command authority as the PIC. I decided not to join Ryan as I had initially intended. I thought he needed the space. Ryan quickly departed, and I turned my attention to the LT.

As far as copilots go, the LT was brand new. Fort Rucker still oozed from her. She was easy to look at, my height, brownish-red hair, and not a drop of makeup to hide all the freckles. The LT was a very book-like person. Got that from West Point I am sure. She had a confidence about her outside the cockpit, but I found her timid and indecisive in the cockpit. She is brand spanking new, and that may speak to her lack of flavoring and spice in the cockpit. Given how she conducts herself outside the cockpit, I am sure that she will grow into an excellent aviator given time. "Why did you direct Ryan to take off the barrier filters," she asked? I smiled to myself. Last time she gave any feedback about the barrier filters was just "okay."

Now, after some reflection and a bit of time to digest, she has more words? I didn't want to haze her for her time delay. Instead, I reminded her of the same systems blocks of instructions that we both sat through in the early part of flight school. Annoying to most, but imperative that each aviator understands the workings of their helicopter. We were taught all about the helicopters mechanical systems; flight controls, electrical, hydraulics, powertrain, and power-plant. It was excellent training actually. I wondered how she did on the exams? I can only guess of her academic accomplishments as a West Point graduate. She undoubtedly aced the check on learning tests, and I am guessing that she flushed that material to make more room in her brain for the pilot stuff. In the classroom understandably, there is no life or death risk that students must process. Out here in the field, however, there are very serious consciences that each of us must consider before making decisions. Since there is no real threat in the academic portion of flight school, the schoolhouse environment may groom a false sense of security. The only danger in the classroom, good grade/bad grade, pass/fail. Out in the real world, it is a totally different story. I think out here the LT maybe having difficulty applying some of those very basic mechanical classes to real-world circumstances.

I may be the PIC, and it may be my call, but equally important; however, I wish to grow her just as much as wanting to grow Ryan. I began to remind her that the helicopters turbine engines air is feed through those barrier filters as well as the partial separator. The engines partial separator had to remain installed as we needed the partial separator installed to ensure we did not Foreign Object Damage (FOD) the engine during its operation, but, because of the partial separator, we could operate the engine safely without the left and right barrier filters. During our flight home, if we get caught in bad weather or icing conditions, the barrier filters would be the first to ice over and ultimately starve the engine of its air and cause a flameout. While she pondered that line of thinking Ryan came back into the room and, while shaking the snow off, reported that he had taken off the left and right barrier filters and had stored them in the aircraft. He did not miss a beat when he reminded me that, "Sir, for your ready reference, you can find that reference in paragraph 8-64 of the -10." I smiled, nodded, and said to the crew, "let's head over to the weather station and get an update on this snow."

CHAPTER 3

USAF Weather Briefing

23 December 1982, ROK. 1030 Hours.

I knew something was wrong, but I could not put my finger on it. Walking over from the Korean operations building to the USAF weather building, I was again approaching numbness from more than the cold. I could not shake this feeling of doom. Maybe the cold was affecting my thinking. We three walked quickly. The LT lead, and Ryan and I followed while conversing about helicopter stuff. I was trying to concentrate on Ryan's questions. He was really interested in how I put together the whole barrier filter thing. If I could have articulated it, I would have told him that I was prompted by the Holy Spirit, but in truth, I didn't understand it myself. I knew that I had a hunch and acted upon it. As we chatted our way through that reasoning, I thought Ryan would be a great candidate for the flight program. He reminded me a lot of myself when I was a CE. I was proud of my professional travels in the military thus far, and I could see that Ryan was the type that the army should invest in. I was glad for the diversion, but our chat was not the focus of my attention. Right now, I was internally multitasking. Our conversation was interrupting what I was really wondering about. The snow that we were experiencing was more than a light shower. I could feel it. I wanted to talk with the weather guy and get the real deal.

I was thrilled that big army and USAF leadership had the foresight to station USAF airmen at most of the remote locations throughout Korea. Wonju was considered significant enough to warrant the assignment of a weatherman as well as an alternate. The posting had to have sucked for these airmen. Wonju barely warranted a dot on the map and was a far cry from the luxuries, by military standards, that most personnel in the USAF were accustomed to. To its fame, Wonju had a short runway that supported the activities of the Korean Air Force. Wonju also had a couple of wind tunnel hangars to protect the two woefully outdated fast movers that the Koreans had stationed there. When I say wind tunnel, I am not speaking to a wind tunnel where aerodynamic testing is conducted.

The wind tunnel to which I refer to here is nothing more than a half-round, arched covering that is open on each end. Aircraft are parked inside. The wind tunnels provided top cover for the aircraft, but the building ends were not closed in. Good top shelter except for the fact that both ends of the building were open, so you had this excellent top cover, but if there was just a breath of wind, it went right through the building. A breath of wind could bring in rain, snow, or dust, hence the nickname wind tunnel. Wonju also had barracks for the permanent party Korean soldiers, if you can call them that. Simple cinder block buildings that were long on utility, short on style or comfort. The outside shower was an interesting design choice. The building had small but functional and infrequent windows. So when viewed from a distance, the barracks might not have any windows at all. As an American soldier, when deployed, I often found myself looking beyond my own windows out of my hooch, daydreaming of being anywhere but there. The few windows of these Korean barracks had had to have created the same sparse and depressing atmosphere I tolerated at the Wonju operations building. I had to wonder if there was ammo box shiplap in there as well.

I was not sure what the mission of the Wonju base was. Most likely an early warning airfield to address an attack from North Korea. There were also fifty-caliber anti-aircraft weapons stationed at each end of the field. I have flown in and out of Wonju many times. With each flight into Wonju, I was always tracked by these weapons. Training for the Korean soldiers who were handling them no doubt, but those were real guns with real bullets that they were pointing at my crew and me during air operations, and it always made me feel uneasy. Thinking back to the Wonju operations building and the single FM radio beseeched with the squelch problems, I had to wonder if that was the same radio used to call for fire missions as well as air operations. A chilling thought. Given the reliability of that radio, one has to wonder how easily a message could become unreadable and incomplete. Fratricide events have happened with less. Concerning the two nations themselves, given the tension between the North and South Korean countries, this was a real-world mission. You could quickly feel the ever-present pressure. Everything was real. Everything.

I was glad to enter the USAF weather building. By contrast, and clearly a different operating budget, there was a stark difference between the Korean operations building and the American USAF weather station. The USAF weather station was set up precisely as it should have been. Well, lit, warm, colorful, inviting, friendly, and it made me feel like home. I'm guessing these airman stationed here did all they could do to make their work environment as pleasing as possible. Indeed, an island by contrast to its surroundings. Ryan found the Joe, but he also found hot cocoa too. With a smile on his face, and while preparing his cocoa, he said, "One marshmallow or two?" It was hard not to laugh with Ryan's antics. The LT opted for more Joe. I was still following the two-hour bladder rule and opted out. Each airman was at their work stations when we came in, and they were genuinely happy to see us. Their assignment puts them well off the beaten path. They were characteristically delighted to host us for our short wait.

Both of them rising, the taller of the two shouted out first, "Hey, welcome to Wonju." KNW is another Wonju designation, but it would have sounded weird to welcome us to KNW. The shorter airmen followed taller airmen with a hearty handshake. Seeing how young each appeared to be made me appreciate the tremendous amount of responsibility the military, regardless of service, places upon us all.

I returned that hearty handshake and said, "Hey yourself. My name is Dean. This is 2LT Boyle, and SPC Duncan over there is trying hard not to enjoy the cocoa." I didn't need to tell him my rank. My WO1 bars were clearly visible as was my last name on my flight suit. I have always been loose with military courtesies. I respect rank, but there is something in a first name. On this cold morning, all were glad to make each other's acquaintances. Mr. handshake introduced himself as Brad, and Brad introduced Bill, his alternate. Looking something like an upside-down Army sergeant (E5) insignia, both were sporting USAF insignias consisting of three stripes, each indicating that they were both E-4's. Neither one looked much beyond 20 years of age. Once again, enormous responsibility for these two airmen. Remotely located, fending for themselves issuing critical weather observations for aviators use and my crew and I were about to get an earful.

Brad remarked that three VIPs stopped in, grabbed a cup of Joe, and headed out to Division HQ driven by a Korean driver. "Are you guys the ride for those guys," Brad asked? I was not surprised by the question. How many Americans are out and about at KNW this brisk morning?

"Yep, that's us all right. Just flew them in. We are scheduled for four hours of ground time so that they can attend their hubbub meeting then we are out of here." You could see the surprise and concern on both Brad and Bills face.

"Four hours of ground time?" they both said as if choreographed.

"In four hours, we are going to be besieged with snow. I think you had already seen its beginnings when you landed. It's going to be a white Christmas for sure." Until just then, I had forgotten that Christmas was just around the corner. This was December 23 already. I had, earlier that morning, debated whether to take the mission in the first place. My wife was visiting from the States, and I have been around army aviation long enough to know that if you have time to spare, fly military air. In other words, if the aircraft can break and leave you stranded, it would. So close to Christmas, I was afraid of breaking down somewhere, anywhere really, like Wonju! I overcame that with the standard reasoning, mission-first attitudes that all good soldiers are ingrained with. Mission first, indeed. My leadership is not out here in the boonies with my crew and PAXs, we were.

"Okay, Brad, what is up with the weather?" I asked. It did not take him long to swing back around to his desk and begin to digest further what was on his computer screen.

Brad said, "It would help if I had a -1 request."

It must be a standard USAF technique when issuing weather forecasts. A -1 is shorthand for DD Form 175-1. The DD Form 175-1 is the standard form used by the USAF to issue a weather briefing. In the business, we just call it a -1. I got a blank -1 from the planning desk and filled in the header information, my requested departure time, an altitude that I intended to climb to, and first stop-over destination following by my final destination assigning both destinations with an estimated time of arrival (ETA).

I was headed back to Osan, with a final stop at Camp Humphreys. Before the mission change this morning, Osan is where I was supposed to pick these guys up at. Hard for me to believe the flag officers would get up that early to travel to the Hump from Osan. They must have anticipated the weather and RONed at the Hump for the early departure to Wonju. The LT watched as I worked the -1 request. Wanting to be a good mentor, I explained each step of the process and why the forecaster needed to know the estimated time of departure (ETD), ETA, requested altitude, and the like. I gave the shell of the -1 that I had filled out along with the -1 that the weather guys at Camp Humphreys had given me earlier this morning to Brad and Brad took them both. It did not take Brad long to build his portion of the new -1, then before he briefed me, he and Bill momentarily left the weather building. I couldn't help but wonder if they had stepped outside to weather guess. They had. I just grinned to myself. All the sophisticated equipment at their fingertips and still, a dash outside to take a look at the conditions firsthand still was a part of the makeup.

"Chief, you may want to make some adjustments to your ETD and requested altitude. The -1 that Camp Humphreys issued for your return flight from here just got overrun by an advancing front out of the north. In fact, if you cannot depart immediately, you may want to consider remaining overnight (RON)," Brad said matter-of-factly. "Chief" was a term of endearment afforded to army warrant officers. I preferred Mr. Doudna, but Doudna is challenging to pronounce for some, and using the moniker Chief is a one size fits all warrant officer moniker.

"RON is a non-starter," I told Brad. "I have VIPs who are not going to tolerate a RON. Plus I have a few more hours of planned ground time so the flag officers can get their business done. Can you walk me through the -1 and brief it so that I can adjust accordingly."

Brad didn't look surprised. I was not shopping for a weather forecast nor was I looking for a basement bargain weather brief either. I just needed him to tell me the worst so that I could consider, adjust, and accommodate. The LT, Brad, and I hovered over each applicable block of the -1 as Brad began.

"Block 3: Depart RKNW: 2200Z.

Block 4: Runway Temp: -4.

Block 5: Dewpoint: -7.

Block 7: Pressure Alt: -224.

Block 9: Surface Wind: "VRB06.

Block 13: Takeoff Altitude Forecast: 2SM SHSN OVC 007.

Block 17: Clouds at Flight Level: Yes.

Block 18: Obscurations at Flight Level: Yes.

Block 19: Minimum Ceiling: RTE 007 AGL.

Block 20: Maximum Cloud Tops: RTE 120 MSL.

Block 22: Thunderstorms: None.

Block 23: Turbulence: None.

Block 24: Icing: SFC to 120 Moderate along RTE.

Block 25: Precipitation: Light to Moderate Snow Showers along RTE.

Block 26-31: RKNW 0100-0200Z VRB06 7 SCT004 OVC010 30.20 -05 72.

TEMPO 0100-0200 1 SHSN BKN005 OVC010.

Block 26-31: RKSG 0400-0500 VR06 7 SCT007 OVC010 30.22 -07 -224.

TEMPO 0400-0500 1/2 +SN OVC001.

Block 35: Remarks: Expect 000/0 conditions at RKNW AFT 04Z."

Now I fully understood the weight of Brad's statement when he said, "Chief, you may want to make some adjustments to your ETD and requested flight altitude."

I felt a knot begin to develop deep in my stomach. The weather was horrible, indeed. I never expected to have to make this sort of decision before. But then why wouldn't I? This is what a PIC does. A PIC evaluates assigned missions and then figures out if the mission is doable. As a fledgling PIC, I had yet to feel the weight of what was before me, so I had no real gauge. Surviving flight experiences are always a teacher of sorts. I found myself in the front row of this lesson. And I knew that the longer I delayed, the worse the weather was going to get.

All the stuff they taught us in flight school came crashing down on me, punctuated with safety first. The only safe thing to do with this sort of weather is not to fly at all. RON may very well be the best option. RON, however, only slightly entered my decision matrix. What was front and center to my decision matrix was the charge *mission first*. There had to be a way to work on this problem. The solution had to be right in front of me.

The LT interrupted my thoughts when she asked, "Are we flying or waiting." 2LT Boyle was no dummy. She knew that there was a big decision looming. She also knew that I was the PIC, so the decision to fly or not rested with me. I felt a sense of confidence as I began to take charge of the situation, and I began to unpack the problem. I put on my best mentor hat and asked the crew to join me at the planning table so that we could work the issue. Before doing so, however, I interrupted Bill from his computer screen and asked him if there was some way that I could get a message to my PAXs. I needed him to relay to them that we no longer had the planned ground time and that they needed to return to the airfield for an earlier departure.

He quickly responded, "Sure, Chief, no problem. They are just a phone call away. I will ring them right up."

The planning table in the USAF weather station was big and spacious. Flight planning tables are furniture at waist height that serves as a popular hangout for aviators conducting flight planning. And today's flight planning for the return trip was going to be anything but routine. Like most others, it had a plexiglass top that protected both visual flight rules (VFR) and instrument flight rules (IFR) maps that were spread out along the width and depth of the table. Some alcoves held and stored all volumes of books filled with all sorts of flight planning information about any airdrome you may need to plan for or fly into. VFR and IFR Supplements abounded. A flight planning table would not be complete without instrument approach booklets. These booklets opened from bottom to top for the various airdromes of the area. We called these booklets that opened from bottom to top "plates." The orientation of the plates made it very user-friendly for an aviator in the cockpit to place on his kneeboard for use. A kneeboard is a small desk measuring five-by-nine that straps to the left or right leg of an aviator. I found it almost impossible to fly without my kneeboard. I did all my administrative flight duties on my kneeboard, fuel check computations, time-distance-heading computations, copying both VFR and IFR clearances, just to name a few. Gathering around the flight planning table, we began.

"Okay, crew. In front of us lies a challenging flight. Ryan, thank you for taking off the barrier filters. If we run into icing, we don't need an engine flameout on the way home."

Just as I began, the LT startled me when she interrupted and said, "We're flying?" Her tone was undeniable. She was scared. So was I. As the PIC, I had to separate afraid of from concern, however. Scared people normally panic. Concerned persons unpack the facts that need unpacking and develop them. Once the particulars are unpacked, then a reasonable decision could be made to fly or not. We were going to unpack our weather briefing and not default to the too hard to fly position. I was choking back real fear, but I had my most professional hat on.

I began again, "We may or may not fly, but first, let's spend a bit of time and dissect the -1 and see if we have legal weather." She was shocked that we would even consider breaking down the -1. I wondered about her. It looked terrible, so don't go. I served a tour in Vietnam, and I happen to know that there were a lot of things that looked bad, but you didn't withdraw from the mission until evaluating everything. Looking at the LT I asked, "What are our minimums?"

She smartly responded, "1000-3." She was quick, smart, and eager and, yes, scared. I acknowledged the 1000-3 statement knowing that 1000 refers to 1,000 feet of the vertical ceiling above the surface of the earth. And I also recognized that 3 means that you have to have three miles of visibility.

Knowing that we were about to split some hairs, I said, "Let's break down some formal definitions. The definition of a ceiling is formally defined as broken, overcast, or obscuration, not classified as thin or partial. Visibility means horizontal visibility as viewed from the cockpit." We were no longer at Fort Rucker attending flight school and flying in a very controlled environment. We were out in the real world on a real-world mission. While handling the -1, I waited for that reality and ceiling definition to sink in. I was trying to defuse her fear and, yes, mine too, with facts. I also wanted to lead the crew. I did not want to exercise my authority as PIC and make a proclamation that we were going to fly regardless.

I continued, "Okay, LT, blocks four to nine is PPC information. We will come back to our departure time in block three in just a moment." Pre-mission planning cards (PPC) are filled out with information charts from chapter 7 of the -10. Every army aviator is required to fill out a PPC card before flying. The information tells the aviator his expected performance of the helicopter's engine as well as what sort of load may be put either inside the aircraft or outside on the cargo hook, mission depending. She nods affirmation. Okay, I can see this is a good tactic. "Block thirteen is a bit more concerning. Concerning the take-off altitude forecast, it says, 2SM SHSN OVC 007. I read 2SM SHSN OVC 007 in plain language, 2 miles visibility due to snow showers, and there is a ceiling defined by overcast to 700 feet AGL. So what I am actually getting from that is that we have 700-2 with snow conditions as opposed to 1000-3 conditions. How are we doing so far?"

The LT acknowledged the 1000-3 reduction to 700-2, and it was Ryan who spoke up with the obvious, "Hey, I may not be a pilot, but even I can see that 700-2 is under 1000-3. Flyable?"

"Yes, Ryan, 700-2 is very flyable," I told him. "The 'why' is still coming," I said to Ryan. "LT, do you remember what the weather was when we departed Camp Humphreys?" I asked.

"I was more focused on flying," she said. "The ceiling was low as I remember and the visibility was flyable," she reported. "I know 1000-3 is FAA VFR, but what does the Red Baron Standard Operating Procedures (SOP) say our VFR minimums are?" We were assigned to the Red Barons, 201st Aviation Company (Assault Helicopter). The Red Barons was a utility lift company that was commanded by a major. The unit consisted of two platoons of UH-1H helicopters. The UH-1 is also known as the Huey. I had grown to love the Huey. I was a Cobra crew chief in Vietnam some eleven years ago. The unit that I served with in Vietnam was a Cobra unit called Blue Max. The unit had ten AH-1G Cobra helicopters and one Huey. I crewed two of the Cobras as well as the units only Huey. While crewing the Huey, I filled one of the two door gunner positions when we flew the Huey. Since Blue Max was an attack unit, I pretended to tolerate the Huey. After all, the Huey performed utility missions and was not near as flashy as the Cobra that performed attack missions. Now eleven years later and as an aviator, I loved the Huey. It has been very good to me. It was very forgiving to fly, and over the years, the Huey has turned hundreds of thousands of fledgling aviators into masters in their own right. I found that there was nothing wrong with the utility mission at all.

The unit that we were assigned to was commanded by a major. Commanders are afforded a tremendous amount of authority. By army regulation, they are responsible for the health and welfare of those under their command. Part of that command responsibility goes to risk mitigating the operating conditions and missions of their commands. When commanders deviate from a known standard, they do so legally by creating and approving a standard operating procedure (SOP). As long as a member of his command follows the SOP, then they are not in violation of a known standard spoken to elsewhere in other regulations. Concerning our flight, 1000-3 is a known FAA standard, and aviators generally fly to that standard. However, and in this case, our commander has determined that the mission of his unit will not be able to be fully realized if 1000-3 remains the only standard. So in the case of minimums, the commander acknowledges 1000-3 as standard VFR weather. But as the commander of the 201st, he has lowered that 1000-3 minima to 700-2 as acceptable VFR weather conditions with a further restriction of 500-1 for Special VFR (SVFR) conditions.

Leading my crew to understand block thirteen of the -1 better, I return to my line of reasoning when I refocus the block thirteen discussion. "The Red Baron SOP says our VFR minimums are 700-2. LT takeoff weather when we departed from Humphreys was accurately recorded as '2SM OVC007,' and no mention of precipitation, either rain or snow. The temps were dangerously close to freezing conditions, however. As defined in our SOP, we flew in legal weather to Wonju. Admittedly, the remainder of the reported blocks on the -1 look terrible. Our requested flight level is now IFR. I recommend this that we make some adjustments to our flight plan. We ask for seven hundred feet en route for the return flight. Doing so will keep us in 700-2 flight conditions. What say you?"

Since there are freezing conditions out there, we have to stay out of any precipitation. The Huey is prohibited from flight into known icing conditions. As a precaution, this is the very reason I asked Ryan to take off the barrier filters. The aircraft is not equipped with anti-icing equipment. Once iced over, Huey's main rotor blades will lose their ability to perform an autorotation. If the icing is bad enough, the engine will flame out from oxygen starvation at the barrier filters. A flameout would thrust us into autorotation, and because of the ice, we will be unable to do so safely. At the end of the day, icing is a lose-lose scenario for a helicopter. Icing was one event that I did not want to encounter. This was supposed to be a milk-run mission. No hassles, in and out. As it turns out, it is has become anything but a milk run.

The LT agreed to the adjustments, and Ryan acknowledged the line of thinking. So collectively, we were okay. Now, only if we could leave right now. I continued to plan as if the PAXs were already here. I gave Brad a new departure time of 1100L (0200Z) as well as a new en route altitude of 700 feet AGL. We arrived at Wonju at 0900L and planned for four hours ground time putting use out at 1300L. We have already been here for 1+30 hours. We have got to go! I need my PAXs and an adjusted -1 to the new requests. It did not take Brad long to adjust the previous -1 with the amended en route altitude and departure time. He called me over, and he began to re-brief it. "Chief, you have a very narrow window to get out of here. If you are not out of here by 1145L (0245Z), you are going to get caught up in this huge front that is headed right for us." He invited me to come back behind his desk so that I could see his computer screen. Crap, it looked like a substantial opaque mess moving south and was almost on us. He was right if we did not leave soon, we were going to RON. We walked back to the counter so that he could brief each adjusted block of the -1. My stomach was in knots.

"Block three. Depart RKNW, 0500Z 0200Z.

"Block four. Runway temp, -4.

"Block five. Dewpoint, -7.

"Block seven. Pressure alt, -224.

"Block nine. Surface wind, VRB06.

"Block thirteen. Takeoff altitude forecast, 2SM OVC 007.

"Block seventeen. Clouds at flight level, no.

"Block eighteen. Obscurations at flight level, no.

"Block nineteen. Minimum ceiling, RTE 007 AGL.

"Block twenty. Maximum cloud tops, RTE 120 MSL.

"Block twenty-two. Thunderstorms, none.

"Block twenty-three Turbulence, none.

"Block twenty-four. Icing: SFC to 120, moderate along RTE in precipitation.

"Block twenty-five. Precipitation, light to moderate snow showers along RTE, none.

"Block twenty-six to thirty-one. RKNW 0200-0300Z VRB06 7 SCT004 OVC010 30.20 -05 72.

"TEMPO 0200-0300Z 1 SHSN BKN005 OVC010.

"Block twenty-six to thirty-one. RKSG 0100-0200 VR06 7 SCT007 OVC010 30.22 -07 -224.

"TEMPO 0100-0400Z 1/2 +SN OVC001.

"Block thirty-five. Remarks: Expect 0/0 conditions at RKNW AFT 03Z."

CHAPTER 4

The Decision Is Made to Fly

23 December 1982, ROK. 1035 Hours.

I wanted to get sick, all while feeling relieved and suddenly rushed. I was happy and terrified at the same time. Like someone who possessed right thinking, I quickly proclaimed, "We are flying." The LT, I realized, needed more than a proclamation.

"How did we go from a possible RON to flying out in this?" the LT asked.

Fair question, I thought. Before I answered, I asked Bill if there was any word on my PAXs. He told me to stand by. Then I shifted my attention to Ryan. I asked him to get the aircraft ready for a departure within the half hour. He knew these instructions went very formal quickly. He quietly left to ready the aircraft. I turned my attention back to the LT.

"Okay, LT, let's look at blocks three, thirteen, seventeen, eighteen, twenty-five, twenty-six to thirty-one, and thirty-five of the -1. Block 3, to account for the impending weather, we moved our departure time back three hours, enabling Brad to build a new -1. Block thirteen, previously, we had 2SM SHSN OVC 007. With the earlier departure and adjusted -1, notice that the 'SHSN' is now gone. The new block thirteen reads 2SM OVC 007. The snow showers are now gone because of the three-hour adjustment that I just made. That means no precip and, ultimately, no icing. Block seventeen, previously we had 'clouds at flight level, with the time adjustment, we have no clouds at flight level. The precipitation is gone. Again, no icing. Blocks eighteen and twenty-five likewise removed precipitation and, again, no icing." I knew this was a lot for her to take in.

She asked, "What about blocks 26-31? I'm seeing 400-feet ceilings. You said we had to have 700-2 by SOP?"

I had to reexamine the -1, and at first look, she was right. But I remembered and reminded her why I discussed the formal definition of a ceiling earlier. "Remember that the definition of a ceiling is Broken, Overcast, or Observation not classified as Thin or Partial. The scattered that you are reading at 400 feet is not a ceiling." I realized I was making myself feel better while briefing the new -1 to the crew. Saying the academic stuff out loud made it sound better than it really was.

"And block 35 says were are going to have zero/zero after 0300Z here at Wonju," she says.

"Not going to sugarcoat that," I tell her. "That is why we have to get out and get out fast."

CHAPTER 5

Ryan and I Discuss the Circled-Red-X's

23 December 1982, ROK. 1040 Hours.

Ryan returned carrying the aircraft logbook. He had that look that CEs have when they have terrible news to deliver. Having been an enlisted aviation crewmember for ten years, I was very familiar with that look. "What?" I asked.

"Mr. Doudna, remember when we conducted the preflight this morning and we had the circle-red-x conversation?"

"Yes," I said.

"We still have those circle-red-x conditions, sir. The aircraft is restricted from IFR operations," he said matter-of-fact. Ryan was being a competent and engaged CE, and I appreciated that.

"Ryan, as long as we do not go IFR, we are legal. There is no plan to enter IFR conditions," I reassured him.

I could have used the counsel of someone with more experience. Enjoying the mentorship of a senior or master aviator right now would have been great. Unfortunately, we were out at a remote site working problems associated with the accomplishment of a mission, and I was the decision guy on site. In review, a scary thought. I am reminded, however, of the tremendous amount of responsibility that the military allows their service members to take on. Was I up for it? The weather may be sketchy, but it was academically still fly-able. Ryan was right in his saying that we have drawn an aircraft that was restricted from IFR operations. The helicopter does not have one gyro that is failing, but two gyros that are failing. Really? *Well, we just won't go into the clouds that's all,* I reason to myself. "Ryan, let's see the logbook." A quick review of the DA Form 2408-13 reminds me that both the attitude indicator and the radio magnetic indicator (RMI) is written up as precessing. Because of the precessing, neither are reliable for flight in an IFR environment.

Precessing is a change in the orientation of the rotational axis that drives a card in each instrument. Each instrument has gimbal bearings inside that help stabilize the information sent to the card face of each device. Remember, the RMI's heading is corrected by rotating the heading synchronization knob in the lower right corner of the gauge. Remember too that the attitude indicator is stabilized and or adjusted by the adjustment of either, or both, of the knobs on either side of that instrument. The real problem with precessing is that neither instrument will hold its last reference made by the pilot by any amount of time. The preponderance of attitude and heading information during a flight in cloud is made upon on these two instruments. A crew in cloud with instruments that will not hold their pilot assigned references could result in disorientation and result in a fatal crash. There are many accidents discussed in the army's flight fax magazine, a monthly army safety publication, where army flight crews have lost their orientation in cloud with instruments that are in proper working order. Contrast that to our situation. We actually have two primary instruments that are unreliable. Taking an aircraft into the clouds with faulty instruments is a fool's errand. Ryan's concerns would prove prophetic.

CHAPTER 6

I First Meet the Commander

1 February 1982, ROK. 1300 Hours.

As a previous enlisted guy, and news to me, when a newly assigned officer is assigned to a unit, it is customary for that officer to meet with the commander. It is a tradition that I was unfamiliar with. I had been in the military eleven years to this point, and I had always met with the first sergeant and only the commander if the first sergeant felt it was necessary. It was never needed. But this assignment was different for me. This was the first assignment where I was now a company grade officer and reporting into a unit, I would learn, was different for me now.

Once I got to the unit, I made my way to the orderly room. Either officer or enlisted, everyone finds themselves at the orderly room sooner or later to begin their in-processing into the unit. The orderly room was busy, and I was barely noticed when I entered. Several clerks were working at different desks scattered about the office. Once one of the soldiers realized that I was an officer, he quickly introduced himself and took my records and very quickly in-processed me into the unit. He was very polite and asked me if I wanted some Joe while he directed me to a comfortable chair. Really, I thought? This was quite a change from previous enlisted assignments. He took my personal file, also called a 201 file, and my finance records, and he processed them first. He barely made eye contact with me as he seemed to already know the answers to questions…that he did not ask. There were a few questions of course, but compared to other in-processing enlisted experiences, he was lightning fast. There were a few outlier tasks from the orderly room that I needed to in-process, like the motor pool, post office, chapel, and PX for my rations card as well as the central issue facility (CIF), to name a few. The CIF was always a problematic place regardless of grade. At the CIF, I would draw all my army warfighting gear, also known as TA-50. Everyone who has ever served in the army is well aware of TA-50 and the drama that is involved in drawing that equipment. Harder still is turning it all in when you depart for another assignment. Those out-layers were still ahead of me, but as I said, as an officer, I was going to be meeting with the commander this time, and that would be very interesting. I was not the least bit intimidated. Since I was a seasoned soldier and now a company-grade officer, it made me feel like I had finally grown into the next level of my career. I was looking forward to meeting him in fact so that I could lay out my career path as I saw it and how I wish to proceed with fulling that path during this assignment. Seasoned or no, there was a lot about this new status that made me very naive. I did, after all, volunteer to come to the ROK, and I expected a lot of gain for the pain of my family separation. I was finding out that learning the officer ropes wasn't always a bad thing. Along with these new life lessons, I would soon discover just how naive I was.

I completed all that I could with the clerk. After he had set up my appointments for the outliers that I had yet to accomplish, he directed me to the staff sergeant (E-6) who was in charge of the comings and goings of the orderly room. The staff sergeant was not particularly impressed with my WO1 status. He had seen many a WO1 come and go. I was just another WOJG to him. He was not disrespectful, however, only direct. He looked at the commander's calendar and said, "Sir, can you see the commander today right after lunch?"

"Sure," I said. "Did I do anything wrong?" I asked.

The staff sergeant looked at me strangely and said, "No, sir. Miss this meeting, however, and it may be another thing altogether." He smiled, and I did too. Again, processing in as a company-grade officer was way different for me. The commander, I came to understand, was a very kind man. But I would soon learn that he was, however, a commander who was in full command of his command.

Since it was lunchtime, I secured directions to the mess hall and departed. The mess hall was a short walk away. Been to many. I found the food functional. New command or no, it was just a mess hall. I saw a few other WOJGs and, after getting my food and drinks, went over and sat down and introduced myself. They were glad to meet me. They were just like me, freshly minted from Fort Rucker. If there were a meter that existed, one could easily measure the energy that all us WOJGs put off. We just wanted to get in an aircraft and fly. It really didn't matter when and where—only that we get into the air. These guys, I found out, we're only a few classes in front of me at Fort Rucker. At Rucker, that meant something. Senior classmen and all that. Out here in the field, it means squat. I shook their hands and forgot their names three minutes into the conversation. Thank goodness for flight suits and name tags.

The one to my front seated across from the table was named William, or Bill, but he preferred to be called Red. It looked as if his hair was on fire.

"Hello, Red," I said with a firm handshake. "Guessing it is the red hair?" I pondered aloud.

"Hey, you're quick," he said teasingly. He went on to introduce his sidekick as Bob.

Bob quickly spoke up and said, "My name is Robert, and don't call me Rob."

I measured the tension and simply said, "Hello, Robert-don't-call-me-Bob."

Robert smiled and said, "I think I am going to like you."

I almost introduced myself with the nickname I was given in Vietnam, but I thought better of it and just introduced myself as Dean. They were both very chatty and were eager to fill me in on the comings and goings of the unit, all that they knew anyway.

"Have you met the commander yet?" Robert-don't-call-me-Bob asked.

"1300," I said.

They both became animated. They both began to exclaim who he was and some of his background. Apparently, he was a war hero. He flew the OH-6 in Vietnam and got shot down…was the crust of what they told me. I could tell that there was much more to the story. They wanted me to formulate my own option about the commander, so they stopped telling me about him at the shootdown point in the story. I thought the whole exchange was odd. I changed the subject and asked each of them what track they were interested in.

"Track," Robert-don't-call-me-Bob said. Both Red and Robert-don't-call-me-Bob were high-school-to-flight-school guys. Neither—other than basic training, WOC, and IERW—had much of a military background. They were as green as they came. Frankly, their lack of military experience was always entertaining fodder and why we WOJGs are so quickly dismissed by NCOs and other officers as well. I was aware of this and did not hold it against them. Instead, I tried to mentor them. I told them that there were three career tracks for warrant officers to choose from standardization, maintenance, or safety. Standardization was reserved for those wishing to become IPs and IFEs. That group of warrant officers was responsible for teaching other aviators their flying skill sets. Next, the maintenance track. The guy who tracked maintenance was more in-tuned with the maintenance and logistics needs that it took to keep the aircraft flying. Warrant officers tracking maintenance became maintenance test pilots. Finally, there remained the safety track. Safety officers were those group of officers who ensured for the commander that all portions the command was conducted within the army's safety guidelines. I watched their eyes gloss over. I knew they were still at the point in their career where the only thing that mattered was getting in the air. Knowing that I had done my very best with Red and Robert-don't-call-me-Bob, I looked at my watch and saw that it was approaching time to head to the commander's office for my meeting, so I excused myself and headed out of mess hall for the Red Baron operations building where the commanders office was co-located.

During my tour of duty with the Red Barons, I served under two Red Baron commanders. The commander I was meeting today was in the latter portion of his tour and had only a few months left before he headed back to the states. He would be handing his command over to another commander soon. As a prior-enlisted member, I was well acquainted with the comings and goings of commanders and their changes of command. So, being aware of the commander's upcoming permeant change of station (PCS) did not place me off-center. Meeting him, however, was another story.

I knocked on his door that happened to be open. He was seated at his desk, and his back was to me. He was reading a regulation from a cabinet behind his desk. "Come," was all he said. He kept his attention in the regulation that he was reading while I came in. He knew I was going to approach his desk, and I did. I positioned myself some three feet in front of his desk and waited at attention.

Moments later, he turned around, and the moment he began to rotate around in his chair to face me, I sharply snapped a salute. The commander had done this initial meeting many times before me. When he fully turned around, what I saw in his face was difficult to describe. He saluted me back and told me to sit down. The commander, who happened to be a major, got up and slowly came around his desk and stood quietly for an uncomfortable moment or two. He said, "I know my appearance is shocking. I'm used to it. I am used to the shock that others go through the first time that people meet me. Have a good look," he said. He turned his head and looked left and right so that I could see both sides of his face. He turned around so that I could see the back of his head, and then, while I was looking at the back of his head, he looked up so that I could see the crater in the top-back of his skull. He turned sideways, and then turned to the other side. When he felt that I was finished, he then took the seat beside me. I suspected that he had choreographed those moves and had introduced himself that way many, many times before. There was just a small coffee table between the seats that were to the front of his desk.

"I was badly burnt in an aircraft crash in Vietnam," he began. "I was flying an OH-6 and was shot down four months into my tour.

I was a young lieutenant, knew everything, and was indestructible. I was flying a hunter-killer mission with Cobras. Are you familiar with that mission?" he asked.

"Yes, sir. I did a tour with the Blue Max, a Cobra unit out of Bearcat, Vietnam," I replied.

"Good, then you are familiar with the mission," he said. "It was awful. The Cobra that I was working with orbited over me a good ten minutes looking for any signs of life. There was fire everywhere, and we were still in the middle of a firefight. My fuel cell ruptured upon impact. I didn't have a chance. I knew the crew that was flying the Cobra overhead. They must have anguished as they surveyed the crash site looking for any signs of life. Understandably, they finally decided that they were looking down on a dead crew. I would have left too. From my vantage point, it was an inferno. No way I could come out of that alive. My gunner was decapitated, so I knew he was dead. Other than God's good graces, I have no idea how I got out. I crawled my way out of the flames and up three hundred feet to the top of the knoll. We were defending that knoll. I was shot down and crashed at its top, then rolled to the bottom as soon as I hit. I popped pin flares from the top of the hill and was picked up by the med guys supporting the firefight. The rest is history. They flew me to the 24th Evac and then on to Brooks Burn Center in Texas from there. I spent years in rehab. See my left hand?" he said. He held up a claw of a hand and said, "I am most proud of this hand. This reconstructed claw allows me to fly today. With this claw of a hand, I can pull and push on the collective as well as manipulate the throttle," he said.

I looked at it and had to take his word for it. Looking at it, I had no idea how he could have done that. I tried not to feel sorry for him. It is only natural, I guess. You could instantly tell he had a powerful will. There was a lot for him to overcome. When viewing his face straight on, the left eye was higher than the right. There were no eyebrows. One eyelid was partially gone, and the other was overexaggerated from the corrective surgery. His skin was two-toned. There was a deep tan side and a light tan side that seemed to run together haphazardly. Both colors joined at a seam that seemed to wonder on its own. You could easily see that the reconstructive surgery he endured was sewn together with donor skin. His right ear was missing. The left was only partially there. His smile was crooked, and his bottom lip looked like it was having a horrible Botox day, all while forming a very inviting smile. When his smile joined his laugh, he was totally disarming. As he reported, he was difficult to look at. If things weren't odd enough, he had a wig in his desk drawer. "I have a wig. Would you like me to put it on? I normally wear it to parties to disarm people," he said with a smile. "Sometimes, it is easier for others to see less even when talking with me."

I politely told him, "Sir, I am sure that you look dashing in your wig, but no need to wear it on my account. You are a soldier and my commander. You don't need a wig to improve upon that," I said in earnest. I felt myself choking up just a little as I felt sorry for him, all the while admiring him.

He smiled from ear to ear and said, "Mr. Doudna, I think I am going to like you."

I replied, "People have said that about me." And with that, we began our meeting in earnest.

"Enough about me, I want to know all about you. You are not the typical WO1 I can see. Looks like you have some seasoning," he said.

"I do, sir," I began to tell him. As I spoke with him, I was surprised at how little I saw of his scars and surgeries. I only saw my commander and desperately wanted to tell him all he wanted to know.

I told him that I came into the army in June of 1970, right out of high school. I was a leap-year baby, so I did not have a draft number. I volunteered for the draft. I married my high school sweetheart and was still married to her. I rose in the ranks and was picked up for E7 while in the flight program. I told him that, before going to flight school, I held the following MOSs: 67A10, 67Y20, 67N20, 67G30, and 67W30. I told him that I had been a mechanic, crew chief, technical inspector, section sergeant, and platoon sergeant. I felt that I was being promoted off the flight line and wanted to go to the flight program so that I could stay in the hangar.

He interrupted me and called out to the first sergeant. "Top," he said. "Cancel my next meeting. I will be here with Mr. Doudna 'til finished."

"*Hoo-ah*," replied the first sergeant, and he closed the door.

Then he returned his attention to me and was as happy as a commander could be. "I am so glad that you are in my unit. The operations officer told me that he had to rescue you at H201 from the 2ID. Glad he did," he said. The commander then began to tell me about his maintenance program and that he could use a good maintainer. As he was speaking, I felt like I had had this conversation before in other units. Commanders *always* wanted useful maintainers. Maintenance personnel kept his aircraft in the air. If they were in the air, then his mission would be uninterrupted. Plus, valuable maintainers made sure that aircraft did not fall out of the sky. These are all excellent reasons to be a maintainer, and given my enlisted years, I fully understood where the commander was coming from. I really wanted to help him and the unit. I wanted to do what I always did, maintain aircraft, but during this assignment, I wanted things to be different. This assignment was something of a rebirthing for me. I was an army aviator now. The army spent a lot of money on teaching me how to fix and manage army aircraft. I did not want to abandon that effort. I wanted to enhance it. I eventually wanted to track maintenance as a warrant officer. I, however, volunteered to come to the ROK to learn how to fly, communicate, and navigate, not to maintain and test fly aircraft. I volunteered to be separated from my family, not to rescue the commander's maintenance program, but to learn how to fly, communicate, and navigate. I had to somehow get this through to him. I told him that even though I had grown up as a maintenance guy, I was really interested in standardization. I wanted to be an IP, or at least give it a try. I told him that, upon graduation from the flight program, I had orders to Bragg, but I went on and told him that I traded those orders for the ROK.

"On purpose?" he asked, almost giddy.

"Yes, sir," I said. "I knew that the ROK would be a condensed and intense assignment. I knew that if I had stayed in the States that, between family and other requirements, I would only have eight to ten hours a day to devote to flying and learning about my new aviator status."

At some point in the conversation, I realized that we had been chatting for almost two hours. I think the commander came to that realization too. He was honest at least when he began, "Mr. Doudna, I appreciate your dreams and desires, but I cannot let you simply turn your back on your maintenance background. Our unit's mission depends upon everyone doing their very, very best. I cannot allow you the time that you think you need to find yourself in this new career direction. You have ten solid, successful years as an aircraft maintainer and supervisor. I have to exploit that to the success of the mission of this unit." At that point, I stopped hearing the words that he was saying. It no longer mattered what I wanted. I could hear the needs of the army raging in my head as he continued to outline my duties. I felt like I was watching an episode of *The Charlie Brown and Snoopy Show*, the *Peanuts* cartoon where Charlie Brown only hears his teacher say, "Wah, Wah, Wah, Wah, Wah, Wah..." The commander was right about one thing. I was a seasoned soldier. I realized that I was going to go to maintenance, not standardization.

While he was wah-wah-wah-ing on with his dialogue, I came up with a scheme that seemed entirely fair to me. So, I waited for him finish all the wah-wah-wah-ing, and when I felt the time was right, I sprang my idea on him. "Sir," I said, "You're right, of course. I am an accomplished maintainer. I didn't make it to E-7 without getting something right. It remains true that I did come to the ROK to learn my new aviator's skill set, and with that in mind, might I suggest that if I go to the hangar, I am just going to get lost over there in maintenance. I am not going to see the light of day all while ensuring that your aircraft is properly maintained. If I may propose, sir, that I go to the hangar and be allowed to select four missions of my choice a week to exercise and develop my aviator skills..."

There fell an uncomfortable silence between us. He looked at me squarely, or squarely for him, and he blurted out, "Two missions a week of your choice..."

I considered my options and smiled and bravely said, "Three missions a week of my choice..."

He cut me off and firmly repeated, "Two missions a week of your choice…"

Instinctively. I knew that the deal was struck. I was going to maintenance, but I also knew that I was going to be freed twice a week to fly missions of my choice. I knew that I had to strike while the topic was hot.

"Sir, I have to ask. Will you walk down the hall to operations and tell the operations officer that I will be able to walk in twice a week and place my name on the mission board for two missions a week of my choice? Let's face it, I am just a WOJG, and he is a captain. We both know how that conversation is going to go…" I braced and waited, knowing that I had really stretched my luck.

The commander stood up and embraced me and then escorted me down to operations. The operations officer was out of the building at the time, but the commander pivoted and wrote on the mission board, "Mr. Doudna will select two missions of his choosing per week. Questions? See me," and signed it, "Commander." We parted when he said to me, "Mr. Doudna, you better fix the bejeebers out of my aircraft. I knew I was going to like you the moment I saw you," he said as he slapped my back with that claw of his. I watched him walk down the hallway back to his office. His laugh was heartfelt. He stopped and pointed to the other end of the hall and said, "Out that door and to the right, you will find the hangar. I will take care of the operations officer. Welcome to the unit," he said as he disappeared into his office.

That memory raced through my mind as I was speaking with Ryan about the circle red x's on this aircraft that we had drawn. Had I fixed the bejeebers out of the aircraft assigned to the unit as the commander had hoped? Not my fault that the instruments were precessing. The aircraft was still flyable…VFR. As I saw it, we were still VFR. I would soon realize, however, just how skewed that reasoning was.

CHAPTER 7

We Have Got to Depart Wonju

23 December 1982, ROK. 1045 Hours.

"Bill, what is up with my PAXs?" I asked. I was becoming more anxious by the moment. Just as I saw Bill shrug his shoulders, in burst MAJ Burns. MAJ Burns was one of my PAXs and was the aviation liaison that was assigned to the two flag officers that I had dropped off. Wow, was I glad to see him. That star on his wings was a welcomed sight. That star means that he is a senior aviator. Maybe he might provide a mentor moment or two to the flight decision?

I was about to brief the major on our weather dilemma when he said matter-of-factly, "We have got to get out of here right now. There is a big storm coming, and we may be able to beat it if we hurry!" I was both stunned and pleased. Amazed because I was questioning myself about my decision to fly. After all, we were squeaking the bottom of all minimums. Happy because the guy with a big star on his wings, a senior aviator, affirmed my decision as PIC to fly as the correct decision. He was not here to witness or participate in the decision matrix that we ran through to come to a fly decision; he was here to depart! His unbiased fly opinion confirmed my decision to fly. His support made me feel much better. "Go, go, go," he directed. "Get your crew to the aircraft, get it started, and I will wait for the flag officers. They are minutes behind me. Go, no time to spare." He was right, of course, no time to waste. After I made a quick stop at the latrine to recalibrate my two-hour bladder, my crew and I were headed to the door.

CHAPTER 8

Just Before Departure from Wonju

23 December 1982, ROK. 1050 Hours.

Ryan, the LT, and I moved quickly to the aircraft. In these conditions, almost two hours on the ground was two hours too long. We needed to get in the air and start heading south and beat this front moving in. We quickly cleared the aircraft of light ice that had formed on its surfaces. It was odd seeing the barrier filters off. A quick check of fluid levels and confirmation that there was no debris around the flight controls, and we were strapped into the aircraft. The LT began to get back in the same seat that I had allowed her to fly here in, but I thought better of it and asked her to move her stuff to the left seat. All the primary instrumentation for the flight was on the right side of the Huey. The left side of the aircraft had backup instruments. The aircraft could be flown in instrument conditions from the left side, but I wanted to stack the cards in my favor if we got into weather trouble, so I took the right seat. Flying into intimidating weather conditions, I felt better being on the right side. An interesting footnote; in the fixed-wing community, the opposite is true. The left side is normally where the PIC would sit as all the primary instrumentation is on that side. Also, rotary-wing personnel call their helicopters airplanes. In all my years of army aviation service, I never understood where those conditions and traditions began but were always amused when in conversations with my peers and we would speak of our helicopters as airplanes. I knew we were not in an airplane, but the sentiment was not lost on me.

We ran through the checklist quickly. After the engine roared to life, the rotors began to spin up to operating revolutions per minute (RPM). It was not snowing, but there was plenty of loose snow about, and the rotor wash stirred all that up. We remained at flat pitch while the snow debris slowly dissipated. Fortunately, this run-up was considered a through-flight, so I did not need to do a health indicator test (HIT). HIT checks are performed during the first flight of the day. We accomplished the HIT check this morning before departing Camp Humphrey. Had we needed to do a HIT check in these snow conditions it would have been a snow mess for sure. I would have been pulling pitch with the collective thereby increasing pitch in the blades to set the conditions for the HIT check, and the surrounding snow would have been greatly affected. I preparation for takeoff, and before the PAXs arrived, I did pull collective pitch to blow as much of the loose snow away as possible. Ryan sensed that I was getting the aircraft light on the skids. There were mixed crew signals.

He grabbed the logbook and asked me, "Sir, ready for the HIT check. Since we have already accomplished our HIT check this morning, are we doing another because the barrier filters have been removed? Must be because the barrier filters are off, huh, sir?"

I really liked Ryan. Again, I thought of him as a good candidate for the army's flight program. "No, Ryan, I am getting the aircraft light on the skids before the PAXs get here. In preparation for our takeoff, I want to blow away as much of this loose snow as I can. I also want to make sure the aircraft is not frozen to the ground. Dynamic roll over, we do not need. We have enough complications with this lousy weather to contend with as it is." I smiled back at Ryan over my left shoulder and continued to raise the collective until the aircraft cross tubes deflexed, indicating the weight of the aircraft was being absorbed by the rotor system. The snow was a mess, and we were in all but whiteout conditions because of the increased airflow through the rotor system. Once the aircraft was light on the skids, I also moved the left and right tail rotor pedals a couple inches each way. If the skids were frozen to the ground, I wanted to break them free all while being sensitive for dynamic roll over.

"What's dynamic roll over," Ryan asked.

As I moved the collective and tail rotor pedals, I pondered the answer. Did he want the short version or the long version? I wanted to be a good mentor, but I did not want to kill him with facts. I decided on the short version.

"Ryan, the full answer is in the army's *Fundamentals of Flight Field Manual*. When we get back, I will be happy to cover the full definition for you. The short answer is this, and I know this is hard to believe, but if one skid is stuck to the ground or becomes a pivot point while I am pulling pitch, if I do not immediately correct for the rolling motion with collective, the aircraft will rollover. The instability is best fixed with collective rather than cyclic. The cyclic is a player, but the collective will reduce the thrust while the cyclic directs the trust. Let's not forget about the snow. The decreased visual acuity is a big player too."

After I had completed manipulating the flight controls and was made satisfied that we were not frozen to the ground, I returned the collective to flat pitch and looked back at Ryan. I could tell he was digesting what I had told him. He was the type who took in all information, digested that information, and then validated the information with doctrine. I fully expect him to chase me down later with that field manual and continue the discussion when we get home. I was looking forward to going over it with him at home base, but right now, I was looking forward to seeing the PAXs. I rolled the throttle down to engine idle to conserve fuel.

The Huey has typically four radios installed—VHF, UHF, and two FM radios. There are also three navigational radios—VOR, ADF, and a localizer. All those radios are sent through a signal distribution panel C-1611. There is a C-1611 dedicated to both the pilot and the copilot. The C-1611 has six-pin switches. Four are dedicated to the radios, and the other two are dedicated to internal communications, otherwise known as hot-mike, and the last pin switch is dedicated to the navigation radios. Pin one is dedicated to FM no. 1. Pin two is dedicated to the UHF radio. Pin three is dedicated to the VHF radio, and pin four is dedicated to FM no. 2 radio. The C-1611 also has a selector switch. When the selector rotated to the number one to four positions, the aviator can transmit out of the aircraft. The C-1611 is a user-friendly and much-needed piece of equipment to manage the array of radios. Once the receivers are correctly tuned, the pilot who is on the controls only has to say to the other pilot not on the controls, "Put me up no.—with the selector." Once the selector is rotated to the correct position, the pilot on the controls is then able to communicate outside the aircraft while he continues operating the flight controls uninterrupted. The pilot not on the controls remains prepared and ready to listen when their pin on their C-1611 is placed in the on or forward position but will not be able to transmit outside the aircraft without their selector being rotated to the desired radio position. The PIC is responsible for briefing all flights and missions.

During the briefing, the PIC divides and assigns duties. I have always felt that the guy on the controls should also speak on the radios. Additionally, the aviator not on the controls backs up all information coming into the cockpit, to include recording information if needed on his or her kneeboard. With a little practice, not forgetting the world-class flight instruction offered at Fort Rucker, what was impossible to comprehend my first day of flight school I find now moving around inside an army cockpit is no more foreign to me than the operation of my own car.

While waiting on our PAXs, I directed the LT through the cockpit setup. I was reading off the instrument plate for Wonju (KNW) and was reading the desired radio frequencies to her for programming. "Please ensure Wonju Operations, 38.50, is still in our FM no. 1 radio." Since we had spoken with operations upon arrival that radio was still tuned. "Please ensure ground, 121.7, is in the VHF no. 3."

"Dean," the LT began, "all the radios are set. We flew in and haven't adjusted anything."

"LT, humor me. We are getting ready to launch into crappy weather. We will be busy enough once airborne. We have time. Let's continue with the cockpit set up."

"Roger, ground 121.7 is in the VHF," she reported.

"Great, please put tower, 257.6 in the UHF, no. 2, then on your kneeboard, record Poncho radio frequency, 327.125. Once we finish with the tower, and after departure, I want you to spin Poncho's frequency in the UHF no. 2. All I will ask for after that is that you ensure that placement of the selector switch on my C-1611 is correctly selected before I transmit."

Pleased with herself, she reported, "All set."

We were ready, and we waited, and waited, and waited some more. As time passed, there were not a lot of words spoken between us three. Since we had time, I asked the LT to call operations and get the frequency for the weather station. Might as well get a weather update while waiting. She did so. While she was communicating with operations asking for the weather station frequency, I had to ponder. Was I that clumsy when I first learned how to talk on the radio? Utilizing the following format for radio comms—who you are, where you are and what you want—is a simple format to use and remember. The IPs at Fort Rucker usually did the heavy lifting radio work, and it was showing now as she stumbled through stage fright while on the radio. Even though I wanted to, I did not interrupt her. We had time. She needed the practice. I was no better when I first was assigned. She got the frequency and dialed it in to the no. 1 FM. She looked over at me and said, "You're up."

"No, I am not up until you rotate my selector to the no. 1 position. Once you do that, then I will be up. Go ahead and get the weather update, LT," I directed. She put her selector up no. 1 on her C-1611 and began again with the stage fright. My no. 1 pin was up, so I could hear Brad tell her that the -1 remains unchanged. He issued a new weather void time and wished us a safe flight and Merry Christmas. The LT responded in kind and returned the no. 1 FM back to the operations frequency.

All of us knew precious fuel was being burned while waiting. Even though I had reduced the throttle to engine idle, we were still consuming dinosaur juice. Looking to the north, we sat quietly, watching the front loom closer and closer. It was very imposing. All total, we waited an additional thirty minutes at engine idle. What a killer. Had I known the flag officers were more than minutes behind MAJ Burns, I would have shut down and topped off the fuel. But when dealing with general officers, things seem to run on their time table, and that always seems different than usual. Where are the PAXs, I wondered. The fuel was burning. I needed them to get here.

While waiting, I briefed the LT on our cockpit duties for the flight. "LT, if it comes in the cockpit over the radio, the person not on the controls will record everything," I began. "Given the weather conditions, I will most likely be doing most of the flying. Navigation wise, I know pretty much that we will be headed south through the Wonju Valley, then we will make a right turn at the Wonju Highway and a left turn at the Seoul-Pusan Highway. From there we will take railroad transition to Osan, drop off the PAXs, and continue south to the Hump. I would like you to follow along on the map and make sure that I make the checkpoints along the way."

That did not settle well with her. The weather was crappy, granted. Since I charged her with navigation responsibilities, I knew she felt that she bore the brunt of the obligation to get us home. I had been in her shoes many times before. Truth be known, I did not need a navigator. I would not have passed the map duties to her if I did not know exactly where I was and how to get home. I thought I would let her talk on the radio some more all while working the map. She needed the practice.

"Mr. D., I see the PAXs coming down the hill," Ryan said.

"Finally," I said. "Ryan, get out there and salute them. Get them on board and strapped in. Give me a shout out when your station is secure." I asked the LT to get the checklist out and call out the before-takeoff checks. I did not want to spend another moment on the ground. We needed to get airborne. Not long later, Ryan slapped my left shoulder and gave me a thumbs up. I asked the LT to make the ground call and I would make the tower call. She placed her no. 3 pin up and her selector on the no. 3 position. As briefed, she put my no. 3 pin up so that I could listen in as she made the call. It was awful. While flying up to Wonju together, I shared with her what a friend taught me a long time ago about radio usage. During the hour flight up, she did not take to the radio like a duck to water, but she did get the basics out for what we needed out. I think ground understood. Again with the stage fright. I just held my breath.

Most students and newly minted aviators are awful on the radio for all the wrong reasons IPs in flight school typically make the radio calls. They do not want their call sign mutilated. I was constantly reminded by my IPs to listen to their example when they transmitted. They often said that it will come to you eventually. Call signs are very personal. I remember when I was new to the Red Barons. The commander at the time believed in battle-rostering crews for the first month that you are in-country. What is battle-rostering crews? Battle-rostering crews mean that no matter what, you were flying with that same aviator, learning the area and how to work in the cockpit as a crew. I was battle-rostered with WO1 Todd Tanner. It was an odd mix. Todd had been in country for eleven months and was a month from going home when I was assigned. He was a high-school-to-flight-school guy, had blond hair, and was always in need of a haircut. He was tall and really lean. He had a carefree spirit about him. Must have been a surfer, or if he wasn't, he sure had that persona. The last thing he was worried about was peer pressure. The CEs liked him, and being an old CE, that told me a lot about him.

By contrast, I had spent ten years in enlisted time before going into the flight program. There was a maturity gap between us, sure, but there was no denying the fact that Todd could fly the pants off a Huey. We first met about the same way that 2LT Boyle and I met. He had drawn a training mission, and I was assigned. We met at the aircraft to preflight. The preflight was beyond the routine. As a maintainer, I answered a ton of systems questions that Todd had for me. We hit it off right away. He assigned me the right seat during the flight briefing, and when he got done with the briefing, I shocked him with a request.

I told him, "Listen, Todd, I can motor skill the flight controls well enough to get through flight school and my ARL training upon assignment. During this month that we are battle-rostered together, what I really want to do is to learn to communicate and navigate," so I requested the left seat.

He was dumbfounded. "You mean that you just want to talk and navigate and that I get to fly?" he asked.

"Yep, pretty much."

He was beyond happy, and the training flight began. Our only mission that day was to burn holes in the sky. Our aircrew training manual (ATM) required that we fly thirty hours semiannually. Getting thirty hours semiannually in Korea was a piece of cake. We averaged thirty hours in a few months. We all needed flight exposure, and training missions were plentiful. Todd happily jumped in the right seat and me in the left. We went through a standard cockpit set up; he cranked the aircraft and looked at me and said, "Call ground for hover taxi."

I was awful, awkward, and could barely speak, and everyone on the net listening to Todd's call sign, RB93, knew it. He was very kind. "Relax," he told me. "Stop worrying about butchering my call sign. I am out of here next month anyway," he said.

I asked, "When you go, Todd, can I have your call sign?"

"Well, you will have to make PIC before they assign you a call sign. I don't think the unit is going to keep my call sign on hold or anything. Anyway, as far as I am concerned, you can have RB93 after I leave. Now let's figure out how to communicate."

I genuinely liked the guy. You could tell he was an excellent listener. He heard every awkward word I spoke, thought about it, and summed up a fix for my awkwardness with his straightforward phrase that I use to this very day.

"Dean, tell them who you are, where you are, and what you want to do. It is that easy. No matter the call, it will pretty much flow in that order. Once in a while, you will find that not to be the case, but it almost always is." For a high-school-to-flight-school young person, I could see real potential in this kid. Well, I can only hope that Todd would be proud of me as I did just what he said and I told my LT tell them who you are, where you are, and what you want to do. When I heard her all but unintelligible radio call to ground, I cringed. The weather conditions pushed the stakes up pretty high for this flight. I realized, less teaching, more performing.

CHAPTER 9

Departure from Wonju

23 December 1982, ROK. 1100 Hours.

My fuel status and imposing weather forced me to move the
LT and the cockpit along a bit faster. Ground gave us hover
taxi instructions; however, for the life of me, I had no idea how they
understood the LT as I surely did not. Remembering how kind Todd
was with me, I was as gentle with the LT as I explained that our
weather is going to move us along a bit faster and I asked if she would
not mind if I took over the radios just to get us out of Wonju. Like my
first experiences with Todd, she was totally okay with surrendering
the radio. With a nod, I asked her to put my selector up no. 2, and
I made the call to tower. I was flying helicopter 67-15782 but, like
the flight up to Wonju, I filed under RB93. We were hover taxing to
hold short of the active. Since we were still hovering and moving, it
made no sense to me at all to stop. No one else was out here anyway,
and I wanted to keep the momentum going for the blowing show.

"Wonju Tower, RB93 holding sort of the 18 runway ready for a
VFR departure to the south."

"RB93," they responded, "surface winds variable at six, altimeter 29.92 cleared for departure. Merry Christmas and safe flight,"
they said.

"RB93 cleared for departure to the south, on the go," I repeated. With that, I likewise wished them a Merry Christmas, and just like that, we were on the go. I hovered fast enough to stay only to the front of the snow cloud we were creating while transitioning to take-off. The departure was something akin to a running takeoff from the hover. I did triple check before taking the active. We were taking off from a Korean air base after all. Plenty of room for communication errors. Again, we were the only ones dumb enough to be out here anyway, so transitions from hover taxi to running takeoff putting that whiteout takeoff behind me happened quickly and naturally. I barely noticed the almost hover whiteout conditions upon departure because we promptly flew out of them.

I kept revisiting in my mind the flight decision. What had possessed me to depart Wonju in the first place? We headed southbound along the river bed. I looked out of my side of the windscreen and realized that I was in total denial about what I was seeing. Save the meandering river flowing southbound, all I saw was white snow covering everything without any definition at all. The mountains that surround this valley were all white, and they disappeared at 700 feet into the clouds and snow. Moisture in these freezing conditions invites ice. Below 700 feet, there were no snow showers. Check, no precipitation and ice, I thought to myself.

I was flying in icing temps, but as long as I stayed out of any rain of any kind, snow included, then I was legal to fly. We did have 700 feet just like the weather guys said, and though it was difficult to judge with all the white snow out there, I am guessing that we had the 2 miles that the SOP called for. So far, so good. We were in the air and flying south along the Wonju Valley. I could clearly see the river. Given the lack of definition from the snow on the ground and mountains, the river is all I could see. All we had to do was follow the river through the southern cut in the mountains, make the right turn at the Wonju highway and the left turn on the Seoul Pusan Highway, and we would have for the most part beat the storm. I was glad to have that plan in my head. I was fighting off fear and trying to replace it with proper cockpit management. Sure the weather sucked outside, but it did not suck in here. All things were going as planned; everything was orderly and calm. Things were manageable.

I was on the controls for the departure and soon planned to pass the controls to the LT. I wanted to look at the radio setup and confirm that the LT had updated Poncho in the no. 2 position. I also wanted to forward plan and get other go-to frequencies in place just in case we got into any trouble. I wanted to establish our route of flight and start a fuel check before passing the controls. One typically flies the cyclic with their right hand, leaving the left hand dedicated to the collective. Because I am right-handed, I choose to attach my kneeboard on my right leg. To record my fuel check, I bound the collective in place with my left knee and took the cyclic in my left hand, freeing my right hand to record the fuel check. I quickly double-pushed the stem of the eight-day clock, then another push to start the second hand running. I promptly log 1,000 pounds of fuel on my kneeboard at the top of the hour.

I called that number out and confirmed that the LT recorded the same thing. 1,000 pounds, I thought. I would have liked to have more fuel than 1,000 pounds. Running the engine waiting on the VIPs hurt our fuel status for sure. Usually, the Huey burns 600 pounds of fuel an hour. Some quick math at 1,000 pounds puts us less than a 2-hour flight. Following the highway makes the flight usually a 1-hour flight. Had we gone direct, it would have been a 45-minute flight. I needed to follow the highway so that I would have the definition of the road against the snow conditions, so I elected to say with the valley to join the motorway. It would have been better to have a full bag of gas, but we can still do the mission with 1,000 pounds. We would closely monitor the fuel burn along the way. If we needed to divert for fuel, we could divert to K16, Seoul Air Base. I do not want to put that into play unless we have to. With the crappy weather, diverting to another Korean air base was not ideal. K16 happens to be one of the Koreans big bases, so that was a plus. In size, it is their Osan Air Base. That thought was comforting. We will see how things shake out as the flight continues.

I felt okay. I had talked myself off the fear ledge, so I passed the controls to the LT. There is something of a ritual involved in passing the controls. A human must fly the Huey at all times. It is a very forgiving aircraft, but it does require flight control manipulation all the time. The Huey has no computer to control the aircraft, there is no autopilot. There is, however, force trim. Force trim is a pilot aid. Force trim, when engaged, will hold the cyclic in place relieving the pilot on the controls. That does not mean that the force trim flies the aircraft. If just means that the cyclic will remain at the last station referenced by the pilot. In flight, even the slightest bit of air movement about the aircraft will affect the aircraft, and if the pilot is not paying attention, the aircraft will develop a roll. I only use force trim in instrument flight. In VFR conditions, not so much.

So when I passed the controls to the LT this is how the ritual is played out; I stated to the LT, "You have the controls."

She responded, "I have the controls."

Then I complete the transaction by repeating, "You have the controls." That ritual of, "you have the controls, I have the controls, you have the controls" is taught to us in flight school and, frankly, is a smart thing to follow. They show us a bunch of great stuff at Fort Rucker, and over time in the field, some of that stuff trained may become tempered with best field practices, always ruled by the ATM of course. The ritual of passing the controls remains unchanged and in place to this day. That is how important it is to ensure that someone is always responsible for motor skilling the flight controls.

Once I passed the controls to the LT, I directed, "Give us your best altitude and fly the river. Eighty knots is a good airspeed. I am going to be inside the cockpit for a few working the radios."

"Roger," she replied. "I'm outside. Dean, concerning our cloud clearances, are we repeating our flight up by keeping the rotor just under the ceiling?" She astonished me. Should I drag the skids along the ground to maintain FAA cloud clearances? I did not want to be cross, so I kept that emotion to myself.

"LT, fly the river, keep the rotor just under the ceiling. We have 700 feet working for us. Let's break the cloud clearance rule as safety as we can for the conditions." I tried hard not to be cross. Indeed, I was not mad, but I was irritated that we should be having that sort of conversation. Cloud clearance, really. The best we had was 700 feet. Okay, I didn't need to be reminded that we were not in compliance with FAA cloud clearance requirements. To her credit, however, I am glad that she at least considered them.

If I could have replayed the entire day, I would have refused the mission for weather in the first place and had been done with it. Fact, I didn't. So here we are stuck. Cloud clearances? Now there is a conversation to have with the IPs when I get back. How does the SOP play into and consider the FAA cloud clearance requirements? In the FAA world, above 10,000 feet, the cloud clearance is 5 miles visibility, 1,000 above and 1,000 below the cloud with a 1-mile vertical separation of clouds, otherwise known as 5111. Below 10,000 and in controlled airspace, the cloud clearance is 3 miles visibility, 2,000 feet above and 1,000 feet below, with 500 feet vertical separation of clouds, otherwise known as 3215. And finally, the uncontrolled airspace is very similar to the controlled airspace definition. The difference between the two is its visibility. Uncontrolled airspace is one-mile visibility. The remaining clearances are identical to controlled airspace. Uncontrolled airspace then finishes out with 2,000 feet above and 1,000 feet below with 500 feet vertical separation, otherwise known as 1215. Unit SOP definitely trumps all others, so I am going with the SOP. The commander has determined that he needs 700-2 to launch his aircraft and complete his assigned missions. We have launched from Wonju, and we are definitely flying in 700-2 conditions. I felt pretty good about digesting that. 700-2 is good.

While I was inside working the radios, we progressed along the valleys floor slowly. I passed the controls, holding the airspeed of no more than eighty knots indicated airspeed (KIAS). The LT was doing a good job. She was maintaining the slow airspeed. The great thing about a helicopter and lousy weather is that if you find yourself in real trouble, you can simply slow your forward airspeed all the way to a hover if need be and safely negotiate the aircraft to the ground and wait out a storm. That fact was buried way back in my line of thinking. It was still okay to fly. After all, I was trained to be an all-weather, day/night army aviator. Surely a little snow was not going to drive me to make an emergency landing for weather? We had 700-2 weather, the LT rightly was poking along at eighty KIAS, and I successfully confirmed that the LT had dialed up Poncho at 327.125. What could go wrong?

CHAPTER 10

Six Hours before Going into IMC

*23 December 1982, ROK. 0600 In Red
Baron Operations Building.*

I graduated flight school in January of 1982, and after a thirty-day leave arrived in the ROK in February. Ten exciting months later, I was becoming a short-timer. Upon my initial assignment, like everyone else, I arrived in the ROK by way of Osan Air Force Base. While at Osan awaiting follow-on orders, assignment personnel arrived at Osan and began to sort through the one hundred or so newly arrived soldiers. I observed a staff sergeant (SSG) and a butter-bar lieutenant (2LT) armed with clipboards quickly finding those that were either assigned to units or who they thought would be great candidates to go to the Second Infantry Division (2ID). They were shopping really, and the shopping was good. Going to the 2ID was not a good thing. That was duty way up north on the demilitarized zone (DMZ). The harsh conditions of the 2ID were well known and, as if it would do any good, everyone that the SSG and 2LT looked at quickly began to turn away from their gaze and tried to melt into the crowd, hoping they would select others rather than them, me too. I quickly learned it was hopeless. The 2LT saw my WO1 Bar right off, and the deal was sealed; I was headed for the 2ID. From Osan, the 2ID bussed me and others to Seoul, otherwise known as H201, for my assignment and placement into a line company within the 2ID. As a soldier, I had long learned not to question the orders, I just went where I was told to go. In reality, I was really assigned to an aviation lift company called 201st Aviation Company (Assault Helicopter), the Red Barons at Camp Humphrey, which we affectionately called the Hump, comprising of two platoons of Huey helicopters, the UH-1H.

I loved the Huey. It was easy to fly and very forgiving. The unit had a huge World War I Red Baron model biplane for their mascot. It had a wingspan of five feet. It was pretty cool. One could easily imagine the World War I Red Baron flying in. The unit was as proud of that model as if it were a real aircraft. It hung in the officer's club at Camp Humphreys over our designated table. I knew nothing of that, however, because the 2ID had cleverly whisked me away to the north. This was my first assignment as an officer. I was very excited. While I was moving north, I was told to find H201 and to wait at H201. H201, I later discovered, was just a small landing pad south of Seoul and north of the Han River with some administrative offices. Wasn't told anything else but to wait. And so I did. I didn't know it then, but our executive officer (XO), who also happened to be the operations officer, a captain, and his crew, had found out about the hijack and was flying up from Camp Humphreys to fetch me back to Camp Humphreys. He was not happy at all. The 2ID was very good at spiriting away soldiers newly arrived in country, and our XO was having none of it this day. I was just waiting like I was told at H201.

Not long after arriving at H201, I heard the familiar sound of an approaching Huey that seemed to be lining up for a landing at H201. I always loved to watch these marvels fly through the sky ways. I was imagining myself at the controls making the landing. I had heard hundreds of times from my IPs in flight school, "Okay, candidate, where are you planning to touchdown?"

"At the Maltese," was always a safe answer.

"Okay, once you find your point of intended landing at eye level to the windscreen, intercept that angle and maintain your angle with collective. Continue to adjust your apparent rate of closure with cyclic. With your pedals, keep the aircraft in trim, and when arriving at fifty feet AGL, align your heading with pedals and adjust your controls to effect a smooth touchdown," the IPs would always say. The exact same procedure for landing a helicopter seems to be universal. Fort Rucker does an excellent job in converting all the wannabe aviators into real aviators. I was one of their products and was proud of it.

I was watching the approaching Huey and was going over all that in my mind's eye. In my mind, I was all but flying the Huey that was landing at H201. It was a great mental exercise. Watching the aircraft all the way to the ground, I amused myself thinking that I had made a pretty good landing. Watching the Huey now landed, I wondered what their mission was. It remained on the pad for an awfully long time. Then without warning, it moved off the pad to a grassy area just to the east of the pad. I looked to the sky wondering if it moved to make way for another landing aircraft. There was nothing in the sky that I could see. Then I heard the crew lower the throttle from flight idle to engine idle and saw a soldier get out of the back. Tossing his headset to the CE as he departed the running aircraft, he began to make his way to the headquarters building where I was standing. He was a trim gentleman and walked as if he had someplace to be and was late getting there. He had a notepad that he took from his back pocket, opened it, and looked at me once he got close enough. I knew something was up.

I wondered if I had done something wrong when all of a sudden, he barked, "You Doudna?"

"Yes, sir," I replied as I stood at attention and saluted.

"See that Huey out there?" he said.

"Yes, sir," I quickly answered.

"Get yourself and your bags on that aircraft right now, I will be right there."

Without waiting for my reply, he was gone in a flurry. When a captain tells you to move, you move. I approached the Huey, and the crew chief saluted, grabbed my bags, and threw them on board and hollered over the rotor for me to get in and buckle up. I was pretty sure that I was either being kidnapped or rescued, wasn't sure what was which at the time, but I was up for the adventure. It was not long before the captain joined us, and off we departed for the Hump.

Entering into operations the morning of our mission to Wonju, I fondly thought back to the rescue flight ten months prior and smiled as I looked over at Captain Rushing. The unit was very fortunate, indeed. He had extended his tour for another tour. He was being considered for promotion to major and wanted the command time. His time spent as the operations officer as well as the XO would be a great help to his promotion and career. He was on a call to the States, guessing the upcoming promotion, and just threw up his hand and pointed at the mission board. Thinking of my forthcoming permanent change of station (PCS) in February and subsequent move with the family to Fort Carson, Colorado, I considered not taking the mission. But that move was still many months off. I shook off what I was feeling and elected to keep my head in the game, almost Christmas Eve or not, I was taking the mission. Actually, it was December 23, and that was close enough. HQ had assigned the mission, and I intended to carry it out.

After packing up those earlier remembrances, I began to review the mission sheet. The operations board led with team spirit coordination and transport of three PAXs to Wonju. All that information matched the mission sheet that I had been given the night prior. Okay, we were to fly an aviation major up to Wonju and an American major general as well as a Korean rear admiral to begin team spirit coordination. The major was the aviation asset assigned to the flag officers. The officers were assigned to Osan, but due to a mission change, they would join us early thirty on the Humphreys ramp for the departure to Wonju. Gratefully and, against all odds, our operations officer secured a mission adjustment for weather allowing for an earlier departure from the Hump rather than Osan. That mission change was prophetically helpful.

Every year, the United States and Korea would jointly conduct simulated combat operations called Team Spirit. For this mission, I was just the taxi driver responsible for getting my crew, the aircraft, and PAXs to Wonju. The flight was very routine. With our three PAXs, we needed three headsets. Instead, we were issued only one headset. I tried to interrupt Captain Rushing's phone call to ask about the other headsets. He was having nothing of it. I made a decision to go with the one headset that we had. We were in the army, after all. The CE would make the best decision as to who got the single headset. The flight was just a little over an hour when flowing the roads. Direct it was forty-five minutes or so. I preferred flying direct, but since we were flying with a low ceiling, I elected not to go cross country, but instead, I decided on following along Route 1 northward that ran north and south then turn eastbound along Route 2 that ran east and west. Twenty minutes after traveling east along Route 2, we would begin a northern leg and fly along the river into the Wonju valley and on to Wonju.

On a 1000-3 VFR day, it would have been quite beautiful. This morning, however, we had only a 700-foot ceiling with 2 miles visibility, so the trip would be short on sightseeing but long on some decent training. The mountains all around Wonju are 3,500 feet, and a river runs north and south along the western side of the Wonju Valley. The only relief from the Wonju Mountains is a north-south river and a two-lane road that wanders alongside. Piece of cake mission, I thought. I had been in the Wonju Valley many times and, save the weather, foresaw no real difficulty for the mission. An hour and some change for the flight up, grab lunch while the general officers work Team Spirit, reverse flight back, return the PAXs to Osan, put the helicopter to bed, end of mission (EOM). What could be easier? The operations board had assigned Helicopter 67-15782 to the mission. I knew that aircraft. Lots of avionics issues as I remember. 2LT Susan Boyle was my assigned copilot. 2LT Boyle was newly assigned to the unit. She had just completed her aviator readiness level (ARL) progression. Interesting factoid, when a new aviator is assigned to an army unit, the commander's guide requires that he, or she as the case may be, demonstrate their ability to fly a helicopter to standard to one of the units IPs. The ride is designed to evaluate his or her ability to perform cockpit duties. Depending on the aviators' experience level, it can be as simple as a records check all the way to many training flights followed by a check-ride. As recent graduates of the flight program, we newly minted aviators always drew the extended version. To the best of my knowledge, 2LT Boyle did okay with the ARL progression. Just looking at the mission board, I would not have known anything to the contrary. What I did know, however, was that this was her first mission in country. So she had to have been successful in demonstrating her abilities during ARL progression. I'm guessing she was selected because we were so close to the holidays. Lots of folks were either on leave or just enjoying some well-earned downtime. I love the military. Work hard, play hard as the saying goes. We were a lift unit. Assault may have been in our official name, but we did more utility missions than assault missions. When we did insert the Koreans and American soldiers into landing zones. Considerable energies were expended—work hard. When we're able to step away from the GI Joe stuff, we played hard. Except for the possibility of getting stuck somewhere, I had no issues flying this close to the holidays. The mission was pretty straightforward. I was ready to fly.

CHAPTER 11

My Co-Pilot Reports, "Mercy"

23 December 1982, ROK. Somewhere South of Wonju.

I had finished confirming that the radios were set correctly. A necessary action should we need to communicate quickly. Looking outside, I was made satisfied that the LT was poking along at a slow airspeed, remaining just below the ceiling and following the river. Things were manageable. I moved my scan from the river along the mountains to the sky in one continuous scan and realized again that I could not differentiate between the surface of the earth and the sky conditions. It was like trying to peer through very sheer white lace fabric that was covering a white floor and reaching up to a white wall and ceiling. The background, as well as the foreground, was blending together.

I felt a prompting from the Holy Spirit. We were in real trouble, but I did not know what to do with the prompting. I rotated and twisted my body to the left in my seat against my seatbelt and shoulder restraints so that I could better communicate with MAJ. Burns. I could have just keyed the mic, but I wanted to see his facial expression while I was talking to him. I had planned to tell MAJ Burns, who was sitting in one of the two jump seats facing forward, that the weather was not going to allow us to continue. I wanted a couple of things from him. I wanted affirmation for my decision, and

I wanted him to brief the flag officers that we were turning around and to prepare for a RON. While I was twisted in my seat, I never got to articulate one word because the LT interrupted me when she shouted. "*Mercy!*"

Many phrases are routinely used in the cockpit. Accomplished and experienced crews practice constructive communication whenever flying. When miscommunication occurs, it undoubtedly becomes causal errors found during a review of every aircraft accident investigation. There was an entire block of instruction dedicated to cockpit communication in flight school. I remember being lulled to sleep by the academic instructors as they droned on how crewmembers are to communicate and that words should be carefully selected. "Are the words action words or are the words just informative?" they would rightly say. They taught that minimizing personal comments in the cockpit during peak workloads, such as takeoffs and landings, is an excellent thing. I thought the academic instructors nailed that part of the block. Maybe there should have been a discussion dedicated to how PICs respond to crewmembers who deviate from industry standards? John and I, another candidate in my flight class, were the only combat veterans of our flight class. John and my combat service were mutually shared between as well as our in-service time. We were both over ten years in army aviation service and combat vets. As measured by John and my service standards, our other flight school classmates were just babies in the military. Still, with all that exposure to army aviation, I thought that block of instruction on communication was long on an academic standard and short on real-world application. I mean if it was clear blue and twenty-two out, I could have cared less what words the LT had chosen to describe what she was seeing. But we were not clear blue and twenty-two, we were in minimal weather conditions, and tensions were very high. The word "mercy" did not get my attention. Upon hearing it, I did not think mercy to be an action word. I was having difficulty determining what sort of information word "mercy" really was. The word did, however, interrupt the conversation that I was about to have with MAJ Burns. I elected to turn in my seat back to the front and investigate the meaning of the word mercy. While I was turning from my left to my right, and seeing the LT in the left seat, I could not help but notice that the LT was frozen on the controls. As I continued to rotate my torso entirely to the front and scan the windscreen, I immediately understood. All I saw out through the windscreen was white. We had flown into a snow shower. Mercy, I realized, was an action word!

CHAPTER 12

Seconds into Inadvertent Meteorological Conditions (IMC)

23 December 1982, ROK. Somewhere South of Wonju.

Oh my gosh! What had just happened? I immediately took the controls from the LT. While doing so, I shouted, "I have the controls." Contrary to cockpit protocol, there was no response from the LT. My terror meter just pegged out. We were IMC in a valley! Seconds ticked by. I held my breath, and then as quickly as we entered, we were back out flying in our previous conditions. Since we were out of IMC, *amen* is all I could think of. Thank you, God. I just held onto the controls to calm myself. We were flying. We had not flown into the mountains nor had we flown into the ground. Let's not forget I have two failed or precessing gyros to manage. Thus far, we were still alive. 80 KIAS. Flying just below the 700-foot ceiling. The breath I had just taken felt better than the one I had taken before. Still alive. Still able to reason. I had good reason to fear up. I was responsible for the crewmembers and PAXs. It was my responsibility to get them home safely. I owed that to their families. They needed me to figure this out. I would love to have a freeze button in the cockpit to push right now. But I didn't. I needed to fix this on the fly all while moving along at 80 KIAS, just below the ceiling. Just land, how hard can that be, I pondered applying the helicopter's best option of slowing down and landing escaped my reasoning, or at least it was so low on the priority I had mistakenly displaced that reasoning. I did think about landing but reasoned it out. I was getting nothing from the LT either. To her credit, I have to remark that there was not a lot of conversation anyway. I was still lost in thought as to what I was going to do next.

I remembered the -1 and the TEMPO weather observation that Brad had given before we departed from Wonju. I needed to review that briefing. I passed the controls back to the LT. "You have the controls," I said.

"I have the controls," she responded.

"You have the controls," I finished up. "Okay, LT, keep that river in sight. That river will take you southernly toward the split in the valley. You cannot see it with this mess we are flying in, but trust me, the split in the valley is there. Once we go through that split, we will make a right turn and head westerly along the Wonju highway." I knew I had already given her those instructions, but it made me feel better to repeat them out loud. "I'm inside the aircraft, you have the outside. Keep us on course."

"Roger," she responded.

Once again, I came back inside the aircraft and began to root around in my flight bag for the -1 Brad had issued us. Relieved to have found it I retrieved the -1 from my flight bag. After a quick review, I choked, gasped, and had trouble containing the fear that was overcoming me as I realized what I was reading. Don't panic, I told myself.

Calm heads can figure things out, just don't panic. I reread predominate weather in block 26-31 of the -1, that said, RKNW 0200-0300Z VRB06 7 SCT004 OVC010 30.20 -05 72. Flyable, But I forgot the TEMPO. The TEMPO condition was clearly stated following the predominate weather line. It read, TEMPO 0200-0300Z 1 SHSN BKN005 OVC010. The words now have a real impact. I realized that we had just flown through the 1-mile visibility with snow showers as well as experienced the broken ceiling at 500 feet. I didn't care about the overcast altitude at 1,000 feet since I was not going to be able to get to that altitude anyway. Oh my gosh. It was a snow shower we had flown through. If there was one, there could be another. God help me.

TEMPO conditions are just that, temporary. Army Regulation 95-1 is the gold standard regulation for all army aviators who fly army aircraft, rotary or fixed-wing. The AR 95-1 tells me that I follow predominate weather. I honestly do not remember what it said to the TEMPO conditions. Silent? Did it really matter? We were out here in it now. No matter now. I was in a pickle. The 95-1 was academic at this point. I did not fly through a page and paragraph number, I flew through a real snow shower. Even if I could recall what the 95-1 says to TEMPO conditions, what matter would it make? As I glanced outside, I still saw the weather conditions, and I was fully aware of the peril that I had placed everyone onboard this aircraft into. PICs are supposed to use their best judgment when considering and applying all weather conditions, including TEMPO conditions, when faced with flight into adverse weather conditions. Flight into predominate weather is legal filing weather, I continued to remind myself.

How stupid was I? I was so focused on accomplishing the mission that I failed to use good judgment in deciding to fly in the first place. When I made PIC, my commander made a statement to me that I thought was profound. He said that maturity and judgment were the cornerstone elements that he drew from before elevating an aviator to PIC status. He felt that I possessed maturity and judgment worthy of PIC status. The responsibilities that went along with that decision were not lost on me. I had eleven years to my army aviation credit to date. I understood the responsibility of the flight. All those on my aircraft were under my charge and relied on me to bring my very, very best to the cockpit every time. Today, I may not have brought my very best. Indeed, I failed in exercising the judgment my commander so believed that I possessed. What do I do now? No freeze button today. Real lives to preserve today, and I will preserve those lives if it is the last thing I ever do. We have to turn around and go back to Wonju.

CHAPTER 13

We Have to Return to Wonju

23 December 1982, ROK. Somewhere South of Wonju.

We had to go back. This possibility gave me great concern; if we turn around and fly back to Wonju, we would fly through the same snow shower that we just flew through. We would also be flying north, and there was a considerable front barreling down on us from that very direction. We were not very far south out of Wonju; maybe with a little luck, we could make it back before the front closes everything down. But there was still that snow shower that we would have to negotiate. We survived the snow shower once, could we do so again? It was brief, I reasoned. I believed the risk was worth a run for it. I was arguing with myself the pros and cons of the decision, trying to reason out our best course of action. Done, I decided. We were going back to Wonju. I instantly felt better. It may have been nothing more than a placebo moment for me, but I had made a decision to return to safety, and having a course of action made me feel better. I studied the terrain as well as the weather conditions to our immediate front. Same, still bad. Unknown conditions south, known conditions north. Going back seemed like the best thing to do.

"LT, I am back inside. I am going to turn around and brief our PAXs that we are going to return to Wonju. Continue along the river. I will be back with you in a couple of minutes."

"Roger," she said. Maybe I should have picked up some cues from her performance thus far. Everyone knows I had made some foolish decisions today, but I was still engaged. If I were copiloting with another PIC, I would have been pretty chatty. Who, what, when, where, why, and how quickly come to mind. Come to think of it, I had been hearing a lot of "rogers" out of the LT and not a lot of conversational engagements. Crew engagements keep us all honest… and alive.

After finishing with the LT, I again turned in my seat to address the major about my decision to return to Wonju. As I said earlier, the last time I wanted affirmation for my choice, and I wanted him to brief the flag officers that we were turning around and returning to Wonju. This time, however, was different. My decision made, we were turning around. I didn't need a debate nor his approval. I was prepared to take my ass-whooping from the PAXs once we returned safely to Wonju. Now I turned around and in eyeball contact with Major Burns, I was about to let him know my decision when I heard the LT say again, "*Mercy*."

CHAPTER 14

We Reenter IMC

23 December 1982, ROK. Somewhere South of Wonju.

"What are you doing? You are going to kill us," screamed the LT into the intercom. Upon hearing *mercy*, I knew that was her action word. I spun in my seat, leaving MAJ Burns mid-sentence, and I took the controls from her. No time for control passing protocol. 2LT Boyle had learned the same IMC lessons that I had learned in flight school, and even if she was not the PIC, based upon my demonstrated immediate action while entering IMC, the LT knew that I had either flipped out or that I was intentionally trying to crash the helicopter. I was grateful that she was not trying to wrestle the controls from me. She was as terrified as I was. She could quickly have wanted to fight me for the controls. She was so newly minted from flight school that she didn't even know how to disagree with another aviator within a cockpit structure professionally, so she chose not to, and for today's flight, her underperformance may well have saved our lives. I didn't need her fighting me for the controls. The LT had no idea that I was as terrified as she was, but I was steadying myself. We had a lot of flying yet to come. Unlike her, I simply could not allow my terror to manifest. I had to command the helicopter. I was responsible for the welfare of the crew and passengers. Aside from the calamity upon us, I was working on my own issues. We were both newly minted aviators. I only had ten months on her. Right now, those ten months felt like a lifetime. As compared to a stateside assignment, I volunteered to come to the ROK because I knew that I would advance quickly. The ROK had real-world missions, and the entire tour of duty was compacted into a one-year envelope. Since I was prior service, I felt like I needed a fast track. I was busy catching up.

I graduated Warrant Officer Candidate (WOC) Training I with class 81-11. After WOC training, I entered the Initial Entry Rotor Wing (IERW) flight program and joined fifty-six other wannabe candidates. Together, we made up the flight class 81-27, Orange Flight. A year later, when we graduated those fifty-six candidates that we started with on start day had been reduced to thirty-six other candidates, and on graduation day, flight class 81-27, Orange Flight, birthed thirty-six graduates who were appointed as warrant officer (WO1). Of the thirty-six graduates, I was among thirteen original class members. Meaning that, from start day to finish day, thirteen of us survived both WOC Class 81-11 and IERW flight class 81-27 training without being recycled. Because of my enlisted time, I found myself consistently in leadership roles during WOC and IERW. The only bragging rights that I really cared about from flight school was that I made the program without being recycled. I was grateful to be in that small group of persons. Not counting holidays, each IERW flight class was programmed for eleven months of intense flight training. Depending upon individual circumstances, during the lifecycle of a flight class, the class size may swell or shrink. For one reason or another, our class roll-call adjusted by twenty-three other WOCs along the way. Each time a flight class size changed its size, it caused an administrative train wreck for the class behind. A recycled IERW student would bump a student, and that shuffle would reverberate throughout the system and create havoc for the cadre as well as the students. It never seemed to stop, and the process seemed to have something of a life of its own.

Flight deficiencies, by far, were the most common reason for a candidate to be recycled. Becoming recycled was not a badge of honor. Some were recycled for medical reasons, sprains and or fractures the most common reason to be medically recycled. I narrowly escaped being recycled during flight school for an injury myself. During contact flight training, training devised to introduce a student to the flight characters of the helicopter, I stepped irregularly off the right side of a Huey that I was preflighting for that day's flight and badly twisted my ankle. Oh my gosh, did it ever hurt. Since my limp caught the IPs attention, I was not successful in keeping it from my IP. Not only is he a trained IP but also prepared to watch for anything that may inhibit a flight student from motor-skilling the helicopters flight controls.

"What's up with the limp, candidate?" the IP was quick to ask.

I was caught and felt the weight of my career as I summoned all my courage to respond. "Boot lacings to lose, Sir," I said.

"Fix it," he retorted, not having time to get into it further. Well, I did fix it. I laced those boots so tight that I thought the laces would break. With my combat boots now very ridged, they steadied my weakened ankle and got me through the flight period. I suffered in silence with each push of the helicopter's tail rotor pedals. Funny now as I look back and realize how many times I would repeat that kind of pain management throughout my career.

Graduated now with all the flight training behind me, and no longer a WOC but a real WO1 and PIC responsible for the conduct of my mission, all the bragging rights that I had earned in the IERW program meant diddly squat right here in the here and now. I found myself in a fight for my life as well as the lives for whom I was responsible. While fully engulfed in my first real emergency procedure, an emergency procedure that was totally my fault by the by, one had to wonder as to how I ever made it through the IERW program. Just before graduation, my class drew assignments that scattered us all across the Continental United States (CONUS) and two to the ROK. I did not hold one of the two assignments to the ROK; instead, I drew a transfer to Fort Bragg, North Carolina. I did not want to go to Fort Bragg.

I wanted to go to the ROK. A tour to the ROK was a one-year unaccompanied tour, which meant that only the soldier deployed while the family stayed in the States. I love my family and did not want to be separated from them, but this was a chance of a lifetime, and I had to take it. I remember well that day when I stood amongst my classmates holding my Fort Bragg orders high in the air like a trader on the New York stock market exchange floor and shouted, "Got a Bragg assignment here. Anyone looking to trade for a ROK tour?" I knew there were two guys out there that had orders to the ROK. Well, it did not take long for either of them to realize that they had an out for their ROK assignment. Both classmates holding the ROK orders charged at me from either side of the assembly area that we had mustered in. You could see the drama play out as each tried to get to me first. The class began to make room and were shouting as a hole was made for each WO1 turned sprinter to pass. The drama of the moment was not lost on anyone. In the end, the WO1 who was farther away got to me first.

Wish I could remember his name. It is lost now to time, but he grabbed my arm with a death grip and was not letting me go. The two of us made our way over to our Training Advising and Counseling (TAC) Officer so that we could trade assignments. Since we were both WO1s, we both possessed the same military occupation skill (MOS) (100B) IERW skill set, and it mattered not to the army the name of the assigned officer, only that an able-bodied 100B WO1 fill the slot. My TAC officer was interested in why I wanted so badly to go to the ROK. He knew I was a prior-enlisted soldier and presumed that I knew what I was getting myself into. I did.

I entered IERW from the army's enlisted ranks. I was a promotable staff sergeant (E6P), which meant that if I just waited out the promotion list that I would soon be promoted to sergeant first class (E7). My enlisted MOS was a 67W30. That meant I was an aircraft quality control supervisor and aircraft inspector. To date, I had invested ten years in the army. I had become an accomplished aircraft mechanic and inspector. I knew my craft well and was ready to move from the back seat into the front seat. I applied for and, much to my surprise, was accepted into the IERW program. I was elated. Knowing what I knew of an army flight line, I knew that everything was accelerated in the ROK, which is why I wanted to swap orders with whoever was willing to do so.

Compressed indeed, four months into my twelve-month tour of duty, I had earned PIC status. Earning PIC status at Fort Bragg would have taken a year and a half easy. Today, and now IMC, a lot of things had gone horrifically wrong. Even I had to wonder how I got signed off for PIC status so quickly. During this mission, I had made some serious errors. I had to take full ownership of that. I was determined that not a single soul would be lost this day. How long could I take the stress and maintain control? God help me, please.

"Standby, standby, standby" was all that I could say to my copilot as I took the controls from her. Where did that calmness come from, I wondered? I wanted to puke, yet I had said it so calmly, so reassuringly. Even I felt better, and I found that I could not stop saying it. I was a mess of emotions, but those words seemed to work. I was wondering all the while if the LT would consider wrestling the controls away from me. What was she thinking, I had to wonder. If she was considering challenging me for the controls, she never let whatever she was thinking translate into action. But I had no time to think about that now. I had to work through my IMC denial before I could really begin the process of aircraft recovery. It took five full seconds for me to say anything at all after entering IMC, and "standby" was the best that I could muster…and it worked at keeping everyone in a calm demeanor.

The freeze button fantasy was a safe thought. In the simulator, we often pushed the freeze button. My actions were always critiqued and debated. My IP did an excellent job of developing training to fit the circumstance of the flight. When something was amiss, a touch of the freeze button would allow for review. In flight school, we spent hours and hours flying approaches under the watchful and critical eye of the IP. Attitude, heading, torque, airspeed, and recovery" was the IMC emergency procedure that was drilled into our very being.

"Attitude, heading, torque, airspeed, and recovery, attitude, heading, torque, airspeed and recovery," he would drone on and on while in the simulator. With each word that the IP spoke, he would extend a pointer and reinforce and associate each word with its corresponding instrument. "Attitude" and the attitude indicator got a snappy tap with his pointer. Upon entering IMC, the IP expected to see wings level on that attitude indicator. "Heading" and the heading indicator became the next object of his attention. The IP was reinforcing the need and importance for a constant heading. "Torque." Not only could I feel him pull up on the collective, but the torque gauge also got some pointer consideration. The IP expected to see a snappy climb, so the torque gauge and vertical speed indicator got a few taps as well. "Airspeed." Then I could feel the IP help me adjust the cyclic forward all while tapping the airspeed indicator. What he expected to see was an adjustment of the cyclic to drive the aircraft to proper airspeed management. This was my big flaw. Like most students, I always sucked the cyclic into my gut. It was natural, he would remind me over and over again.

"At first, most do that, pull the cyclic into your gut thing," he would say. Not an aggressive adjustment mind you but slowly and steadily pulling the cyclic aft. "Fear is absolutely normal," the IP told me time and time again, but we have to recognize fear for what it is, work through it, and believe in your instruments and fight through the fear so that you are prepared and ready to make rational decisions. "Simple mechanics," he said. "It's a fight or flight emotion that most humans deal with when challenged," he said over and over. "Army aviators," he reminded me, "fought through the fear...period!"

"Recovery. Okay, Candidate Doudna, how and where are we going to recover?" asked the IP. I always looked up. "Nothing for you in the windscreens candidate," remarked the IP. Nothing was ever in the windscreens I quickly learned while in the simulators. All the action was with the instruments. My IP would talk me through the many varied approaches that were at my disposal, and by the end of the simulator training period, we always recovered somewhere.

Today's flight in the Wonju valley was not a flight training simulation. Not a training exercise at all. This was the real deal, and I was the PIC. What have I done? I have surely killed us. "Standby," I heard myself say again to the LT I was doing the best I could to compartmentalize my emotions. Focus, Doudna, focus.

On the one hand, I was very grateful that the LT had not begun to wrestle the controls from me. She knew full well that I was not exercising the proper IMC emergency procedure. The appropriate emergency procedure for IMC was…don't go IMC. But if the worst happens, attitude, heading, torque, airspeed, and recovery is the prescribed emergency procedure…or not.

CHAPTER 15

Three Minutes into IMC

23 December 1982, ROK. Somewhere South of Wonju.

"Stand by, stand by, stand by," I continued to say to the LT while combating her very vocal attacks.

"Why are you banking the aircraft? What about the attitude? And our airspeed? Stop it!" she kept shouting.

Again I said, "Stand by, stand by, stand by." I calmly squeezed the mic switch on the cyclic to the first indent so that the comms would stay inside the aircraft rather than be transmitted outside. My own calmness with the comms surprised even me. I could take her shouting, but I could not tolerate a fight for the controls. Had I been in her shoes, I would have thought that the PIC flipped out and would have addressed who needed to be flying the aircraft, but surprisingly, she did not. She felt volume was enough to combat my perceived foolishness. She didn't need to key her mic; I could hear her screaming at me just fine.

We were not out of control at all. We were IMC in a valley! I had no idea where in the valley we were, and frankly, I had no time to break down for her why I had elected to modify the emergency procedure. What I needed to do immediately was to keep us alive. I would break down the emergency procedure modification as soon as I had time. Until then, I was grateful that she was only vocal and not trying to take the controls from me as I elected to lay the aircraft over on its side with the cyclic and pull the collective with all that I had. We were corkscrewing up. At this point, safety is in altitude, and right now, I wanted plenty of altitude.

I had not flipped out at all, although I did want to puke. I fought that back just like I fought back the fear. Finally, I stopped saying standby and very abruptly took my left hand off the collective and rotated my own C-1611's selector to the number two position and made the most crucial radio call of my entire career. Squeezing the mic switch on the cyclic to the second detent, I peacefully and professionally transmitted the following, "Poncho, Poncho, RB93 inadvertent IMC south of Wonju passing 2,000 feet for 5,000 feet. Request immediate radar vectors for a no-gyro approach to Osan AFB." Oh my gosh, what a relief to get a lifeline out there. My world may have been pretty crappy right now, but getting that lifeline out made all the difference.

Without any hesitation at all, Poncho returned my call. "RB93, climb to 5,000 feet, turn to 245 degrees direct Osan."

"Roger, 5,000 feet, turn 245 degrees direct Osan," I echoed back. I could have burst with excitement. I was overwhelmed and was glad that I still had 3,000 more feet to climb before turning toward Osan. I needed that time to fight back the tears that were welling up inside me as well as get my other emotions in check. With the radio call to Poncho, the LT got quite as she just watched the altimeter tick off the climb. I didn't take time to look at the torque gauge.

I was not only a PIC for my unit, but I was also a maintenance test pilot (MTP). While becoming an MTP, I crossed swords with our standardization pilot, CW3 Stan Help. When I was assigned to the unit, the commander made sure that I went to the maintenance platoon and I flew with CPT Harris, our maintenance officer. During four months' worth of maintenance test flights, he became very impressed with my flying and comprehensive abilities in troubleshooting broken aircraft both while flying and on the ground as well. CPT Harris was well aware of my enlisted maintenance experience and happily trained me. Months later, he was satisfied that I could test fly as good or better than he. He took me to see that commander and asked the commander to sign me off as a test pilot. The commander brought in the standardization officer to confer. Stan was livid. He, as politely as he could muster, told the commander that I was just a WO1; how possibly could he sign me off as a maintenance test pilot? Stan had only barely begun the work of developing me to become a PIC. CPT Harris retorted and reminded the commander that he was losing a test pilot candidate who could rapidly return his aircraft to service if he joined Stan's myopic position by not signing me off. CPT Harris argued that "Dean may be a WO1, but his experience makes him the exception. He has ten years of maintenance experience and comes to his aviator status by way of that background." The commander weighed out each argument and elected to sign me off as an MTP and told Stan to pick up the pace for my PIC training and eventual sign-off. Great for me; I was an MTP three full months before I was a PIC. As an MTP, I was restricted to the traffic pattern and test flight valley. As an MTP, I would regularly test fly aircraft that had been repaired and awaiting their return to service. It was my job as an MTP to certify repairs made by maintainers to the aircraft by taking the aircraft out and shaking the aircraft out. Stan was greatly troubled by the commander's decision to sign me off as an MTP. Actually, I was an excellent MTP. I excelled in the VFR environment. It was just me and the aircraft when I test flew. As an MTP, I am all about the engine instruments and how things would fall. Today, however, was another story. I was fighting through the conditions that I had created for myself. It was enough at this point that I was in a controlled climb, corkscrewing up to my requested altitude. Even though I had an armpit full of collective, the engine was still doing its thing. Did I over-torque the aircraft's engine doing so? At this point, the altitude was enough for me.

CHAPTER 16

The Reality of the Circled Red Xs

23 December 1982, ROK. Somewhere South of Wonju. Five Minutes Into IMC.

At 5,000 feet, I reduced the collective and attempted to level the wings with the cyclic. I was immediately reminded of those circle red x conditions that Ryan had mentioned to me of before we departed. I felt flush. I leveled the wings as best I could with references made to the attitude indicator now fully knowing that the attitude indicator was wildly off. I was trapped. I knew the attitude indicator was off. That, however, was not all I had to work with. Internally, I was raging with conflicts. Trying to work my current dilemma all while being angry with myself for getting us here in the first place. Wondering where in the hell that stupid freeze button was and fully realizing that I was a mess of emotions and was in sensory overload. I didn't dare seek help from the LT…yet, anyway. I knew she was dealing with her own issues. Her first mission and then this happens, wow!

In milliseconds, I began to break down what was happening. I knew that, if I could just understand the problem, with God's help, I could work out a solution. "God help me" was a constant prayer that I offered up. Not a lot of time for a full-blown conversation with

God as I had my hands full, but I knew that I was not alone. Even in the confusion of the moment, that thought gave me comfort. I knew I needed to engage with the LT soon, but first, I needed to understand what was going on. I needed to create and then break down a plan into manageable segments to get us safely home.

I realized that my inner ears sensed that we were still in a turn. There is a host of illusions that were working through me and against me right now. If I did not do something fast, we were going to become a statistic. I desperately searched my memories of my aero-medical training from flight school. I was having difficulty recalling the formal name of the illusions that I was experiencing. I quickly remembered, however, what my instrument IP demonstrated over and over again in actual cloud conditions. Anytime an aviator attempted to fly in cloud by external reference, in other words trying to look outside the aircraft while in cloud, somatogravic and somatogyral illusions would have to be dealt with. It would be much later before I would recall the formal names of these and the other illusions that I was dealing with. But for now, remembering the instrument mechanics, my IP taught me was enough. My IP said some of the illusions affected some more so than others. Apparently, I proved during flight training that I was one of those who was greatly influenced by illusions. I would stray from my instruments and begin to fall prey to one of many illusions that seemed so real. In training, it would not be long into the flight, and I would have us in a spiral. My IP would take the controls, correct the unusual attitude that I had flown us into, and would bark at me and drill me over and over again, "*Believe your instruments, candidate.*"

This Wonju flight was no different. My inner ear was in conflict with what my eyes were seeing. I was trying to reconcile the situational understanding of the aircraft's attitude and speed when I first leveled the wings. The only fix—*trust your instruments*. All humans have an inner ear, and that inner ear communicates with their brains. It is how God wired their use. Particularly during this flight, right now, I had to discard information that my inner ear was sending to my brain. If we were going to live, I had to *trust my instruments*. I had to believe what my eyes were telling me when evaluating what my attitude, altitude, and airspeed indicators were showing me. Not forgetting that my attitude indicator and RMI were precessing and telling me false information. That confusion left me physically sick. God help me. Becoming physically ill is a real side effect of spatial disorientation. Instead of puking, I fought back the sensation and did not get sick. How would that have gone down? PIC throws up while on the controls in IMC! Had to combat that impression too.

To add to the misinformation that my brain was digesting, there also coexisted proprioceptive sensations. You do not have to be a pilot to experience this. All humans experience proprioceptive sensations. Proprioceptive sensations in the aviation business is called seat-of-the-pants flying. And my proprioceptive sensations were raging. I had become a reasonably good seat-of-the-pants aviator. In VFR conditions, it is an excellent skill to develop and master. I could fly almost exclusively from looking outside of the aircraft and not paying much attention to the instruments. On VFR flights, I would glance at the airspeed indicator occasionally to set my airspeed. But once established, my seat-of-the-pants sensations would take over. Using sounds and my seat-of-the-pants sensations, I could tell differences in my airspeed and would correct to my original airspeed to within five knots of the original setting. The same was true for altitude settings. While VFR, I would use the altimeter to confirm and set my altitude, but once arrived at the altitude, I rarely referenced the gauge again.

I was able to sense altitude changes to within fifty feet. I did so by looking and sensing what was going on outside. The attitude of the aircraft was always referenced by viewing the horizon through the windscreen. Frankly, I thought that my seat-of-the-pants flying could get me through anything. But now IMC, flying proprioceptively (seat-of-the-pants) was also at war with the inner ear. My inner ear was at war with the somatogravic and somatogyral illusions, and regrettably, I found myself caught in a vicious cycle. I had to believe my instruments. Should I believe my eyes? The instruments that I were seeing were precessing—giving me false information. Should I believe my inner ears? They were spinning still and, like my instruments, sending incorrect information to my brain. Should I believe or even consider my seat-of-the-pants flying signals? If VFR, no problem, but I was IMC and could see nothing out of the windscreen. So I return to the two primary instruments, attitude indicator, and RMI that were both precessing. If we were going to live, I had to discard my natural sensations, the same feelings that God wires all humans with, and believe the instruments. You know those two broken ones. Try that out for size. How do you unplug wires in your brain and consider what your eyes are telling you? Frankly, my seat-of-the-pants sensations made me a good aviator in VFR conditions. Discarding the signals because of the somatogravic and somatogyral illusions and the seat-of-the-pants feelings became the greatest challenge of my young aviator career. All with failing gyros, yet it became the most important thing I had to do, and I only had seconds to do so. God help me.

CHAPTER 17

A Pilots Technique Is
Discovered and Developed

*23 December 1982, ROK. Somewhere South
of Wonju. Six Minutes into IMC.*

Spending all that time, purposefully spiraling up to 5,000 feet was a real blessing. This long in cloud without reliable instrument guidance typically would have resulted in a crash. Because the upward spiral was so controlled, the climb to altitude bought me some time to figure things out. The first instrument that I went to was the turn and slip indicator. This instrument has a vertical bar that freely moves left and right. There is a fixed marker at the twelve o'clock position customarily referred to as the doghouse. On the bottom of the instrument's face was a black ball trapped in fluid. The fluid tube houses a black ball and looks sort of like a carpenter's level, except either side of the fluid tube was tilted up ever so slightly, making a slight smile. When the pilot correctly adjusts the tail rotor pedals to an in-trim position, the ball would then be centered. If the black ball were to the right of the center, then that told the pilot to push the right pedal to return the black ball to center. The same is true if the black ball is on the left side. We call that stepping on the ball. Doing so places the aircraft in trim. Flying in trim was a primary flight fundamental. Keeping the aircraft in trim made the aircraft much more efficient. Therefore, the aircraft did not work as hard. The aerodynamic drag and fuel burn is also optimized when the aircraft is in trim. The turn-and-slip gauge has a heading component as well as a trim component. Using this gauge to remain on a selected heading was quickly done by placing the gauges freely moving bar under the center dog house. While the freely moving bar was under the middle of the dog house, the aircraft would maintain an assigned heading. This was a backup instrument, as the RMI was primarily used for heading control. The RMI was also backed up by the mag compass. I am sure that the nickname of dog house at the top of the turn-and-slip gauge came from student pilots whose experiences with their IPs landed them in the doghouse. Just keep the bar in the center doghouse to stay out of the doghouse with the IP, I suppose the conversation went. There were also markers on either side of the doghouse that indicated a four-minute turn. When the cyclic was displaced laterally, the aircraft would bank in the direction the cyclic was moved. To maintain a coordinated turn, the cyclic remained neutral during the bank. Meaning neither moving the cyclic left or right nor forward or rearward. Doing so meant the aircraft would neither accelerate nor decelerate. A coordinated turn would be confirmed when one witnessed the black ball centered in the fluid tube just below the center doghouse and bar. The doghouse and the freely moving bar and ball trapped in the fluid were all in one instrument called the turn-and-slip indicator.

To keep from flying into a mountainside, I deliberately corkscrewed upward. At 5,000 feet, I leveled off. At this time, the turn-and-slip indicator became my go-to instrument to get us in trim, wings level, and headed in one direction. The next instrument I visited was the vertical speed indicator (VSI). The VSI is a very user-friendly instrument. It has a movable needle that points to the left and moves both up and down. If the aircraft is straight and level, then the VSIs needle will point straight left to zero. If the aviator incorrectly adjusts the cyclic, both the altitude and airspeed are affected. While I was corkscrewing upward, I adjusted the collective as well as the cyclic to effect an indicated 1,500 feet per minute coordinated climb as shown on the VSI. In other words, I held the cyclic slightly to the right to produce the right bank. Then I pulled on the collective to increase power for a climb, and I adjusted that power to settle on a 1,500 feet-per-minute climb. I needed to climb, but I did not need to do so out of control.

Contrary to the IMC emergency procedure, it was a coordinated climbing corkscrew maneuver executed with great care. Concerning the VSI gauge; once I arrived at 5,000 feet, I adjusted the power to ensure the VSI needle pointed to zero at all times. Doing so ensured the aircraft was not climbing nor descending. The next instrument I visited was the altimeter. The altimeter indicated that I was remaining steady at 5,000 feet. Fortunately, neither the turn-and-slip, VSI, nor altimeter was affected by the precessing dilemma of the attitude indicator and the RMI. I still needed to work out alternates to those nonfunctioning primary gauges. I was struggling to unplug the wiring in my head. I had to believe my instruments. It was imperative that I not act upon what I was feeling. Neither could I act upon what I was seeing when I viewed the attitude indicator and the RMI. Wow was this hard! The physiological dynamics were impressive. The two gauges that I desperately needed to work, the attitude indicator and the RMI, at this point, became my primary attention. I needed to figure a workaround for these precessing gauges. The attitude indicator is the primary instrument required for straight and level flight. Mine was precessing. When I looked at the attitude indicator, I saw that the gauge was tumbling down and to the right, though sometimes it would falsely display a spin upward and to the left. In-flight school, we would train to fly without this gauge. The IP would cover over the attitude indicator to force the student to fly the backup instruments. This is called flying partial panel. I was one of those persons who seemed to be deeply affected by the somatogravic and somatogyral Illusions.

Additionally, my instrument IP felt that I gave too much attention to my proprioceptive sensations during IFR flight operations. My IP was determined to address this shortfall in me. So my instrument IP dedicated a large portion of my instrument flight training to partial panel flying, forcing me to use my backup instruments for primary flight. Enduring this instruction taught me to believe in my instruments.

At this point, I was feeling and seeing the aircraft level, headed in a direction, and that we were immediately safe anyway. I was almost ready to engage with the LT, but I needed to get back to my conversation with Poncho first.

"Poncho, RB93 unable to determine my heading, my RMI is precessing, request direction of turn for Osan," I said. That was not totally true. I had an extremely reliable mag compass. The downside to that instrument at this moment was that it was still moving around from the corkscrew climb. Since I didn't have a freeze button, I needed a reliable heading indicator and a direction to turn to right now.

The radio crackled to life as Poncho directed, "Roger, RB93, begin standard rate turn to the right."

Oh my gosh, I was elated. We had survived IMC entry, and the aircraft was not out of control. Neither had we flown into a mountain nor were we spinning to the earth. We were flying on an assigned heading with no gyro and were under the direction of Poncho. Circumstances were grave, but they were better than the initial entry and were definitely looking up. I displaced the cyclic just enough to the right to comply with Poncho's instructions and began the standard rate turn to the right. I knew I had arrived at the correct bank angle because I had successfully moved the movable bar on the turn-and-slip gauge to the marker on the right side. Once there, I adjusted the cyclic again to hold that turn. Not long later, Poncho came back on the radio, "RB93, stop turn. You are now headed direct Osan."

CHAPTER 18

I Am Ready to Brief the LT

23 December 1982, ROK. Somewhere South of Wonju. Seven Minutes into IMC.

"Hey, LT, not ignoring you," I began. "Thanks for not wrestling me for the controls. I know things looked a bit scary a few minutes ago, but we are level at 5,000 feet and headed to Osan." Then I gave her the floor.

"I just don't know what to do or say. I am so pissed. You could have killed us. Frankly, I don't know how we are still alive. You went IMC and did not do the correct IMC emergency procedure upon entry. Who is Poncho? Why are we at 5,000 feet? Aren't we flying in icing conditions? There is so much wrong," she continued. I let her vent a bit longer. I knew it was good to get stuff out. It did take a bit of time for her to vent, and I gave her all the time I could afford, but things were moving along pretty quickly now, and frankly, I did not have the time for it.

I interrupted her and began, "Technically, you flew us into IMC conditions. *But* before you start to holler at me again, I should not have put us into conditions ripe for IMC entry in the first place. It is totally my fault, and I bear full responsibility for our current dilemma. I am not shifting blame. But before we continue slicing and dicing the flight and who did what to whom, let's not forget to fly the aircraft. I know the IMC entry was odd, to say the least." I took a breath and continued, "What is the emergency procedure for IMC?"

She quickly and smartly replied, "Attitude, heading, torque, airspeed, and recovery, recovery being a moving target. Once in cloud, we are supposed to figure out where we are going to recovery to."

"Perfect answer and procedure to follow if we were at Fort Rucker," I told her. "Fort Rucker is flat as a pancake and just a few hundred feet above sea level. We aren't in flatland any more, we were in the mountainous valley of Wonju in the ROK. Do you know the height of the mountain tops in the Wonju Valley?" I waited.

"I don't know," she said.

"LT, had I done what we were taught at Fort Rucker, maintaining an attitude and a climb, we would have flown into the side of a mountain. Let's break down the procedure and see if the modification that I performed best fits the mountainous area of Korea. As advertised, the IMC entry procedure is attitude, level the wings; heading, remain on one straight heading; torque, initiate a climb; Airspeed, adjust the cyclic to a comfortable climb airspeed; Recovery, find an airdrome to recover to."

I could see that she was connecting the dots. We were in a valley. The mountaintops are at 3,500 feet.

"Listen," I said. "I was not sure where in the valley we were when we flew into IMC. After a few moments of denial and hoping that we would pop back out again, and since we did not pop back out, the safest thing was to lay the aircraft over fifteen degrees on its side and grab all the collective I could to get some distance between us and the earth. LT, you saved our lives by not grabbing the controls from me. You sat their bravely as I continued to say standby, standby, standby to your objections."

Between flying the aircraft partial panel and talking to her, I looked at her closely. She realized I was right to modify the procedure to fit our circumstances. She also realized that we were in it now and there was no freeze button on her side either. She was overwhelmed. That was okay. I was pretty busy flying partial panel, and I needed to give her some space. In fact, I wanted to get a good old-fashioned shoulder-bouncing, air-gasping, runny-nose cry myself. Could not do that. The LT did not need to key the mic for me to hear her distress. It was a sobering moment. I am not sure if the VIPs in the very back were even aware of what was going on. I was happy that they had no headsets. Ryan made the correct decision to give the only headset that we had to the major. The generals were conversing, I was positive, but I was hoping they were oblivious to what was really going on.

While the LT was collecting herself, my attention moved between the turn-and-slip gauge, the VSI, and the altimeter. As indicated on the mag compass, Poncho's last attitude correction had me headed on a 245 degree heading. Then I realized the dual value of the mag compass. What a fantastic little instrument. As an MTP, I would swing the mag compass after any significant maintenance event. Swinging the mag compass was nothing more than landing the aircraft on a compass rose painted on the ground calibrated to true north. I would land and make adjustments of the compasses magnets that were in a very tiny drawer within the compass with my non-metallic screwdriver. There is always a non-metallic screwdriver assigned to each tool crib just for this event. Who could ever find one of those? It's a very special screwdriver with an extraordinary purpose, and it was rarely found. As an alternative to the special screwdriver, the army had millions of blackball pointed pens emblazoned with "U.S. Government" on them like anyone would want to steal one. I was rarely successful in finding the proper special screwdriver, so as an alternative, I unscrewed one of the many government black pens. Take out the brass ink container as if it were a refill, flatten the one end of the brass ink container, and abracadabra, I had a brass screwdriver. Worked great. I was a very conscientious MTP. I made sure that all of the mag compasses that I had adjusted were spot on. The mag compass also has a DA form signed by the person who last swung the compass. The mag compass has a card that is smaller in size than a credit card posted to the airframe above the mag compass. I could easily read the name of who last swung the compass. And upon inspection of that card I found…that's right, yours truly. I so appreciated that right now. Knowing that I last swung the compass, I knew it was right. Understanding its construction was a plus because, as long as it was correctly adjusted, it was very accurate...once it settled down from spiraling maneuvers. The mag compass is constructed with a magnet on the bottom of the card that sets parallel with the surface of the earth. That magnet senses the earth's magnetic field and correctly and independent of any power source indicates north, south, east, and west and all heading in-between. For the purpose of this flight, the part of its construction that most interested me now was the fact that the card was suspended in a liquid mixture consisting of distilled water and part pure ethyl alcohol. The liquid dampens movement as well as resists freezing in extreme weather. It would later prove out that it would be the mag compass upon which I would mostly rely upon. The movement of the compass card was likened to an attitude indicator. I was almost giddy. After confirming the center doghouse was aligned with the movable bar on the turn-and-slip and the mag compass card was steady and not moving around, I freed my left hand from the collective, binding the collective with my left knee, and adjusted the attitude indicator to read straight and level. *Yes!* I was no longer looking at an attitude indicator with a tumbled face precessing into any direction it so close. I quickly followed the adjustment procedure with the RMI, making the RMI match the compass heading. I looked over at the LT and smiled.

"Hey, hero, want to help out?" I asked.

CHAPTER 19

I Now Have Hope

23 December 1982, ROK. Somewhere South of Wonju. Ten Minutes into IMC.

"LT, on my mark, I want you to pull-to-cage your attitude indicator." On her side of the aircraft was the standby attitude indicator. When the standby attitude indicator was caged with the pull-to-cage knob, mechanically, the gimbals were momentarily erected and captured in the null position. It ran independently of my attitude indicator, but it made me feel better to have her included in the drill that I had to perform on my side. I desperately wanted my attitude indicator to look situationally correct. Seeing both the precessing attitude indicator and RMI was really messing with my head. Once again, I checked the doghouse on the turn-and-slip and the VSI and the mag compass, and then I directed her to pull-to-cage her attitude indicator. At the same time, I adjusted my attitude indicator to a wings-level position and the RMI to the correct heading as displayed on the mag compass. I found, for the duration of the flight, this would have to be repeated every ten minutes or so. So worth the extra work to see all the gauges looking correct. Including the LT in the drill, even though her attitude indicator was not affected by mine, paid off in the end because we were teaming to solve a problem, even if her actions was likened to placebo.

We were ten minutes into IMC now, and there were a lot of things we needed to clean up.

"How ya doing, LT" I asked.

"Okay, really, better than okay. You are right, I flew us into IMC, *but* you should not have put us there in the first place. I can see why this aircraft is restricted from IFR flights given the bad gyros and all, yet here we are in the thick of it." I could tell she was still processing the whole thing. She continued, "I would not have put together the whole modification of the IMC emergency procedure thing as you had. I would have used what was taught at Rucker and would have flown us into a mountain." I could tell that it was really haunting her. "You saved our lives back there, and I totally fell apart."

There was a lot for her to process, and I understood that. "Hey, you are a hero for not grabbing the controls, thank you for that," I told her.

We needed to clean up the cockpit and get on with the recovery part. Osan is out there somewhere and less than an hour away. I totally understood the whole dying in an aircraft reality that she was now processing. I knew personally that crashing into the earth really does happen to real people. Death is an uncomfortable reality. I had lost fellow professionals to enemy fire, pilot error, as well as material failure. I also lost my dad and twin to an aircraft crash. Of all the times, if there is ever a good time, now I was having a hard time shaking memories of my dad and twin. I did not need what happened to them to hinder me now. I had to shake the thoughts and get back to flying. Neither was it lost on me that we were no longer IMC but now in full IFR flight mode, flying partial panel in icing, without a flight plan. Crashing into the earth or another aircraft out there legally flying IFR is a bad option for us. God help us.

CHAPTER 20

I Was Fourteen Years Old

Summer of 1966, Hayward, California.

I was well into a good old-fashioned shoulder-bouncing, air-gasping, runny nose cry when I came to myself. My mom had just received word that, along with his passengers, my father and twin brother had just been killed in our family's airplane. My dad and twin were not alone in the aircraft. In Dad's aircraft, there was a pal from work and his daughter also. Four were lost that fateful day. For the life of me, I cannot remember the messenger, only the message. I was in our house when the news came, the house that my father and uncle had built with their own hands. Our home was a comfortable three-bedroom, one-bath home built in the late '40s. I ran out of the house to our garage. My dad had also constructed the detached garage. My dad and my twin and I spent hours there with my dad, where he rebuilt and restored the family's airplanes. I sat at Dads treadle Singer sewing machine, hugged his overalls, and just let it all run out of me. I was awash with emotion, terrified of what happened next and knew that Mom needed me. I just needed some time and space before I had to grow up.

Dad and my twin brother Dan, along with Dad's PAXs, were headed to Nebraska to see my grandma on my dad's side. Dad was supposed to drop his pal and his daughter in a town near to grandma's house. He and his daughter were going to visit their relatives. Dad was to pick them up on the return flight. I was supposed to be on that flight that day. It was my turn to fly. Dan and I annually rotated the cross-country trip. My mom had schizophrenia and, at times, could not fly. During those times, someone had to stay with her. Every year, Dad would fly back to see Grandma, and Dan or I would go. The other would stay with Mom. I disappointed my dad earlier that week, and he abruptly changed me out for Dan. That made me very, very mad; remember, I was just a snot-nosed fourteen-year-old kid. Dan and I were members of the United States Naval Sea Cadets. The Sea Cadets was sort of like the Sea Scouts, but the Sea Cadets were government-affiliated whereas the Sea Scouts, not unlike the Boy Scouts, were civil. It was a great adventure. Should a cadet choose to join the navy after high school, if you did well and kept your nose clean, then the rank you earned, up to E3, could be taken with you into the military. E3, compared to E1 on start day, was quite a jump. The competition was fierce, and the adventure very rewarding.

Dan and my last adventure with the Sea Cadets together were aboard the USS *Coral Sea*. The *Coral Sea* was headed to Vietnam and had scheduled a two-week training exercise off the coast of California. Dad helped Dan and me with our application for the fourteen-day cruise, and we were accepted along with twenty or so other cadets. It was an enjoyable experience. And I was astonished how lonely and homesick I became very early on. Dan was smart as a whip. Because of his aptitude, he was selected to be a blue shirt. That may not mean much to the casual observer. The deck of an aircraft carrier is a busy and hazardous place. Only a very few cadets were allowed on the flight deck during flight operations.

Everyone on deck facilitates the movement, launch, recovery, or maintenance of the airplanes on board. Each deck sailor is assigned a different color shirt. The air boss, who resides in the conning tower during air operations, has total control over the flight deck. From his perch, he can tell by color who was who and doing what where. If there is a misstep, the air boss held the best vantage point to correct what may be going on. He has many under his charge, and I am sure that he delegates to petty officers or chief petty officers the movements of the many different-colored shirts, but whoever the guy was who assigned Dan as a blue shirt set a very high bar for Dan. Dan never stopped working. I know he slept, but I don't when. I barely remember seeing him in his bunk. Always gone living life. I loved how happy he was, and the stories he told when we were able to meet up were lots of fun.

One such story: During air operations a rescue helicopter is always launched to effect an immediate rescue in case a naval aviator has to ditch his plane during a takeoff or landing. Dan was invited to go along with one of the helicopter launches. He told me how awesome it was. Dan watched with great amazement as the helicopter left the deck and then hovered like a hummingbird perpendicular to the ship at deck height while the jets launched. He was so amazed at how the helicopter effortlessly hovered next to the gigantic carrier all while the ship turned into the wind and steamed at sufficient cruise speed to launch the aircraft. After the launch, Dan was beyond himself as he described how the helicopter rose and orbited the ship a few times before landing on the deck. Dan said the mighty *Coral Sea* looked like a toy from above. All the helicopter flight maneuvers he described I now take for granted.

Not all the cadets were assigned to the flight deck. Only a very few were. I was not attached to the flight deck; therefore, I was not assigned a shirt color. I was designated as a boatswain's mate. Boatswain's mates are the ships maintenance guys. It was not a glamorous assignment. I was young and did not know much of anything and would not discover for another fifteen years or so that I had a learning disability. That learning disability followed me like a dark cloud. I just thought I was stupid. Dan knew better, but still, it haunted me. I am sure that it was the very reason that I was a boatswain's mate rather than working the flight deck. I did get to steer the ship once, however. That was an okay story that I got to share with Dan. Just okay? Well, that was a moment for sure. Dan and his stories held most of my attention.

The closest I got to launch was either at the fantail or while trying to sleep in my bunk. I would steal time during the day and would sneak back to the fantail and watch the planes land. Typically, and for safety reasons, during launches, the fantail was off-limits, but I was young and found ways to get back there anyway. No one really seemed to care anyway. It was fantastic watching them land. Every time a jet would come in for a landing, at first, I would run and hide with each approach as each one seemed like they were going to crash right into the fantail. The aircraft was only feet above my head. They did not crash, of course, but it was sure scary. After a while, I became a bit saltier and quit running to save myself from each landing. A crash into the fantail never came. I admire naval aviators to this day. Takes great courage to do a deck landing.

In the beginning, the air operations were conducted in daylight hours during the first few days of the fourteen-day cruise. Then for the last ten days or so, all launch and recovery operations were done at night. The night launch and recovery operations were the worst for me because I found sleeping to be the most difficult during those times. Because we were kids, we were housed in officers' quarters. Our beds really were bunk beds. They were stacked two high and were not the hammocks that I had seen on TV and was expecting to see in real life. Those war movies that had prepared me was long on Hollywood and short on reality. Well, in the '40s there may have been hammocks, but this was the '60s and the quarters I saw had none anyway. Our quarters were very welcoming. The beds were a combination bed and locker as well. We slept on top of our locker, where we stored our clothes. There was a thin mattress three inches thick on top of a box eight inches deep that was the same dimensions of the mattress. All our gear stored in the bed/locker. We just had to raise the lid and mattress, prop it open like the hood on a car, and store or retrieve our stuff. It worked great. Slept hard as a rock, however.

It did not take long for the day operations to end and we moved into night operations. At the first launch, I understood why these quarters were mostly, except for visitors, vacant. We were right under the forward catapults. The catapults on the *Coral Sea* were steam operated. Lying in your bunk, you could hear the steam build, and just when you thought the steam pipes would explode, they were released, launching the planes. The retracting of the traps or launch gear was just as bad, maybe worse, than the launch itself. While the traps were retracted, they clanged and clanged, clanging all while dragging the launch chains with it. *Whoosh,* the launch and then *clang, clang, clang,* the retract. All night long it seemed. Some enlisted seaman braved a visit to the quarters. They were interested in the kids who were living in officer's country. I remember them standing at the doorway, peering in like we were goldfish in a jar. I remember one of the sailors mused aloud and remarked at how lucky we kids were to be bunked in officer's country. I didn't think of myself as a kid and, given the noise of the launches, didn't feel lucky either. I had no reference for how the seaman aboard the *Coral Sea* lived. If they thought we were lucky, what conditions did they live in? I just thought all sailors lived like this and loved it except for the launches.

One evening I was assigned to night duty, or watch. That evening, I was to steer the ship. Apparently, boatswain's mates did that too. Grasshopper was the nickname of the guy training me. It is better said that he was more responsible for babysitting than teaching me. Each of us cadets had a seaman personally assigned to us. I cannot even imagine how bad it would have been for them if one of us cadets got hurt during their watch. Looking back, I am sure we were a thought-provoking distraction for them. All the cadets wore the same uniforms as the sailors. Our uniforms, however, had a United States Naval Sea Cadet patch on our right shoulder so that even the most casual observer would know that we were kids and not really young-looking sailors. I will come back to the night watch event in just a moment, but to that patch: I was walking through one of the many corridors on the ship and met a sailor lugging a weighty box. I stopped and asked if I could help him. He hemmed and hawed a bit and, in the end, did let take me help. We moved the heavy box together and, frankly, could have used the help of a few other guys before it was all done. I was glad to assist and was feeling very much like a sailor. Upon completion of the project, he tried to strike up small talk with me, asking me what division I was assigned to and my rating. I did not know the answer to either of those questions, and it did not take him long to see my patch and, quite dismissively said, matter-of-factly, "You're one of those kids!" I was crestfallen. He disappeared without another word into the bowels of the ship, leaving me lost and stranded. It took me quite some time to find my way back to my quarters. The first thing I did was to remove that patch.

Back to the night watch, Grasshopper had drawn helmsman watch duty. It meant he was to steer the ship. He told me to meet him at the ship's helm at 2045 hours to assume responsibilities at 2100 hours. Finding my way to the helm was a story in and of itself. The ship is massive and very easy to get lost in. It is enough to say that I managed to arrive in time to make the watch. He took me aside and told me that I had to go to the captain of the ship and ask permission to relive the watch before I could start my watch. I had to memorize the current course and speed of the vessel. I was told to stand at attention in front of the captain. I had to salute while asking permission to begin my tour of duty at the helm. The helm, or ship's steering wheel, looked just as I thought it should look. It was a slightly smaller version of one that you may find on a pirate ship. It was almost as tall as I and looked like a sizeable spoked wheel with handles on the end of each spoke. It was easy to see that all the wheels brass was highly shined and well-worn over the years. There had to have been thousands of sailors over time that stood watch at this very wheel. Grasshopper made me practice over and over again before asking the captain. I asked Grasshopper if there was any other way for me to take the helm without me asking the captain, and he said no. So I mustered up all the courage I could and approached the captain. As instructed, I stood three paces from him, saluting, and recited the current course and speed and asked for permission to take the helm. He very slowly looked me over. Despite my missing patch, he knew of course that I was a cadet. Not because of the missing patch, of course; it was because I must have looked like a baby, I'm sure. He stood and returned my salute and simply said, "Permission granted."

I dropped my salute after he dropped his and quickly departed for the helm. I could hear the captain tell Grasshopper to watch me closely and to be ready to step in immediately if anything went wrong. It didn't happen, of course. I dared not move the wheel in either direction without a heading assignment from the captain but, like the movies, wanted badly to spin that wheel and shout, "Aye, Cap'n."

In no time at all, our cruise came to a close and we docked. Unlike the movies, there were no crowds of people, girls, or even a band there to meet us. Even a teenager could see that our docking seemed to be pretty ordinary. Dan and I hiked our seabag over our shoulders and headed to the gangway. We saluted the officer of the deck and asked permission to depart. With permission granted, we each one turned and saluted the ensign, and just like that, it was over. Dad was waiting for us. I was just a kid and had no idea that he had shifted his vacation time waiting for our return from the cruise. But being the dad that he was, he did that for us. The next day, however, Dad and I were scheduled to depart for Nebraska. We did not drive home in silence. When Dan was not recounting adventures, I was. We just bombarded Dad with kid stuff. It was great. When the roar began to wind down, Dad began to discuss what was going to happen tomorrow. He said to me as soon as we got home to unpack to repack for the flight tomorrow. When Dad spoke, he spoke in absolutes. There was not a lot of space given for much discussion. Years later, I would understand the great pressure Dad was under. He worked full time. He kept up with Mom. Schizophrenia was not only a cruel reality for Mom, but for our entire family as well. He kept up with twin boys, and I can tell you firsthand, Dan, and I were a handful. Our bedroom window was a standard exit for us at night as we were out and about on one adventure after another. To relax, Dad spent much time with his hobby—rebuilding and restoring airplanes. He maintained our property, and I can go on and on. It is enough to say that his surviving adult twin of today greatly admires his resolve, but I was not an adult then. I was a stupid kid who thought I was all that and a bag of chips.

True to form, Dad laid out the events that would happen tomorrow. Just off the cruise, I was feeling a bit salty, and I asked Dad if I could have an additional day to rest up. The cruise had been quite an adventure, and after all those catapult shots, a couple of good night's sleep was in order. I loved flying with Dad, but the rest would have been great too. Dan and I had been flying with Dad from the time we were big enough to sit up and strap into a seat. In the early years, Dan and I shared a seat and a seatbelt too. It was great fun.

Dad did not see a salty adult; he saw an insubordinate fourteen-year-old whiner. He was terribly disappointed with me and told me so in quick order. Dad explained that he had shifted his vacation time to accommodate the cruise and that we were going to depart tomorrow as planned…period. He quickly shifted gears and asked Dan if he was up for a flight to Nebraska tomorrow. I was crushed. It was my turn. Dan had gone the previous year. Dan immediately said that he was up for the flight. The switch happened right then and there. Dan was to fly instead of me. Just then, I hated my dad's absoluteness. With my dad, there was never a follow-on discussion. As an adult, I understand now, but I didn't then. I hated him and wanted him to die. How's that for a teenage lash out? It is difficult for me to write that truth, but that is what the fourteen-year-old thought about the solution that Dad had come up with. Of course, I had no idea that he really would die. I have questioned myself to this very day. All of my childhood, as well as my adulthood, has included this guilt… to this very day. Did I cause the crash? Did I will that to happen, and then it did happen? I mourn Dad and Dan's loss to this very day. The details of these sorts of tragedies are always messy and cluttered with questions. How? Why? Why not me instead? What about the others? Others? Yes, the others. Too many years have gone by now for me to remember precisely where Dad's PAXs were going. I do know, however, that their destination was along the route of flight to Nebraska and close to Grandma's. He worked at the Naval Air Station Alameda with Dad, and Dad agreed to fly him to his destination. During the flight, they got as far as Carson City, Nevada, when the aircraft's generator went out. Dad was an airframe and powerplant (A&P) mechanic as well as a pilot, so the day was late when they landed in Carson City and they elected to RON, allowing Dad some time to fix the generator problem. He had it repaired by the next morning and did a quick test flight on the aircraft that following day. Satisfied that the generator problem was fixed, Dad landed, refueled, loaded everyone aboard, and departed. The witnesses reported that he used all the runway to get off the ground. The Carson City airport has hills on all sides, and Dad must have known, during his climb out, that he was not going to clear the mountains. Witnesses reported watching Dad begin a slow turn to return to the airport. He was unable to sustain lift while in his bank and flew it into the ground. I am grateful that the g-force killed them instantly, because witnesses went on to say that the plane burst into flames upon contact with the earth. It was a remote airdrome. There was no crash-rescue at the airdrome. By the time firefighters came in from the local town, the plane has already burnt to ash. In an instant, they were gone.

It took me years to understand that my dad had made a mistake and got caught. It was pilot error after all. Until my own attendance to flight school years later, I had always thought that Dad did not make a mistake—that the plane fell out of the sky for reasons beyond everyone. There was nothing left for the National Transportation Safety Board (NTSB) to examine. The wreckage was ash. The NTSB concluded that Dad was an experienced sea level pilot; however, they believed he was overweight and underestimated the performance of his plane at Carson City elevation of 4,800 feet above sea level. If the 4,800 feet were not bad enough, Dad needed another 1,000 feet on top of that to clear the mountain for his route of flight. He was flying the final aircraft that he had restored. It was a Charlie Model V-tail Bonanza. It was a beautiful plane, and it was my dad's favorite.

During all of my fourteen years, both Dan and I grew up in our garage, helping Dad rebuild airplanes. He would buy one that was in terrible shape for a song and restore it. It may have been odd having a father who rebuilt planes but no different than the father down the road that rebuilt automobiles. Dad would fly the aircraft that he restored for a few years, sell it, and start the process all over again, upcycling with each exchange. Dad had five planes in his lifetime. An Aeronca Champion, or "Champ;" a Luscombe; two Stinsons; and finally, the Charlie Model Bonanza. All Dad's planes were family affairs, but the Champ was where it all began; the Champ was the first after all. During the time of the Champ, we had no idea how many Dad would restore at the time, so we just enjoyed all the firsts offered by the Champ. As with all the planes, Dad rebuilt the motor first. Once the engine was restored, he would preserve it for storage and begin work on the airframe. The Champ, and later the two Stinsons, was cloth-covered aircraft. The Luscombe was a combination of metal and fabric. The Bonanza was all metal. The cloth is called ceconite. Ceconite is a unique polyester fabric that, with the application of heat and a resin commonly called dope, stretches and becomes as rigid as the skin on a drum. Dad called the ceconite paper, and to this day, as did he, I refer to all little airplanes as paper airplanes. After Dad finished with any welding repairs to the tubular airframe, any repairs needed for the flight controls, electrical wiring, and generally anything else that needed to be done before skinning the aircraft, he would then skin the plane.

Even from my youth, I was always amazed at the skinning process. I was too young to understand all the workings of the flight controls, electrical and the like that the skin covered up. But when Dad put the skin on the aircraft, all of a sudden, it began to look like an airplane. He sewed the skin on a treadle-driven Singer sewing machine. For the longest time, Dad sewed it in their bedroom before moving it out to the garage many years later. I suspect Mom had enough of the plane residing in her bedroom, or the shell of it anyway. I remember watching him work the mountains of fabric, pushing and pulling, all without a pattern. He had funny scissors too that were special for the fabric. They were called pinking shears. Pinking shears created a cut that zigged and zagged. Dan and I would cut all sorts of paper and scraps of material and make a bunch of cool stuff...when Dad was not looking, of course. After he would sew the wing coverings, the family, as well as the neighbors, helped hold the wing up while Dad pulled the fabric over the wing likened to putting on a pillowcase over a pillow. After doing that for each wing, we placed the wings on homemade sawhorses that Dan and I would ride everywhere...when Dad was not looking, of course, and he began to dope and heat the wing fabric all while the fabric magically shrunk to fit. You really could play that fabric like a drum. Dan and I did so often...when Dad was not looking of course. When the wings were done, he would hang the wings from the rafters in the ceiling of the garage. Then we would all gather and repeat the process for the fuselage. Putting the fabric for the fuselage on was trickier than the wings because of the rudder. That always reminded me of someone putting on their socks. But with some pulling and pushing, the task was completed, and Dad would duplicate the heating and doping process to stretch the fabric over the fuselage.

Running the restored and preserved engine from time to time was integral to the entire storage process. Every so often, Dad would bring out the motor and mount it to a hulk airframe that Dad had behind the garage for the sole purpose of running engines. It was his test cell, if you will. Of course, Dan and I flew that Frankenstein-ed hulk of an aircraft all over the world…when Dad was not looking, of course. Dan and my flights will have to remain another story for another day, but when it came to bringing the engine out of storage and running the engine, Dad, who called Dan and me "bad-e-boys" when he spoke of us collectively, would say, "Bad-e-boys, go gather your friends. We are going to run the engine this afternoon." Other than being in the aircraft with Dad during stall training, nothing would excite Dan and me more than running the engine. We would gather our friends who were so jealous of us. I mean really, who else had a dad who had an airplane in their garage, who could ride saw-horses, play the drums on airplanes, and fly all over the world in an airplane whenever we wanted to…when Dad was not looking, of course.

The ritual was fun but serious. The adult in me knows that Dad was practicing his propping technique all while he was bonding with his bad-e-boys. The bad-e-boy that was the best bad-e-boy that day got to be on the controls when Dad started the engine. The Champ did not have a starter, so it always had to be propped to start. The other planes did have starters, but by the time the other planes came along, Dan and I were well acquainted with propping. The engine in storage had to be run from time to time, and that was all we cared about. Propping the engine was dangerous. As I said, Dad was practicing his procedures with us. With all of our friends around the hulk a safe distance away, Dad would place the best bad-e-boy of the day at the controls, with Dad on the prop, and Dad would begin. If Dan was in the cockpit, then I was out with our friends giving the play-by-play details of what was about to happen. If, instead, Dad determined I was best bad-e-boy of the day, then Dan would like-wise be with the hordes of kids that we would assemble and give the play-by-play details to. Dad's position on the pop was critical. With the prop parallel with the surface of the earth, Dad would position himself on the left side of the prop when viewed looking at the prop. He would exaggeratedly grab the left side of the prop when viewed from straight on, push the prop upward all while raising his left leg, likened to a pitcher winding up for a pitch and, with a significant release of energy, would pull the prop down all while moving out of the way so that the engine would burst to life, and the prop would not hit him. Not trusting the best bad-e-boy of the day and for his own safety, Dad preset the position of all the necessary switches before putting a bad-e-boy in the hulk's cockpit. The fact that I had come to understand in my adulthood, not in my childhood. As an adult, as I relive those moments, I better enjoy the childhood memories untouched with safety measures taken by my dad. My childhood's drama is captured in my mind, pure and clear, and it all played out in a particular order. This is how it went. Enjoying the excitement of the moment, Dad would shout as if there was a gale:

A. "Fuel Selector Switch," he would cry.
   "Off," the best bad-e-boy would respond.
B. "Master Switch," he shouted.
   "Off," the response.
C. "Mixture," he shouted.
   "On," the response.
D. "Engine Prime," he shouted.
   "Primed," the response. We were not allowed to touch the prime.
E. "Clear the prop," he shouted. Clearing the prop included more than getting out of the way. Dad always propped the engine a few times before actually starting it. He would pull down and release all that wound energy with his left leg. Dad did that first a few times, and then things really got hopping. He came around to the cockpit, moved some

switches on our behalf, and we would begin at the top of the checklist again, only…

F.   "Fuel Selector," he shouted.

"On," came the reply. Since this was a Frankenstein hulk, a collection of all sorts of airplanes that Dad welded and assembled for his test cell, the airframe had no dedicated fuel cell. Instead, there was a tin gallon can suspended high where the windscreen would have been had it had one with a tube and a petcock. The tube led straight to the carburetor. The fuel's petcock represented the off and on switch or, in this case, the master switch. I hate mixing my adult memories with my childhood memories. The safety standards may have been a bit loose back in the day. To Dad's credit, the hulk was tied down, however. I tripped over the tie-down many times during my flights around the world…when Dad was not looking, of course.

G.   "Engine Prime," he shouted.

"Primed," still the response. We were never allowed to touch the prime. Dad always did that.

H.   "Clear the prop," he shouted again. This time, when he wound up and threw up his left leg while simultaneously pushing up as far as he could go, with a mighty effort, he pulled down as hard as he could, and clearing the prop, the engine sprang and rumbled to life. There was no muffler on the exhausts, so the noise was quite loud. Sometimes it even backfired, sending all the kids into an uproar. The other bad-e-boy rallied the mob of kids with hollers and whoops.

"Told ya it would start."

Those days were filled with adventure. Dad got better and better with each aircraft. He loved what he did, and we did too. He was really stepping up by the time he bought the Bonanza. The other four aircraft before the Bonanza needed significant restoration. The Bonanza was more cosmetic. A paint job, interior work, upgraded navigation, some engine work. I believe Dad had matured and was ready to enjoy flying more than working on them. Before he bought the Bonanza, I remember him teasing Mom that he was going to buy a small helicopter next. Mom was ill but saw clearly through her illness when she put her foot down. No helicopter, she declared. I have to wonder, had Dad lived longer, if he would have gotten a helicopter. I would love to converse with him now. I would first ask for forgiveness for my thoughts before he flew. I did not want him to die. He and Dan were taken too early. Tragically and abruptly gone. My family was devastated. My older brother by twelve years and my older sister by ten years, and I lost the counsel of a man who solved problems. My mom lost her husband, the love of her life. The very rudder of her life, in fact. Dad would never meet nor spoil his grandchildren, and Dan, his nephews and nieces. I had my own challenges. I may share them later. It is enough to say for now that I lost Dan, who was my safe place, and my dad, who was my rock. Dan and I had a special connection. That all stopped in the summer of 1966. I will forever be tormented by my last thoughts of Dad when he changed up the crew when Dad had Dan fly in my place.

CHAPTER 21

Time Past to Clean Up the Cockpit

23 December 1982, ROK. Somewhere South of Wonju. Twelve Minutes into IMC.

Dad had underestimated the performance of his plane as well as underestimated his flight conditions. He flew anyway. All the signs were there for an experienced pilot to see, but he flew anyway. Like my dad, I had made errors. I may have been technically correct to depart, but just like my dad had done, I underestimated my conditions. Density altitude (DA) and pressure altitude (PA), combined with Dad's lack of flight experience in high DA, PA, and summer temperature conditions, became Dad's undoing. Not forgetting Dad was on a tight vacation schedule, so he had something of a mission profile to manage. My lack of experience unfolds and presents differently, but the parallels of our stories are uncanny. The same premise exists; my inexperience let me fly anyway. Not fully understanding how weather forecasts, snow, icing, crew mix, and applying the aircraft's mechanical restrictions developed into my perfect storm bringing us right here in the here and now. Flying and crosschecking, flying and crosschecking, I continued to contemplate the comparison of Dad's cockpit and mine. In a flash of time, memories of Dad and Dan surface and recede. No time to dwell on them and how we parallel. The circumstances that drove our decision to fly were different but oddly the same. Bad choice. Missed signs. We flew anyway. So far today, we were still alive. I had to focus on cleaning up my mess. I was determined that this day was going to end successfully. The only tragedy today would be the remembrances of my family's loss.

"Okay, LT," I began. "Let's just embrace the suck and get on with flying IFR to Osan. Identify the transponder and dial in 7700 in the squawk." Dialing in 7700 in the transponder is equivalent to dialing 911 on your telephone. It lets ATC know that you are in trouble. "Identify the pitot heater switch," I continue.

She spent a moment processing that. "Right, icing," she realized.

"Let's get some juice to that pitot tube. If we lose any more instruments, we are going to be in deeper kimchee," I told her. We needed the pitot heater on so that the pitot tube would not freeze. The pitot tube is a tube that measures the ram air that hits the aircraft. The pitot tube for this model Huey is just above both pilots stations on the roof out of immediate view of either aviator. The hole in the center of the tube is very small. It would not accommodate a no. 2 pencil. There is an electric heating element built into the tube that disallows ice from forming. In order to measure airspeed, that hole needs to be free of ice and totally unobstructed.

"Additionally," I continued, "let's get some heat on the windshield via the windshield defroster and some heat into the engine inlet via the deice switches and place them both on." The pitot heater is an electrical function. The defrost and deicing of the engine inlet is a product of bleed air off the engine. I will have to tradeoff engine power by redirecting that bleed air, but right now, I need every system possible working for us while mitigating an icing threat. I gave her some time and followed her as she identified each of those switches and placed them on.

Since I am on the controls, there isn't a lot of things for the LT to do. I knew I was going to have her eventually get the Osan approach plate out and begin to review the instrument approach that we were going to do into Osan, but for now, I wanted to dismantle our problem piece by piece so that we were talking our way through it together. I thought this would help her...and me too.

"Remember what the source of power is for the VSI? How about the altimeter?" I asked her.

She looked at me as if to say, *Are you kidding right now?* "No, I don't remember the source of power for the VSI or the altimeter. Is that something we should be focusing on right now?"

"Sure it is," I tell her. "You turned on the pitot heater to keep the pitot tube from freezing over. That ram air is needed for the airspeed indicator to function properly. The static side of the pitot-static system has no heater. It is not protected from ice, but if the static ports on either side of the aircraft begin to collect ice, then the VSI and the altimeter are going to be adversely affected. We cannot lose those instruments too" The VSI is a gauge that has an eternal bellow with a calibrated leak. The hole in the bellow has been calibrated to leak into the static system. Once the pressures inside and outside the bellows stabilize and relax, then the relaxed position is displayed as zero on the face of the gauge. The altimeter is also part of the static system. It also has a bellows, and the deflection of the bellows is also displayed on the face of the altimeter. The difference between the bellows in the VSI and the bellows in the altimeter. There is no hole in the altimeters bellow. When the aircraft ascends to altitude, the bellows inside the altimeter swells and holds a position. The reverse is true when descending. The aviator gets to benefit from the mechanics of that action as an altitude indication. If the static side ices up on either side of the aircraft, then both the VSI and the altimeter will give false information. Not acceptable for us as we are already down an RMI and an attitude indicator.

"LT, time to pull-to-cage your attitude indicator again. Let me confirm our attitude with the turn-and-slip, VSI, and mag compass and on that mark, pull to cage." Satisfied that the turn-and-slip, VSI, and mag compass are all indicating straight and level, I tell her, "Mark."

At 5,000 feet, it is quite bright. Not because we were anywhere near breaking out of the snow clouds into the sunlight. The last part of lines 26-31 of our -1 read that there was an overcast ceiling at 10,000 feet. That was 5,000 feet above us now. Since we were flying in icing, an option could have been to climb out of the icing conditions. Initially, I elected not to do that. One of the things that I was taught in flight school concerning weather flying was to minimize movements. Turns and banks were the absolute worst thing to do unnecessarily in cloud. Now I am partial panel flying, and turns and banks in cloud partial panel increase our chances of getting into dangerous illusions. Climbing would not have required a change in my attitude. It would have been a straight and level maneuver and, in retrospect, may have been the correct thing to do. I was already flying partial panel and forced to do a mechanical reset of the primary attitude indicator and RMI. We also caged the standby attitude indicator on the LT's side, but only to include her in the crew action. Had I climbed, there was no guarantee that I would break out even if I did attempt a climb, and at this point, I was more interested in breaking free of the icing. Getting out of cloud would remove me from moisture and icing. Lest I forget that the AR 95-1 says that sustained flight above 10,000 feet for more than 30 minutes requires supplemental oxygen. I did not have supplemental oxygen onboard. So my bad decisions thus far that got us into this mess in the first place, a co-pilot who was off her game, and no guarantee to break out was enough to dissuade me from doing any sort of altitude changes. Still, I was surprised how bright the snow made the cockpit. We were not only in cloud, but in a very snowy cloud. Since we were full-on IFR, I had accelerated the airspeed from eighty knots when we were marginal VFR to standard instrument cruising airspeed of ninety knots for the Huey's. The snow was splatting against the windscreen. Some of it was freezing as it worked itself along the side. I could not help but think about the static ports.

A standard SPH-4 flight helmet has a clear and a shaded visor. I elected to drop my shaded visor. It helped with the brightness. I wasn't squinting any longer from the light. Dropping the shaded visor made me feel like I was doing things that bettered our chances of surviving and may have been mental for me, but it seemed to help. I better saw those snowflakes smashing against the windscreen. Given the track of the wipers, there was an ice dam slowly developing one each side of the windscreens. I guarded the collective with my left knee, and I reached up with my left hand into the overhead counsel and recycled the wipers again. Recycling the wipers momentarily cleared the snow and ice. We were flying at ninety knots, and as soon as the wiper moved even an inch, there was plenty of snow to replace it on the backside of the wiper travel. The wipers pretty efficiently snow plowed that snow and broke the accumulating ice dam on either side of the windscreen. I waited a few moments and repeated the maneuver. I was ecstatic.

We were removing some ice from the aircraft and were not out of control. I looked over at the LT and said, "LT, I need you to be the wiper guy. When you see ice accumulate on either side of the windscreen, please turn on the wipers to clear the windscreen. I need to stay inside with the instruments. Eventually, we are going to arrive at Osan, and I don't want to miss seeing the runway environment for the buildup of ice on the windscreen."

She seemed to be okay with that assignment. Every now and then, I saw her hand go up and hit the wiper switch, I heard the wipers swish back and forth, and a rapid glance showed me that she was controlling the ice buildup. This was a good thing. I was doing the lion's share of the work by flying and crosschecking. I needed to be respectful of my copilot and assign duties befitting her station. I asked her to get out the Osan approach plate for the instrument landing system (ILS) approach and begin to review the procedure and be prepared to answer my questions after her review. Instrument plates have a ton of information, and the unpracticed can get easily overwhelmed discerning the info.

CHAPTER 22

An Unsuccessful Annual Proficiency and Readiness Test (APART) Instrument Check Ride

23 December 1982, ROK. Two Weeks before Going into IMC.

I was as nervous as a cat. I was one of those guys who did not take check rides very well. People like me are said to have check-itis. Well, that was me. Some people have white coat syndrome when going to see a doctor. I have check-itis when it came to my annual check rides. For most WOJG aviators, check rides can be grueling. I always performed badly when under a microscope. When not being tested or when not taking a check ride, I was a pretty fair aviator. Maybe better than fair based upon my status thus far. Only ten months out of flight school, and I had already successfully become an MTP as well as a PIC. Ten months into my tour, I had logged a couple hundred hours in the ROK, and I was feeling pretty proficient, except when it came to my turn to take my annual APART check rides. When taking an APART, there is no set order to completing the APART. All components of the APART must be completed during the last three months of your birth month. For example, I am a February baby, so my APART period is from the beginning of December through the end of February. Senior aviators have additional APART check ride components, but for a rookie aviator such as myself, my APART components are broken into the following areas: The annual flight physical, annual written exam or writ, contact check ride, and an instrument check ride.

I elected to begin my APART with the writ. The writ is a sixty-question open book written exam. 80 percent was needed to pass. We were given a stack of regulations, field manuals, training circulars, and the like to use while taking the writ. We also were issued VFR sectionals, IFR en route low altitude maps, and approach plates. I have never ever done well with tests. I don't know why I choke during test taking, but I do and did so during all of my schoolings, flight school included. Concerning the writ, four other February babies and I went into the flight standardization office on the morning of December 2, 1982 and took our seats. The standardization instructor pilot (SIP) briefed the writ. A plus for me…it was an open book exam. One of the reasons I hated tests? I hated it when questions were written in such a way that there could have been other answers. I hated that. One word would often be the distractor. It always seemed to be a gotcha game. Clarity in testing was rare for me. I just endured every event and hoped for the best. After taking a few questions from our group, Stan, our SIP started the time and departed. The other aviators in the room seemed more relaxed and seasoned. That was my take anyway. This was the first writ that I had ever taken, and firsts for anything can always be imposing. I could already feel the apprehension coming on. The other aviators seemed to move quickly but quietly through the exam. You were not required to put a page and paragraph number next to your answer but were encouraged to do so. I took that as a requirement, so I made sure to have found a page and paragraph for each answer. The time dragged along. An hour in, and one guy was already done and gone. That terrified me. I needed to stretch. You could leave for the latrine but were on the honor system not to speak with anyone about the writ while in the latrine. I splashed water in my face, dried off, and returned to the standardization office. I thought I would go through the exam and answer first the questions that I could then go back and begin my research into the ones I did not no know right off. That seemed to work pretty well. Instead of agonizing and stressing over each and every question, I seemed to move along more quickly doing that. I really got into the zone and had not realized that the room had shrunk by two more when next I looked up. Two more had finished and departed. I tried not to hyperventilate. I began my research on the next group of questions that I could not answer off the top of my head. Slowly but steadily, I worked through the majority of the test questions. Suddenly, I was alone in the room. I checked the time. Three hours in, and I felt like I was failing. Still had an hour left. I had to stretch again. Another visit to the latrine. I passed Stan as I headed for the latrine, and he gave me that look as if to say, *Really, three hours? How dumb can you be?*

A fellow WOJG passed me and asked how it was going. He had not taken his first writ either and wanted some intel. I told him I couldn't talk about it. I returned to the standardization office to finish up. I had less than fifteen minutes left to go. I found myself drained and emotionally a wreck. I double-checked a few answers but realized that it is what it is. I found Stan at his desk and gave him my exam.

"Are you sure you are done, WOJG?" Stan asked. If I was not intimidated enough, I certainly was now. WO1s were referred to as WOJGs. It was an acronym for warrant officer junior grade. It was more a rite of passage than a badge of honor.

"Yes, sir, done as done can be," I said. I stood by quietly while he got the master out and compared the master to my answers.

"You pass, WOJG. You got an eighty-six. Want to challenge any of the questions?" he asked. I should have shown more interest, I guess, but I did not want to become a punching bag for Stan; all I wanted to do was exit.

"No, sir, pretty sure where I messed up," I replied.

"Not good enough, WOJG. Let's review the exam and get some training out of this," he said. Stan enjoyed raking me and other WOJGs over the coals. We reviewed every missed question. I have to admit, on another day, it might have been proper training, but this day, it was an endurance maneuver. I just wanted it over. I felt like I was bleeding out.

A few days later, I tackled the flight physical. Frankly, no person alive lies better than an aviator to a flight surgeon. We all face the annual music with the sky doc, and regardless of how we actually feel, the answers to his question are always the same. "I'm fine, doc. Here is my up-slip. Just sign there." That may not be a direct quote, but the sentiment is always the same. Endure the time with the sky doc and get a flight release or an up-slip to fly for another year was the name of the game. The flight physical was broken into two sections—Labs and seeing the doc, or part one and part two. I found that both parts of the physical to be anticlimactic for the 1982–1983 year shot group. I guess I really was in good health. Nonetheless, I joined the long tradition before me and told the sky doc all was well and got my up-slip.

I went back to the standardization office and turned in my up-slip to Stan. Stan Help was our standardization officer. He was a CW3. He and I had already professionally crossed swords when I was challenging the MTP check ride. Three months afterward, he completed my PIC training. He was a real black-and-white guy. I was an MTP and PIC and still had a real fear of tests and check rides. Stan was curt but professional. After filing my up-slip, he asked where I was with the APART. I told him the writ and sky doc was completed. The stands/contact ride and instrument ride remained. To accomplish the instrument check ride, Stan told me to "go and see Roger. When I return from Christmas leave, I will finish up with your standardization ride…be ready."

Be ready…really? I thought.

Roger was out, so I had to come back the next day to get a mission to plan for the upcoming instrument check ride. Roger was CW3 Roger Wills and was a nice guy. He was the unit's instrument flight examiner (IFE). He was short and had a handlebar mustache that only a cavalry soldier could appreciate. I was with the 1st Cavalry Division during my tour in Vietnam. Roger was a reincarnation of one of those cavalry soldiers that I had served with. I would later discover that Roger served in Vietnam with the 101st Airborne. He had the temperament of a solder forged in wartime. I genuinely liked him.

When we met the next day, he greeted me as Dean rather than WOJG. He had a good firm handshake and made eyeball contact with me as he introduced himself. He warmed me up with some small talk. I suspected he knew I was nervous and was trying to defuse that. I can only imagine what Stan had told him about me. It did not take long for him to lay out the mission that I would fly during the instrument check ride. In the simulator, we would depart Camp Humphreys and fly over to Osan and do the ILS, followed by missed and holding, and return to Humphreys for the VOR approach full stop. It seemed pretty cut and dry. The simulator was okay with me. I would learn that the mission he assigned was a classic mission profile that combined the minimum elements of an instrument check ride—a precision approach, a non-precision approach, holding, and then some cross-country instrument flying. The mission was pretty straightforward.

At the time for me, there was nothing basic about it. I was sure of one thing, however; I was pretty sure that Roger would give me an unusual attitude along the way to recover from as well as some emergency work. No telling what he would do. IPs loved to surprise aviators and pull circuit breakers. Those are unannounced maneuvers devised to shock the aviator so that the IFE can determine the aviator's ability to recover from an IMC event or, at least, an unusual attitude while in flight. Not forgetting an engine, hydraulic, electrical, or a host of other emergency procedures he desired to dive into. After getting the mission from Roger, I headed over to the maintenance office to tell my boss, CPT Harris, that I would be out the rest of the day planning my instrument check ride for my APART. He was not there, so I left him a note.

I went back to my room to work the flight plan. My wife was there, and she was a nice distraction. The next day, Roger and I met and got on a bus to Seoul Air Base (K-16). K-16 is where the simulators were stationed at. We bussed over because the weather was too bad to fly. There were snow flurries, and Roger didn't want to hassle with a marginal VFR flight over and possibly getting stuck for the weather. Ground transportation was the next best bet. It always worked. It did not take long to get to the simulator building.

Roger checked us into the simulator building and told me to go to the cockpit and make ready. It was a nonvisual Huey simulator exactly like I trained in in flight school. My stomach was in knots, but I suppressed it as best as I could. I had gotten into the right seat and was in the process of getting set up when Roger startled me when he opened the door to the left side. I was in the zone setting up the radios.

"Don't let me interrupt you. I am just going to jump in and put us on motion," he said. After he closed his door, he pushed the motion button. Like in flight school, the aircraft began to erect. The cockpit first leaned back and then tilted to the left and to the right while ascending some twenty feet. Since all the windows were blacked out, we could not actually see the rise in altitude from the inside of the cockpit, but you could quickly feel the increase. I had watched dozens erect over my time in flight school from the outside. The movements forward, back, left and right, and then back to neutral when viewed from the exterior was quite dramatic. From the inside, however, you did not feel the dramatic shifting. You were aware of the movement, however, and even more so when the simulator was fully erected and stationary. If we opened the door, as a safety measure, the aircraft would come off motion and settle back into its cradle, so you were very careful not to do that. While in flight school, other candidates often opened the door and suffered friendly banter from classmates as well as corrections from the IPs. I was not immune to the error.

In no time, Roger and I were up and ready for the flight. Roger told me to relax. He also said he would be handing all ATC duties. Familiar with that technique from flight school, I simply acknowledged the instructions. I began to go over the cockpit set up with him. I have clearance delivery in the no. 3 and ground in the no. 2. I asked him to put tower and, later, the victor frequencies for departure control in the no. 3 once I had finished with clearance delivery. I had the ILS frequency of 109.3 set in the ILS and the initial approach fix (IAF) 371 tuned into the non-directional beacon (NDB). I had the runway heading tuned into the bug of the RMI for now but advised him that I would update that with first turn information once that information was received. Operations were dialed up in the no. 1 position and weather in the no. 4 position for a weather update before departure. I wanted to brief the ILS approach now followed by holding, but he waved me off as too soon. I was pretty satisfied that we were ready to go.

"ATIS?" he asked. Automatic terminal information service, or ATIS, is what he was referring to. ATIS is a continuous broadcast of recorded airdrome information. It is updated as new information is added, and once updated, it is assigned a new alphabetical designator. It is designed to arm aviators with pertinent airdrome information as well as weather. Armed with this necessary yet repetitive information, aviators then contact ATC for follow-on information. It is bad form not to use ATIS, and during the first radio call, it always becomes apparent if the aviator has missed that step. The tower will have to repeat all the repetitive information, and it just looks bad for the aviator. As soon as Roger asked about ATIS, I realized that I had made a basic error.

Roger was nice enough to say, "Let's continue as if you had contacted ATIS. Had you included ATIS in your setup, this is what ATIS would have told you, 'Humphreys information uniform. Time, 12:50, automatic. Runway 22 in use. Ground is open, delivery is closed. Expect a VOR approach. Surface wind 250 at 14 knots. Visibility 10+. Scattered 2,400 feet, broken 4,600 feet. Temperature +19, dew point +14. Altimeter 29.92. Work in progress in Apron Alpha—taxiway. Juliet closed between papa and alpha. Acknowledge receipt of information uniform and advise aircraft type on first contact.'"

I saw his teaching point right off. Since on this day there was no operational clearance delivery, I would not be able to receive my IFR clearance from them. Satisfied that he had made his point, instead of waiting for me to reset the cockpit, he said, "Don't reset. Let's move past it. I know the ATC guy," he said with a smile. Roger was satisfied with my cockpit setup and copilot brief. He acknowledged that he would do everything I asked of him. He also said that he would not interrupt my flow but would join it. Not interrupting my flow but joining it was not only a surprising statement for me, but I found that I liked that statement so much that I used it on every flight after that. Joining other success stories had become a staple for me. Any violations that I may make in cockpit procedures or with protocol Roger said would be debriefed at the end of the flight so as not to interrupt my flight. I appreciated that. At this point in my aviator career, every error I had made was always digested in great detail and was always immediate and disruptive. Roger's approach was refreshing. I gave the instructors plenty of opportunities to digest my errors in great detail, and it always upset my rhythm. I appreciated just being left alone to excel or not on my own merits.

Roger could not help but look over at my kneeboard and saw that I had the CRAFT acronym already prepared and ready for his clearance. In flight school, my instrument instructor would not accept anything short of the CRAFT acronym used. Clearance fix, route, altitude, frequency, and transponder (CRAFT) is what it meant. To the practiced aviator, it worked very well. I always completed every test flight with a VOR approach into Humphreys, so I had lots of practice using CRAFT in the real world.

I called ground (Roger) for my clearance and hover taxi instructions. Desiderio was the name of Humphreys's airfield, so I began, "Desiderio Ground, Army 12345 parked on Delta Row, IFR clearance on request," I said into the microphone.

Roger quickly and professionally responded, "Army 12345 cleared to Osan as filed, fly runway heading, climb and maintain 3,000, expect 5,000 one-zero minutes after departure. Departure frequency one two four point six five, squawk two seven one three, hover taxi hold short of the active for IFR release."

I was required to write all that down and Roger, as briefed, also backed me up by also recording the clearance on his kneeboard. Before I responded to ATC (Roger), I waited for a thumbs-up from him, indicating that he had satisfactorily recorded the clearance. I, however, missed the altitude part of the clearance, so I asked, "Desiderio Ground, I understand that Army 12345 is cleared to Osan as filed, fly runway heading, climb and maintain 3,000, expect, say again altitude, one-zero minutes after departure, departure frequency one two four point six five, squawk two seven one three, and hover taxi hold short of the active for IFR release."

"Roger, Army 12345, that expect altitude 5,000 feet read back correct. Hover taxi hold short of the active for IFR release. Contact tower one two seven point three five when ready for departure."

Roger sounded pleased when he said, "Hey, Dean, great job. You missed the climb to altitude, but you went back and corrected the missing information. Well done. There I said I was not going to interrupt your flow, but I could not help myself. Glad you got that straightened out while on the ground instead of trying to fix it in flight. Okay, I am out of your business now, and we will chat after the flight. Let's continue," he said.

Since you cannot really hover in a nonvisual simulator, I did what I had been trained to do. I simulated hovering to and short of the active by bouncing up and down in my seat. Roger surprised me, and he bounced up and down too. A moment that only those who flew in a Huey simulator can really appreciate. After a few moments of bouncing around in our seats, we stopped indicating that we had arrived short of the active. I smiled. As briefed while we were bouncing in our seats pretending to hover, Roger performed his briefed duties as he placed tower frequencies in the no. 3 position. With this done I knew that he would likewise put up departure control into the no. 3 once finished with the Tower.

"Desiderio Tower, Army 12345 holding short of the active for IFR departure," I said.

"Roger, Army 12345, line up and wait," Roger responded as ATC.

This was not unexpected. In flight school, we sometimes would wait as much as thirty minutes waiting for our turn to depart. IFR traffic is not released into the system all at once. IFR traffic is sequenced into the airspace for ATC management. At times, it can be a frustrating wait. Roger added the lineup and wait for instructions so that it would give me a chance to catch my breath and make sure I did not forget the simple things. I confirmed my hover power as thirty-two pounds. Information that I would need for the instrument takeoff (ITO). I also made sure that the attitude indicator was adequately set up for the ITO. I told Roger on the climb out to take the transponder out of standby and begin the fuel check. Once we were in the air, I would back him up with my own fuel check and confirm that the transponder was on.

"Army 12345 cleared for release, contact departure control one two four point six five passing through 1,000 feet."

"Roger, Army 12345 on the go." I had already done a hover power check while hovering to the active and saw that my RMI would begin to free up at thirty-two pounds of torque engine power, indicating that I was light on the skids. This was a simulator thing and not really true in the aircraft. For the ITO, I added ten pounds to my hover torque that had just recorded as my hover power. I pulled on the collective while slightly applying forward cyclic, allowing for the transition into transitional lift. The wings were steady on the attitude indicator, the VSI had a positive climb, and the airspeed indicator was accelerating to and on its way to ninety knots. Things were looking good. While Roger was placing the transponder into operation and beginning the fuel check, I contacted departure and said, "Departure, Army 12345 passing 1,000 for 3,000."

"Roger, Army 12345, contact approach control on two four seven point five."

"Roger, thanks, Departure," I responded.

Roger had already put me up the no. 2 for the new frequency and simply pointed at me.

Understanding the unspoken communication, I visually confirmed I was up no. 2 and keyed the mic. "Approach Control, Army 12345 passing 1,500 now for 3,000."

"Roger, Army 12345, state intentions." Not an unusual bit of communication at a military airdrome. My flight plan may have already stated my intentions, but a lot of things change quickly in the IFR environment. So I was not surprised by the comms.

"Approach, Army 12345 requests the ILS six, followed by the published holding."

"Army 12345," Approach (Roger) responded, "receiving the OSAN locator outer marker (LOM), cross the beacon at 2,500 feet, cleared for the ILS 06, missed approach instructions as published. Contact departure control on the missed." Knowing now that I was no longer going to 5,000 feet, I began to level off at 2,500 feet and made my level off call.

Looking for the no. 1 needle to start to become alive, I begin the push-and-pull dance to move the head of that needle direct it to the LOM. By the clock, I had approximately ten minutes before crossing the LOM, so I needed to pass the controls to my copilot so that I could get the plate out and set the cockpit up. I passed the controls to Roger and instructed him to maintain 2,500 feet, ninety knots, and push-or-pull or track the no. 1 needle as needed to get us to the LOM. I got busy looking over the plate. With my attention directed inside, Roger banked the aircraft slightly. I looked up and watched as he recovered. I just assumed that he was making heading corrections to get us to the LOM. A short time later, he very slowly and gradually banked the aircraft five degrees, and once he did that, he pulled the circuit breaker to my attitude indicator and then leveled the aircraft using the standby attitude indicator.

Now the primary attitude indicator was stuck five degrees to the left. Of course, I was unaware of this as I was still studying the plate. Roger asked if he could pass the controls long enough so that he could make an adjustment to his kneeboard.

"Sure," I said.

The moment he passed the controls, the aircraft or simulator began to operate erratically with intermittent surges of power. I initially thought I was experiencing a high-side engine failure but was unsure as it was erratic. I increased power slightly to study the effects of the engine. Seemed fine 'til I reduced power, and then the engine again continued to operate erratically. I shifted my thoughts from a high-side to a low-side engine failure. I was stumped. I realized that I was in a left bank. I began to correct that and found that my altitude was no longer at 2,500 feet but that I had lost 700 feet while troubleshooting the engine. I also noticed that I was off course to the left by 25 degrees. I decided to call Approach.

"Osan Approach, Army 12345 declaring an emergency. Currently at 1,800 feet and 25 degrees off course."

"Roger, Army 12345," Approach (Roger) replied. "State intentions."

"Army 12345 requests vectors for a no-gyro approach into Osan full stop," I replied.

"Army 12345, turn left and intercept the LOM inbound. Report LOM," Approach (Roger) reported. Those instructions just aggravated my left turn failure. I asked Roger to identify the emergency governor switch and place it into the emergency position. He did so without me leading that action with throttle reduction. When Roger placed the emergency governor switch into the emergency position, it suddenly and rapidly delivered fuel to the fuel control putting this manageable emergency over the top.

Since I had no further instructions for Roger, he just sat and watched as I tried to regain RPM and control of the aircraft. The rotor almost spun off the aircraft before I had pulled enough collective to catch it. The throttle was still full-on as well, and once I reduced the collective, both the engine and rotor began to highside…again. To make matters worse, I was in a full-on left spin and heading quickly to the earth where not even crash rescue could help us. Before we made a fiery hole in the earth, Roger pushed the freeze button, and we became awash with silence. He was busy writing out his debriefing notes on his kneeboard. I knew it was terrible, and I sat there quietly waiting for him to finish. He opened the -10 to make sure that his observations were correctly documented.

"Okay, let's start at the top," he began. "Your mistake not to call ATIS from the get-go was very redeemable. I thought you worked through that teaching point well. Your radio work is above average. Your cockpit set up and copilot briefing and duty assignment were better than okay. I might have done somethings differently, but all in all, still satisfactory. Your ITO was textbook and nicely executed. Your transition from tower to departure and then approach was smooth and understandable. Again, I might have changed a few things, but you got the job done nicely. We were headed to the LOM at the right altitude. Were we tracking or homing to the beacon?"

As soon as he asked, I remembered that when you track the needle, you push or pull the head of the needle to maintain an assigned heading. When homing the needle, you place the head of the needle at the top of the RMI and wait to arrive at the beacon. Knowing that I was struggling for the answer, Roger referenced my clearance from his kneeboard, and he repeated my clearance. "Army 12345, receiving the OSAN locater otter marker (LOM), cross the beacon at 2,500 feet, cleared for the ILS 06, missed approach instructions as published. Contact departure control on the missed."

After hearing the clearance again, I gave him what I thought was the correct answer when I said, "Since there was no heading assignment, we were homing to the LOM."

"Then why did you tell me to push or pull to track the no. 1 needle as needed to get us to the LOM?" I had no answer. "Let's talk about the emergency procedure," he said. "What kind of emergency were you experiencing?"

"One of many," I said. "It could have been a high-side then possibly a low-side. Engine surges possibly. I honestly don't know."

"Let's review what the -10 says. Paragraph 9-9 b(4) says, should the engine malfunction during a left bank maneuver, right cyclic input to level the aircraft must be made simultaneously with collective pitch adjustment. If the collective pitch is decreased without a corresponding right cyclic input, the helicopter will pitch down and the roll rate will increase rapidly, resulting in a significant loss of altitude. The *warning* on the same page says:

> Warning. Do not close the throttle. Do not respond to the rpm audio and/or warning light illumination without first confirming engine malfunction by one or more of the other indications. Normal indications signify the engine is functioning properly and that there is a tachometer generator failure or an open circuit to the warning system, rather than an actual engine malfunction."

"Dean," Roger continued, "I failed your attitude indicator in a left five-degree bank and gave you a tach failure. Your engine was fine, you overacted, and I had to freeze the aircraft to keep us from crashing. It is an honest new guy error. This is what I see all the time. You are at the rote level of learning. He went on to explain the four levels of learning—rote, understanding, application, and correlation. You have a good rote foundation. Sometimes that rote foundation manifests at the next level, understanding, but you are away yet from the application and correlation stages. You are not far from where you need to be, but we still have some work to do. Hey, let's turn this flight into a training flight instead of an instrument check ride, and we will come back another day when you are not so tense."

He should have given me an unsatisfactory and grounded me from performing any other mission flights until he trained me to standard. Instead, he made the nice-guy call and called it a training flight. He should not have allowed me off that easy, but I appreciated it. He was a nice guy after all, and I know that he had intended to return me to the simulator to address these training deficiencies. But that did not happen as planned. The workload and the Christmas holidays got in the way. A few days became a few weeks, and here now, on December 23, I was out on a mission in the thick of as many errors as one could count. I had to wonder how Roger was feeling knowing that I was out in full-on IMC conditions knowing full well that he had turned my instrument ride into a training ride rather than busting me.

CHAPTER 23

Haunted by My Failed Instrument Check Ride while Continuing to Clean Up the Cockpit

23 December 1982, ROK. Somewhere South of Wonju. Thirteen Minutes into IMC.

I continued to monitor the LT's hand on that wiper switch. A quick glance at the windscreen showed me that she was controlling the ice buildup. I could have told her to let them stay on, but they were very distracting and noisy. Frankly, my plate was pretty full. I had enough distractions going on, and I didn't want any more distractions. Imagine the crew's vote of confidence in me if they knew that only a few weeks prior, I had failed an attempt to successfully fly instruments in a flight simulator during my APART instrument check ride. If I were them, I would be terrified to be in the same aircraft under the command of someone who choked during a simulated instrument flight. I couldn't say anything to my crew about me failing my instrument check ride. Whatever confidence I was trying to inspire would be for naught. Roger was a master of his craft as he had absolutely distracted me by pulling a circuit breaker for the attitude indicator as well as failing the tach, giving me the impression that we had engine trouble. That position in and of itself is one of a person looking to shift blame onto Roger. I was deceived by Roger right enough, but I am not shifting blame to Roger. I messed up during the check ride, mostly by choking.

Hell, I was deceived by real-life occurrences during this flight. The deception is not the issue. How I reacted is the issue. I was just moments from crashing the simulator, and I fell apart and had to be rescued by Roger when he depressed the freeze button. No freeze button here while IMC for me to push. If we crash, I will be repeating my dad's flight, and I wanted more than anything for my dad to be proud of how I handled this flight's circumstances. Even though I was responsible for the errors, I had to rise above the mistakes and get us all home safely, something I failed to do during my instrument check ride under flight simulation…

No distractions, only flying now. If I can understand this problem one bite at a time, then we should be okay. Safely arriving and landing at Osan was my only mission at this point. Here we were in it now. Feeling the need to purge myself and beg forgiveness for my faults by telling my crew that I busted my instrument check ride just a few weeks earlier would do no good at all. How would that make them feel anyway? Here they are, stuck with a guy making life-and-death decisions on their behalf. I owed them a sense of hope. A vote of no confidence is counterproductive. No time to clutter the problem with these facts, so instead, I will have to choke the simulation event down and do the best that I possibly can to deal with the reality of this flight. My head inside continued to spin with self-doubt.

I wanted the LT to get busy doing two things; (1) tune the VOR and (2) tune the ILS.

"LT, have you an IFR en route low altitude chart in your flight bag?" I asked. She gave me a startled look. I had seen that look many times on the faces of my stick buddies in flight school.

"Ryan, can you reach into my flight bag and give the LT my IFR en route low altitude chart?"

Ryan smartly rummaged through my flight bag and found it and passed it to the LT.

"LT, Osan is in there somewhere." Since she was not familiar with the area, it became something of an Easter egg hunt. I was not about to pass the controls to find it for her. Given her performance thus far, I did not need to recover the aircraft if she inadvertently fell prey to one of the many illusions haunting us both.

"LT, lay the map out over the center console."

She began to unfold it, and I could not help but think of the movie *1941* starring John Belushi. John Belushi was a swashbuckling aviator winging it, sort of like we were. There were plenty of hilarious scenes throughout the film, but one of the funnier points of the *1941* movie was playing out before me as the LT grappled with unfolding the map and getting it laid out between us. Funny film...not funny here. Hey, I am human. Excuse my mental relief as I ponder the LT's parallel experiences with the film. I am just glad it was too cold to open her the side window. In the movie, John Belushi opened his canopy with the map fully opened, and the entire map was sucked out. Had she opened her side window, we could have lost the map for sure. Finally, she had it between us, and between my flying and scanning the flight instruments, I helped her search for Osan. It was taking too long. I asked her to flip it over. She did, and again, we scoured the map for Osan.

"Not there," I said. "Flip it over again," I asked. A short search on the first side again produced the reason that Osan was so challenging to find. Osan was inside the Songtan VOR compass rose. Osan was printed in a light brown, and in the poor light, it was difficult to see. She pulled the map closer, and she confirmed Osan was inside the Songtan VOR compass rose.

"Great," I said. "With Osan found, what is the VOR Frequency for Songtan VOR?"

"116.9," she said.

"Dial it in," I told her. It was reassuring to see the no. 2 needle on the RMI turn around and point to the Songtan VOR. I asked her to flip up my nav switch on my C1611, and when she did, I faintly heard the Songtan VOR identifier as dot, dot, dot, dash, dash, dash, and finished up with a dash. All stations are all assigned a Morris Code identifier. We call it tuning and identifying. The LT had correctly tuned the frequency, and I had correctly heard and recognized the assigned dots and dashes confirming that we were heading to the right place. With the no. 2 needle pointing at the station, I looked at its tail. The tail of the no. 2 needle sat on 065 degrees, meaning that we were sitting on the 065 radial out of the Songtan VOR on a heading of 245 degrees inbound to Osan. What a victory that was. Navigationally anyway, I felt that things were looking up. We still had a way to go, but I had a radial to navigate if radio problems developed. I was currently under radar control and was following those instructions.

Next, I asked the LT how she was doing with working the approach plate for Osan. She was slow but responsive. The entire time I spoke to her, I rarely left my instrument scan. I continued to maintain head discipline by not moving my head any more than absolutely necessary. Flight school was still fresh. I appreciated now, not then, the efforts and lengths that the IPs went to to instill flight lessons and develop behaviors. Becoming familiar with the instrument plate construction was one such drill. My IP would hold the plate and drill me on every approach that we were to fly during each flight period.

I had to recall the construction of the plate, and I had to direct him through the approach plate correctly. It was a great drill. He told me that, one day, I would be flying with a copilot who would require that sort of attention. Knowing the construction of the plate could save my life. I thought that all IPs did that. I was wrong. When speaking to my other classmates, they would not complain about that at all. They would complain about other aspects of the instruction, but not of the construction of the plates. In later years, I would come to understand that this was an instructional technique used by my IP to press a point. My IP apparently found the need for that sort of plate knowledge intensity during his own flight experiences, and he was making sure that I fully understood plate construction as well. Like I said, during flight school, I did not appreciate that technique, but his insistence upon using that technique was paying off huge today. By contrast, the LT IPs apparently did not feel that plate construction was that big a deal. I felt that I was leading her block by block through the plate to find things just as my IP had suffered as he taught me to do. Wherever you are, Mr. IP, thank you for that training. You were right, it may have indeed played a large part in saving our lives today.

I had the construction of the instrument plate fixed in my mind. All instrument plates are constructed the same. It is a standardization thing. Standardization is a core element to the flying business. Strange the things that come to mind during times of stress. I remembered the children's television show where there was a purple creature by the name of Barney. My daughter was raised watching Barney. My wife hated Barney. At the end of the show, the creature would sing some sort of see-ya-later song, and when it mercifully got to the end of the song, before my wife could change the channel, Barney was back with another episode. My wife would complain to me when I got home about this Barney creature and would relent how it never went away, it just kept coming back time and again with one show after another. Our daughter loved Barney and would sing along and laugh with all its antics even though she had seen the show hundreds of times.

I thought I would show off about stuff that I was learning during one of my wife's rants about Barney. Now that I was in flight school, I was learning much about the importance of standardization. I thought that she would appreciate what I had learned and how standardization worked. How it may, in fact, be related to Barney. "Do you know why the kids love Barney so much?" I asked out of the blue.

"No," she said, and I suspected she didn't care. But after being married to me eleven years, she knew there was more to my story. "Well, why?" she impatiently asked.

"Simple," I said. "Standardization, that's all. The kids know all the words to the songs, all the jokes, they know they are going to have fun and not get hurt. They feel safe wrapped up in a purple creature called Barney." Now I knew every word of that was accurate. My wife, however, was not the slightest bit impressed with my burst of brilliance.

She stomped off and turned around long enough to tell me, "You're home now. You enjoy Barney. Maybe you will learn more about standardization. I need some relief from that creature," and then disappeared into the back part of the house.

Barney was pretty stupid, but the fact remains that Barney and standardization have a lot in common. I could have used some of the safety offered by the receptiveness of Barney stuff right now. I wanted all the standardization stuff that the LT and I had learned thus far to gel and lead us through this flight to a successful ending. Just deal with logic, I kept telling myself. Dissect the problem and solve that piece and then go on the next problem set. Enough was going wrong with the flight without doing anything extra. Running the wipers intermittently removed additional stress from me and gave the LT something essential to do. I had my hands full flying and cross-checking, flying and cross-checking, flying and more cross-checking. Thanks, Barney. This I was content to repeat minute by minute as we lumbered on. As long as we were flying, we were alive, and it never seemed to stop—flying and more cross-checking. I was okay with it. So when I had developed my mental picture of the Osan approach plate, I asked her to walk me through it. Roger was correct when he proclaimed that I was at the rote level of learning. I knew all the plates were broken down into sections. those sections: the heading, plan view, profile view and, lastly, the minimums.

The heading is packed with ATIS, ground, tower, departure, and approach frequencies, just to name a few. Missed approach instructions were also found there. The plan view, to me, was the most important, because in one glance, you could see all the components of the approach. All the views were important, but the plan view showed the approach to the airdrome as if you were hovering directly above the airdrome looking straight down. It had the direction to track to the airdrome, the navigational aid frequencies, as well as holding diagrams if holding was applicable to the approach. The plan view was distinctive to the type of approach as well. NDB approach as opposed to a VOR or ILS approach, for example. Water features shown on the plan view were also drawn to scale. It showed clearly the direction of turn during the missed as well. For me, the profile view was kissing cousins in importance the plan view. The profile view shows the approach as if you were looking at the approach perpendicular to the airdrome. When looking at the profile view, one could easily imagine watching the aircraft leave altitude to arrive at the airdrome. While dropping in altitude, you have to have a direction to fly. Handy indeed as the direction of flight is also published in this view.

Along with altitude changes and direction of flight, the navigational aids are also addressed. Finally, the minimums section at the bottom called out the different categories of approaches with their associated airspeeds and altitudes for each approach, e.g., ILS, NDB, VOR, etc. The plate to the casual observer could be a confusing place, but while in flight school, if I did not learn anything else, I learned of its construction. I would just tune out the bombardment of information provided by the plates and focus on the stuff needed for the approach that was filed for.

And that is precisely what I needed now. I only required the information necessary for the approach. I knew I was going to ask for a no-gyro approach, so realistically, we didn't need a plate at all. I was planning on asking for a no-gyro approach because my RMI and my attitude indicator were unreliable. Asking for a no-gyro approach also took more work off me. During a no-gyro approach, the ATC controller watches me on radar and, based upon what he sees, is responsible for bringing you into the airdrome capture zone. He controls your direction of flight as well as your altitude. During the approach, the ATC controller will hand you off to a final controller. The final controller is responsible for my heading as well as my bank angle. He is responsible as well for keeping me on the decent angle needed to track my approach to the runway centerline. The final controller will talk you all the way to the actual touchdown. As you are descending and before he takes you to the ground, he advises that you are at decision height (DH). It is at DH when the PIC makes a decision to continue with the approach to the ground under his control or break off the approach and complete the approach visually. I was sorely looking forward to breaking out of this snow and completing the approach visually. I did not want to take the approach to the ground under the controller's directions. We were still thirty minutes or so from that, however. I needed to keep it together another thirty minutes or so, and we would be home free. I was planning to overlay the ILS approach to the no-gyro approach that I would be asking for. Before beginning the no-gyro approach, I would ensure the LT had correctly tuned the ILS so that during the no-gyro, we would have all the aircraft's navigational instruments tuned and working in our favor. I wanted to see my instruments correctly responding to the instructions of the controller. This was a technique taught in flight school. Why not stack the deck in my favor, I was thinking. I just wanted to break out and get this flight over with.

The LT took another swipe with the wiper switch, and then she took my task at hand. Visualizing the heading of the approach plate, I asked her to confirm that she was looking at the approach plate for the ILS 9 into Osan. She acknowledged so and held the book over the center console to show me. I waved her off. Told her I was too busy with my part of the mission, flying and cross-checking, flying and cross-checking, and asked her to continue reading me the information in the heading slowly. I wanted her first to tell me the frequency for Osan approach control. She found that information and said to me that it was 125.4 on the victor radio and 270.35 on the uniform. I asked her to put 125.4 into victor radio, no. 3 position. Then I asked her to write down 270.35 on her kneeboard.

Once we were finished with Poncho's frequency of 327.125 in the uniform, no. 2 position, then she could tune up Osan approach control frequency of 270.35 in the uniform, no. 2 position. Since I was still monitoring Poncho on 372.125, I needed that frequency to remain right where it was for now. It was our lifeline, and I did not need that radio fooled with right now. On that note, the uniform radio no. 2 came to life when Poncho came on the radio with a position report for me.

Poncho reported, "RB93, you are maintaining course and altitude, and you are making your way to Osan. You will be leaving my airspace in another ten minutes or so, state intentions."

I was immediately awash with gratitude. Poncho was kind enough to give me exactly what I needed. We were still flying toward Osan. We were still alive. We were flying straight and level on the last attitude correction he had made for us, and we're heading for Osan as if it were a routine IFR flight. I had to smile as I embraced the Barney moment and replied, "Roger, Poncho. RB93 will be requesting a no-gyro approach at Osan. If you can notify Osan that we are on our way, that would be a great help."

"Roger, RB93, will pass that along. Talk with you again just before you leave my airspace." I know it was nothing for an experienced aviator to do, fly IFR. But I had entered IFR and icing via IMC and just weeks before I busted my instrument check ride in the simulator. This unplanned event, coupled with the ice, non-responsive instruments, and a crew that was a terrible mismatch would have been a challenge even for an experienced PIC, so I was so very grateful for the typical conversation with Poncho as, if only for a moment, it seemed all was normal, even from his seat. That was a comforting Barney moment.

"Okay, LT, back to the radios. Have you the Osan Approach control frequency ready to tune into the no. 2 position once I am done with Poncho."

"Yes, 270.35 standing by for the no. 2."

"Great," I said. "How about ATIS on the victor? What is the frequency?"

"123.2," she reported.

"Great," I said. "Let's put that in the victor no. 3 position. We are not using the no. 3 right now, and maybe we are close enough to get their ATIS automated service."

She turned it up, and we listened. Nothing. Listening…nothing. I would like to have heard something. We were still thirty minutes out of Osan, so maybe it was a range thing. I explained that to the LT and asked her to keep that frequency in the no. 3 position while we flew closer and closed the distance.

"How about the ILS frequency?" I asked.

"I don't see it," she said.

I remembered from flight school that that could be tricky.

"In the heading information, it is called LOC or localizer. The plan view also calls it localizer. The frequency should be in both the heading as well as the plan view."

I got caught more than once on instrument check rides in flight school with that one. The IFE would ask, "What is the frequency for the ILS." The plate name is ILS blah, blah, the localizer is the frequency that will allow you to fly down the ILS dart. It can easily be confusing. Add some real life and death stress, and one could quickly get it wrong. The LT did find the frequency and called it out as 109.7.

"Good. Tune that up into ILS navigational aid."

Out of my highly trained peripheral vision from flight school, I saw Ryan's hand go up and turn the wipers on, then, after a few wipes, off again. During the first two weeks of warrant officer candidate training, we had to eat square meals. When we sat down, we could only look straight ahead and not look at our tray of food. While looking straight forward, using our peripheral vision, we had to pick up the proper utensil and select food we could not see and then, in a perpendicular movement, attempt to feed ourselves. When I asked why we did that, I was told we were training our peripheral vision. Really… That was a very long two-week lesson. I got as much food on me as in me. Every time I see anything now out of my peripheral vision, I smile at the absurdity of those two weeks. At any rate, Ryan was sitting in one of the two jump seats closest to me facing forward just over my left shoulder.

The wiper switch was in the upper console, likewise over my left shoulder. The new duties that I had assigned the LT seemed to disclude those previous and essential wiper assignment. Investigating the plate interrupted the LT's rhythm concerning keeping those windows clear. I did not want to be unkind by reminding the LT that she had missed keeping the windscreen clear of ice. I did not want to miss the runway environment due to ice on the windscreens. Neither Ryan nor I spoke a word but made eyeball-to-eyeball contact, and with a nod, I knew that Ryan would operate the wipers, ensuring that they would be switched on and off as needed to keep the windshields cleared. Another moment that I stole away to myself. I was overcome with gratitude at the accomplishment of this minimal but essential task. I was also grateful not to have to explain why I did not want what them to run. It was important to me that they run internment and my crew just accepted that as reason good enough. To the best of my knowledge and recollection, the LT never again addressed the windscreen with the wipers.

"Okay," I said to the LT. "109.7 for the ILS. How about the LOM?" I could see her study the plate. "Look at the plan view, it may also be called the IAF."

"Yes, here it is. 212," she said.

"Excellent, please tune 212 into the beacon. What is the inbound track for the ILS approach?" I asked.

"091 degrees," she responded. For the first time in a long time, I took my left hand off the collective and put the heading bug on 091 so that I would know the immediate direction of turn when the time came for the approach. I also tuned the heading 091 in the course deviation indicator (CDI) so that I could fly down the localizer while the final controller was articulating his part of the approach.

The CDI was a critically important instrument when performing an ILS approach. It was a round instrument and has two movable bars called pointers. There is a vertical pointer and a horizontal pointer. I don't know what the circle in the very center of the gauge is formally called, but we called it the donut. The vertical pointer and the horizontal pointer, when joined in the middle, looks like a cross through the middle of the donut. If the pilot is on course and on glide slope, then the vertical pointer and the horizontal pointer will be joined in the middle, and it will look like a cross right through the center of the donut. That was my goal for the approach. Easier said than done.

At the airdrome, there resides two signal generators (localizer and glide slope); one in the very high frequency (VHF) range as well as one in the ultra-high frequency (UHF) range. The generation of both the localizer and glide slope signals combined sends a signal three degrees upward and outward from the airdrome. It is commonly called an ILS glide slope and looks like a dart pointing at and directing the flight crew to the airdrome. The fall of the ILS glide slope into the airdrome is typically engineered to 3 degrees, which provide for a 500 feet per minute aircraft rate of descent while the crew directs the aircraft on the ILS approach. The localizer signal generator provides for azimuth navigation (heading), while the glide slope signal generator provides for the three-degree signal fan from the horizon. The pilot is considered on course when the vertical pointer of the CDI is dead center of the donut within the CDI. Likewise, the pilot is considered on glideslope when the horizontal pointer of the CDI is dead center of the donut within the CDI. During the final controller's directions to the pilot during any no-gyro approach, if the pilot hears the final controller say, "On course, on glideslope," then the pilot should see the CDI with a cross in the donut. At some time during the approach, it is hoped that the aircraft will break out of the weather conditions and the pilot will complete the landing visually. There are a lot of moving parts to an ILS approach, but if done correctly, it is advertised to be a precision approach right down the centerline of the runway. Add winds, vertical air, and an obscuration like snow and ice to the mix, and what would otherwise be a piece of cake becomes anything but. For now, things were going along okay, it seemed. ILS or localizer tuned up—check. The beacon tuned up—check. Radiofrequency strategy established as we would eventually change frequencies to Osan—check. How much worse can this flight get?

CHAPTER 24

Icing Manifestation Is Realized— Fuel Check Is in Progress

23 December 1982, ROK. Somewhere South of Wonju. Fifteen Minutes into IMC.

A few minutes went by, and it was easy to see that we were set-tling into a rhythm. The drone and vibration of the T53 turbine engine was ever-present. The snow splatting against the windscreen had become white noise that I had come to accept. I appreciated Ryan's action as he replaced the LT by occasionally clearing the windscreen of snow before it iced over. None of us had much to say. There were many goings-on in my head, but I kept it all to myself. I wondered if the fragile moments of normalcy meant as much to the rest of the crew as those vulnerable moments meant to me? I cherished every ordinary moment if one can call flying IMC/IFR without a flight plan in icing conditions with failing flight instruments normal. We were quiet. I was flying and cross-checking, flying and cross-checking, flying and more cross-checking. In-flight school, we were taught to minimize head movement to keep our inner ear as still as possible. My neck ached from being so ridged. I knew that being too ridged was also bad, so I carefully left my instrument scan to look over at the LT to monitor what she was doing. I found her most often looking at the plate as if she were willing our arrival and safe approach. Didn't seem like much of a task but it kept her busy. I glanced at the center console and made myself satisfied that the ILS and LOM were still correctly tuned. We would have to wait until we were closer to identify them as we were still too far from the station to hear its dots and dashes.

Thinking about that, I asked the LT to put on her kneeboard a remark to check the identifier when we were closer. Also, I asked her to close out her fuel check. I chose to run mine another five minutes. We were fifteen minutes into the fuel check, and I wanted to know how we were doing on our fuel burn. She put down the Osan ILS plate and began working her fuel numbers. While she was working the numbers, I was doing some beer math in my head. A full bag of gas is charted at one thousand three hundred and forty-two pounds. But staying with the beer math, typically twelve hundred pounds is used for a rule of thumb. Discounting a fuel reserve that must be maintained, considering a Huey's standard burn rate of six hundred pounds an hour would give us a two-hour flight. We did top off when we got to Wonju, but we sat at Wonju with the engine running at ground idle for thirty minutes waiting on the PAXs. That cost us in fuel. We departed Wonju with one thousand pounds of fuel. I remember wishing that we should have topped off before leaving, but waiting on the PAXs and the quick escape for weather did not allow for that. We are too far into the mission to look back now. At fifteen minutes into this flight I can see that we have eight hundred and fifty pounds of fuel, putting us down by a hundred and fifty pounds of fuel, so I am hoping the LT will tell me that we are burning one hundred and fifty pounds on the quarter-hour making for a six hundred pound burn on the hour.

I waited. I waited. I waited. "LT how's that fuel check coming." She was spinning her E-6B Flight Computer, aka a whiz wheel, much too slowly and studying it for far too long. Finally, she said we are burning six hundred eighty pounds per hour. She began to give me the burn out times with reserve, and I interrupted her. How can that be right? We burned just under six hundred pounds per hour during the flight up to Wonju. The conditions were colder on the leg back for sure, but colder means a better fuel burn typically. What has changed, I wondered? I couldn't tolerate the math distraction right now, still too busy flying and cross-checking the instruments. "Okay, LT work up the fuel burn and our reserves. Record it on your kneeboard and restart your fuel check. Let's make sure the number are the same. Six hundred eighty pounds per hour is a heavy burn rate. Let me know when you complete the second check. I will close my numbers out soonest," I tell her.

It was time to cage the attitude indicator again. Fifteen minutes into IMC and five minutes past the last time we pulled to cage the attitude indicators. We were getting pretty good at this. I got the LTs., attention. She was still writing stuff on her kneeboard when I interrupted, "LT it is time to cage the attitude indicators again." As before, I waited for the mag compass to be perfectly level and still. I checked the dog house on the turn and slip as well as ensuring that the VSI was sitting at zero and once satisfied that the attitude of the aircraft was level I said "Mark" to the LT and she caged her attitude indicator, and I adjusted my attitude indicator to wings level. That went well, I thought.

Ryan tapped on my shoulder, keyed his mic, and said, "I think I know why we are burning more fuel on trip back versus the trip up."

Intrigued, I asked, "Why?"

"Ice, I believe," he said.

Over each pilot's head is an upper windscreen commonly called a greenhouse. We call it a greenhouse because…well, it's green. It is akin to a moon roof on a car, except these do not open. They allow the pilots to see above. With your flight helmet on, you really have to crank your neck to see much of the aircraft, but still, you can see some. The greenhouse was not designed for aircraft inspection; instead, they were there so that the pilot could clear themselves overhead. The green color helped with direct sunlight from above. The ice had heavily impacted the windscreens and was only removed where Ryan had faithfully operated the wipers. The greenhouse and the windows in the doors were still relatively clear as the slipstream was moving ice debris rearward. Through the moving ice debris on the greenhouse, you could just make out the top of the wire strike protection system (WSPS). The WSPS is designed to provide 90 percent wire strike protection on the Huey. There is duplicate WSPS on the very bottom of the aircraft. Part of the WSPS system, there is a serrated metal member that runs up through the center of each windscreen. That serrated metal member has hacksaw like teeth that begin to cut the wire and direct the cable into the WSPS where the final cutting action happens. If a crew flies a Huey into power lines, the thought process is that if the wire is struck in the windscreen area, the cable will run up the serrated metal cutter in the middle and into the upper WSPS to be cut, saving the crew. Remarkably, it has in fact, over the years, saved many a crew. We were well above any wires, so at this altitude, there was no wire threat. Even so, the WSPS still continued to stand watch for wires as we charged ahead. Instead of ingesting wires, even while cranking my neck looking up through the greenhouse, I could clearly see that the WSPS was now a tower of ice and growing. Looking still through the greenhouse, and with great effort, I could see the very edge of the pitot tube. The heater within the pitot tube was doing its job. No ice on the pitot tube, only its supporting structure.

Before looking back at Ryan, I took a moment to re-cage my brain. I checked the instruments to make sure that I had not inadvertently induced a bank when looking at the WSPS and pitot tube. Sure enough, there was a slight right bank indicated on the mag compass, and the heading had changed some twenty degrees. I very carefully corrected the heading and attitude. My heart raced for a moment, but all in all, the correction was very slight, and once I was satisfied that my wrenching actions to see the WSPS was corrected, I looked back at Ryan.

"You're right," I said. "I wonder how many fixed structures up there are covered with ice."

"There's the extra weight," Ryan suggested.

I agreed, and worse, it was growing with each passing minute that we flew in these conditions. I did not want to speak it out loud. If I kept that to myself, maybe no one else would put that together. I ultimately knew that was stupid. Ryan was the one that directed my attention to the ice in the first place. There was nothing I could do at this point but fly the aircraft. Something many of my IPs taught me. Never stop flying the aircraft, they would proclaim. As long as you are flying, you are in a better place than crashing. I fully understand that concept. I intended to do nothing more than fly this aircraft directly to Osan and land safely. God help me!

CHAPTER 25

Icing Thickens on the Aircraft and Flicker Vertigo Is Introduced

23 December 1982, ROK. Somewhere South of Wonju. Twenty Minutes into IMC.

We are at the twenty-minute mark in the flight, and we have become comfortable with our developed routine. I am flying and crosschecking, flying and crosschecking, and still, more flying and crosschecking. LT is studying the approach into Osan. Ryan is working the wipers, keeping the windscreen from icing over. Major Burns was back in the back, observing and offering nothing. I found that very surprising. He was seated next to Ryan in one of the two forward-facing jump seats just to the right rear of the LT, so he had a good vantage point. His silence was reassuring...I think. The major did have that big star above his wings. To qualify for a big star, otherwise known as a senior aviator, one must be on flight status for seven years and had reached 1,000 hours of flight time. Compared to the few hundreds of flight time that I had thus far, 1,000 hours was a big deal. We fledgling aviators took real stock in those who have big stars on their wings. I take some measure of comfort in his silence and have to hope that he is in agreement with the things I have done thus far. I get it that I should not have gotten us here in the first place, but if I missed something, I would have to think that he would have spoken up by now so. I will take his silence as a positive. It's a Barney moment for me to enjoy. Everyone doing their jobs to a standard meant we were still alive.

Back to flying and crosschecking. During the instrument cross-check, I saw that I was twenty minutes into my fuel check. I remembered that the LT's fuel check had us on the other side of 600 pounds per hour. I have to confirm that. At that 20-minute mark, I calculated that we were burning 220 pounds. That put us at a 660-pound per hour burn rate. That is a significant increase in fuel burn. At that fuel burn, we will arrive at Osan with 340 pounds. Factor in a 30-minute IFR reserve and our adjusted arrival fuel, that leaves 110 pounds to work with. If we were VFR, I would shrug off those numbers, but we were not VFR. We were IFR, and I needed more wiggle room. I announced to the crew my fuel check numbers. The LT agreed that only having 110 pounds of wiggle room was cutting it close.

"Sure is a good thing that we have our thirty-minute reserve to fall back on if we need it," she said.

"Let's hope that we don't need it, that we experience a normal landing at Osan, and that we log this into our very beings as lessons learned," I said matter-of-factly. "I am starting a new fuel check," I announced. "LT, please back me up," I asked. We have to get this fuel thing spot on. Both the LT and I recorded the time as well as the fuel. 780 pounds. The clock was running. It was four-five past the hour on when I started the first fuel check. It was now zero-five past the hour. I will revisit the fuel check at three-five past the hour. I want to get a full thirty minutes on this fuel check.

Out of my highly trained peripheral vision from square meals, I had become aware of an intermittent red glow against the snow sky. I was too busy to notice until now. Now that we had settled into our flight routine and crew rhythm, I could expand my senses into other areas, like noticing the intermittent red glow while I scanned the instruments. It really began to bother me. It did not take me long to realize the source. It was the anti-collision light. Scrolling my mental Rolodex, I brought up a subject from our aero-med classes and gave it a name...flicker vertigo.

Flicker vertigo is a trigger element. Vertigo is dizziness. Spatial disorientation occurs when the aviator incorrectly perceives his attitude, position, and motion relative to the center of the earth. I remember well reciting those two definitions in aero-med classes as well as discussing the topics on multiple occasions with IPs when they were trying to assess where I was at in the training cycle. During my failed instrument check ride of late, Roger's assessment of me was correct, I was still at the rote level of learning. I could recite definitions but only occasionally flirted with the correlation level of learning. At this point of flying and scanning and flying and scanning, I appreciated the mental distraction as I needed to understand every aspect of this flight. It was critical that I not become fatigued flying and scanning, repeat, repeat, and repeat all the way to Osan and the landing and lulled to sleep either by the monotony of the repetitive nature of my tasks. Hard to think that I could get lulled to sleep in these conditions. I didn't think that I was in danger of taking a cat nap. I was in danger of flying my aircraft into the ground; however, if I allowed any condition to go unnoticed or unaddressed, then that mistake could be the straw that breaks this flight. Missing something now could mean life or death. Sort of like missing and misdiagnosing a failed tach in the simulator during my last instrument check ride. So recalling and understanding the ills of the anti-collision light was very important. I knew that my vestibular system was in play, and I also knew that the inner ear and my brain were responsible for balance. I just had to choreograph what my brain was saying with what my eyes were seeing. Maybe that is the reason that my IPs in flight school were so persistent in minimizing one head's position during instrument flight. The flicker vertigo symptoms I remember from aero-med: balance, headaches, ear ringing, and sweating more than normal. I also remember panic attacks, fatigue, and nausea as symptoms of flicker vertigo. Oh my gosh, I have to stop looking at the red flashes. But wait, I can't stop. The flashes continue to invade my consciousness. My highly trained peripheral vision from square meals is ever-present. The anti-collision light is there for one purpose—to warn others of my position. I didn't need to fly into someone nor did I need someone else to fly into me.

Back at Fort Rucker, it was a flight violation to fly without an anti-collision light. In fact, the only way that you knew an anti-collision light was inoperative was when another aircraft or the tower would let you know on the radio that your light was inoperable. If you had forgotten to turn it on, then a quick switch displacement solved that problem. However, if the switch was indeed on and the anti-collision light really was inoperable, then you were forced to precautionary land (PL) the aircraft right there and wait for maintenance to come and fix it. Well, that was Fort Rucker logic in a training environment. I learned great lessons during flight school. The majority of the IPs were battle-hardened Vietnam veterans. That group of aviators built army aviation and the deployment of army aviation from the ground up. Upon their flights, the army aviation doctrine was written. I viewed them as the greatest generation of aviators. PL? I continued to go over the pros and cons in my head about the function of the anti-collision light. I am pretty sure that if they were in my cockpit, they would have simply turned the anti-collision light off. That action best fit my determination of the amount of risk that we were currently in. If I kept it on as taught and reinforced at Fort Rucker, then the possibility was great that I could fall prey to the pitfalls of flicker vertigo. I was pretty sure no one else was flying around out here, and even if they were, I was under radar control, and I doubted that I could be seen anyway because of the snow. The risk was greater to keep it on, I concluded.

I was maintaining head stillness discipline and announced, "LT, identify the anti-collision light switch in the overhead console and turn off the anti-collision light, please." If she looked at me, I could not tell. After going over in my head the ills of flicker vertigo, I was more determined than ever to maintain head discipline. It did not take long for the mic to come to life.

The LT began to exclaim, "But we are supposed to keep the anti-collision light on anytime to rotors are turning." I not only heard her, but suddenly, I heard the voices of many IPs in my head while in training about the anti-collision light.

"Listen, LT," I began. "I do not want to succumb to the effects of flicker vertigo. I am not saying that I am experiencing flicker vertigo right now, all I am saying is that it is bothering me in the same way that the wipers are bothering me. I want that light off please."

I waited, and then she offered, "But I had to PL in flight school because of an anti-collision that was inoperable. Do you plan to PL?"

I wasn't sure if I sensed scoffing or if she was pulling my leg. She knew well that we could not PL. I did appreciate the exchange, however. Questioning is healthy. She has carried out my instructions thus far.

Instead of letting her comment blow up the cockpit I just simply said, "Ha-ha, very funny. Wouldn't I love to PL right now? Turn off the anti-collision please."

"Identified and off," she reported. "How about the position lights? Do you want them to stay off?" she asked.

"The position lights are off?" I asked. Oh my gosh!!! If I wasn't mad enough at myself for getting us into this mess, I certainly had a good right to be angry with her last question. I am the PIC, it is not her fault that the position lights are off, and I am not going to shoot the messenger either. Right after entering IMC, the pitot heater switch was the number one switch to turn on. After redirected engine bleed air for other anti-icing, I should have followed that action with turning on the position lights too. I was just a bit busy laying the aircraft over onto its side and spiraling up above the mountains so that we would not run into the mountains. Given all the circumstances, forgetting to turn on the position lights was an easy mistake to make and, fortunately for today's flight, a mistake that will not kill us.

I did not share my frustration. I smiled instead and violated my head discipline and turned to her and simply said calmly, "Yes, I want the position lights on too. Thank you," and with that, I returned my head front and center and continued with the flying and scanning, flying and scanning. I was pleased to see that the loss of the anti-collision light narrowed my distractions back to the ones that I needed to keep a close watch over. Keeping the attitude straight and level was my primary focus. Keeping the attitudes of my crewmembers in check was a plus too.

Ryan had been very respectful not to interrupt thus far. His attempt at keeping the windscreen clear has proven fruitful. A quick glance at the windscreen shows the snow that has turned to ice. The bad news? The snow was being impacted all around the windscreen by the travel of wipers. The good news? The area swiped by the wiper was clear; that is great news really, actually. Again, missing the landing environment because of an iced-over windscreen is not good. Ryan knew I was swamped. The non-trained eye may not come to a busy conclusion, however. Just looking at me would find me pretty much frozen in place. I was practicing movement discipline. Every now and then, I would move my left hand up from the collective to the attitude indicator and after conferring with the turn and slip as well as the VSI and mag compass, I would adjust the attitude indicator to level. Then in the same movements to adjust the RMI to concur with the mag compass. As I have said earlier, I am flying partial panel, but seeing the precessing attitude indicator in a wings level condition as opposed to watching it fall off its gimble and begin to tumble was too much to manage. It was easier to feed myself a placebo by updating the attitude indicator visually. At least that looked normal, and it made my job flying just a bit easier. That is what Ryan saw from the outside none the less. But his was a trained eye, and he did not see a frozen person at the controls but one who was constantly assessing conditions.

He ever so lightly tapped my shoulder. I was so focused I missed his first attempt. The second was a bit more aggressive. "Hey, sir," Ryan began. "Been doing some reading in the -10 while you guys are flying. Thought you would like to know what the -10 has to say about icing."

"Ryan, I already know it's a bad thing."

"I know, sir, but since we are stuck, I thought I would let you know what the -10 has to say so that you can factor what you need to into your planning," Ryan said.

"I appreciate that, Ryan. Just the highlights. Please do not read the entire text," I asked.

"Okay," Ryan began. "Continuous flight in light icing conditions is not recommended because the ice shedding induces rotor blade vibrations."

I interrupt Ryan, "Well, we are beyond light icing conditions. I have never flown in icing conditions before either from the back seat or the front seat, but based upon what the WSPS looks like, I would have to guess that we are experiencing moderate to heavy icing conditions."

The LT chimed in and said, "Let me drop my window and look at the cross tube outside my door."

I could feel the rush of cold air coming into the cockpit the moment she opens that window. I could easily imagine the cold blast of air and snow hitting her helmet as she stuck it outside to look at the cross tubes. I have to admit, the fresh air was refreshing and stimulating and countered the monotony of my instrument crosscheck. She spent only a few moments with her head outside. When she came in, she quickly raised her window. She did not have ice on her helmet, but the water was dripping when she said, "There must be an inch of ice built up around the cross tube." This confirmed what we were able to see on the upper WSPS.

Ryan continued, "Every effort should be made to vacate the icing environment."

I interrupted Ryan again when I reminded the crew that we had already discussed altitude changes. The ceiling topped out at 10,000 feet, and we did not have supplemental oxygen. Given my second interruption, I could sense that Ryan was speedreading through text that would not be helpful to our predicament.

Having found text that may be helpful to our conditions, Ryan continued, "Ice accumulation on inlet screens can be detected on particle separator systems by the illumination of the *engine inlet air* cat-eye on the instrument panel or the *engine inlet air* caution panel segment light. Sir, before you told me to remove the side barrier filters, I read that section to you so that you would be reminded that the *engine inlet air* cat-eye on the instrument panel or the *engine inlet air* caution panel segment light on the master caution may illuminate if air-intake to the engine is comprised."

"Ryan, I appreciate the background. The good news is that we did remove the side inlet barriers to the engine inlet thereby creating, I'm guessing, a two-foot-by-three-foot hole in the engine inlet allowing for air to service the engine. I concede that I have never flown in icing before, but that is a pretty big hole to ice over. I will, however, be very watchful for the illumination of the *engine inlet air* cat-eye on the instrument panel or the *engine inlet air* caution panel segment light on the master caution panel. Is there anything else of interest that may be helpful for our current circumstances?" I asked.

"No, sir," Ryan replied. "The last point in this section of the -10 deals with ensuring and directing windshield defrosters to the windscreens. Not forgetting the turning on of the pitot heater. You have all the heat that is available directed to the windscreens, so that is a check. And the pitot heater is on and doing its job too. The -10 goes on to say that the windscreens may become obscured with the accumulation of ice. We are keeping that as clear as possible with the wipers. Sir, I find nothing else in the -10 that may help or that you have not considered," Ryan concluded.

"Thanks for that, Ryan," I said. "This is a crew effort, and your contributions are greatly appreciated."

With that statement, my highly trained peripheral vision from square meals, I could see Ryan's hand reach up and again attack the ice on the windscreen. His efforts remain consistent. During this wiper action, he let the wipers run just a bit longer to address the ice buildup. A short time later, I looked up from the instruments and saw that the ice was beginning to back up with each swoosh of the wiper blades. We have to be able to see upon landing, I pondered.

CHAPTER 26

Farewell to Poncho and Hello to Osan Approach Control

23 December 1982, ROK. Somewhere South of Wonju. Twenty Five Minutes into IMC.

Poncho was a call sign for one of the many ground control intercept (GCI) sites operated by air force personnel. I am not sure how many there are throughout South Korea. Poncho's mission is to sit quietly and watch for bad guys. They are real people who, like ATC personnel, sit in front of radar screens and observe the airspace. If a bad guy pops up, they send that information along. Unlike ATC however, they are part of an early warning system. They are not forbidden from speaking with aircrews. Aircrews are encouraged to be respectful of their mission and not call them on their primary frequency. They did have a family FM frequency for other than emergency communications that we all chatted on frequently.

I knew a bit about these sites. I knew there were real people at these sites. Poncho was located in a mountainous region of the country at a place called Salem Top. Approximately four months before going IMC, I was the copilot on a hook mission charged with delivering water to the top of Salem Top. Their water supply had become compromised. I believe the main water line had ruptured. The Koreans were effecting repairs, and while they were doing so, the water was turned off. The renovation was planned for a week to ten days. Multiple military units were tasked to support Salem Top's water needs. Each tasked unit brought to the tasking different services. My unit was tasked with flying water up to them. We did so by filling an M-149 military water trailer, commonly called a Water Buffalo, and cargo hooking it up to the top of the mountain. It was easier said than done. The combined dry weight of the Water Buffalo, as well as its filled weight of water, put the filled Water Buffalo well over the cargo hook's allowable weight limitation of 4,000 pounds. The cargo hook is mounted under the belly of the Huey. For weight and balance purposes, it is just under the transmission in line with the mast. The mast comes out of the top of the transmission and mounts the main rotor. All lift must be well balanced for the aircraft to fly safely. When additional external weight is added to the aircraft, the cargo hook is designed and mounted strategically for that mission. Had we tried to lift a fully-loaded water buffalo, the cargo hook would have automatically opened upon reaching its 4,000 pound limit. To get the Water Buffalo under 4,000 pounds, we let some of the water out. We experimented with the combined dry weight of the Water Buffalo and its water level. Our flight planning for this mission, a significant factor to consider, other than the weight of the Water Buffalo, was forecasting and understanding the presence of turbulence during the weather briefing. We did not need any vertical air. We knew if we attempted to pick up a Water Buffalo that had been drained to just below the 4,000-pound limit, and if there were so much as a breath of turbulence, then the cargo hook would automatically open. This automatic opening of the cargo hook was a safety factor designed into the aircraft. If the load became too heavy or unstable, then the load would have to be jettisoned so that the aircraft did not crash. We were eventually successful in draining the Water Buffalo to a weight of 2,000 pounds. We felt that draining the water buffalo to a weight of just 2,000 pounds, thereby 2,000 pounds under the cargo hooks rating, would best address the problem of automatic jettison if turbulence was encountered. It would require more trips up the mountain, but the reduced weight on the hook was better suited for the mountainous terrain.

Neither the assigned PIC nor I had recently flown a cargo hook mission. The hook was not mystical, it was just not used often. Most of the stuff we carry goes inside the cargo area of the aircraft as an internal load. Both of us had to get the -10 out and do some reading if we were going to accomplish this mission safely. The PIC, of course, was much less intimidated than I was. We found all of the cargo hook procedures that we needed in chapter eight of the -10. The instructions were pretty straightforward. There was a preflight procedure we needed to be aware of as well as a cargo hook operational check. We really needed to get the operation of the hook right. There was an electrical switch located in the overhead console as well as on the pilot's cyclic control stick. There was also a manual release pedal that was found between the pilot's tail rotor pedals. Before the electrical switch on the cyclic can be operated, it must first be armed by the copilot using the cargo release switch in the overhead console. The -10 said that when first picking up the load, the cyclic switch should be armed by placing the cargo release switch in the overhead console on or armed so that if anything goes wrong with the load, the pilot on the controls can readily eject the load with the cyclic switch. Once underway with a stable load, the cyclic switch no longer needs to be armed. De-arming, the cyclic's cargo release switch serves as an insurance policy to inadvertently releasing the load by the pilot. To prevent inadvertent release by the pilot, the copilot de-arms, or turns off, the cargo release switch in the overhead console. Bill successfully completed this ten minutes into our cross-country flight. Now the only way for me to jettison the load; I would have to depress the pedal between the tail rotor pedals intentionally. Turbulence could also trigger the safety release mechanism of the hook by multiplying the weight on the hook.

CW3 Bill Felts was the assigned PIC for the mission. I had yet to make PIC but was being groomed for the rating by Stan. Working the cargo hook on a real mission was a big step in attaining PIC status. Being chosen over the many other WOJG/WO1s assigned to the unit for this mission did not go unnoticed by anyone. All of us WO1s competed for all the best missions. Considering the commander's agreement that he and I made upon my assignment to the unit, this was not one of the two choice missions that I got to choose per week. I was actually selected for this mission, so that told me and everyone else that I was well on my way to making PIC.

Bill was a funny guy—a prankster, in fact. He was very tanned and weathered. Not tanned as one would get at the beach, but there was a natural hue to his skin tone. The weathered look gave him an air of age and wisdom. He was a senior aviator. That big star on his wings spoke volumes to a newly minted aviator like me. He was tall and lean too. He flew with his seat all the way down and back. Even with the extra room that seat adjustment gave him, he filled out that space with legs and arms running over. He smoked like a train too. Whenever he flew, at the end of his missions, his CEs always found his ash receiver, as the -10 called the ashtray, full to running over. He was light-hearted and good at playing jokes. I would learn the full extent of that trait before the mission was over.

Salem Top was along the route of flight to Wonju. Poncho was strategically located at the tallest peak of one of the many mountains that made up the many ridgelines in that area. Radios of the day needed line of sight to be effective. Salem Top was located at the perfect location for line of sight communications. Its only landing pad was on a pinnacle. A pinnacle landing is one of the most challenging landing options for helicopter operators. Someone else may say that the slope was the most difficult or landing in whiteout conditions or to brownout conditions that exist in arid conditions as the most difficult. There are many hazardous conditions that the helicopter pilot must negotiate in the daily operation of his craft. Most of all of those other helicopter operations are well-practiced maneuvers. With practice comes proficiency, and with proficiency comes the skill and expertise needed to overcome the hazards associated with those other operations. Pinnacles, however, are not as commonplace as slope landings. You have to adjust your mission to do pinnacle work deliberately.

To work real pinnacles, you have to operate in mountainous environments. I attended flight school at Fort Rucker, Alabama. To attain my helicopter rating, I had to demonstrate proficiency in all modes of flight, pinnacles too. Fort Rucker is flat as a pancake and only a few hundred feet above sea level. There were many man-made mounds constructed at Fort Rucker that served as pinnacle training areas. We practiced on those mounds all the procedures of pinnacle landings, but nothing at Fort Rucker prepared me for my first *real* pinnacle landing. Couple that with a hook mission, and this flight day was going to be full of challenges.

SP4 Ryan Duncan was our assigned crew chief. We were flying his bird for the mission. Ryan told us that he knew of the mission the day prior and had already checked the operation of the hook to make sure that it was a go. Bill told Ryan how much he appreciated his professionalism, but since all three of us were going to be operating as a crew on this mission, then the rest of the crew needed to see that operation as well. As Bill and I went over the preflight and procedure of the cargo hook, Bill was very courteous. He explained all aspects of the mission. He was ahead of his time as he introduced me to the crew-coordinated tasks needed to complete the mission safely. We completed a normal preflight and then went directly to the special preflight items for the cargo hook as called for in the -10. The last thing we needed was a hook failure while negotiating a pinnacle in the ROK. Bill called out the details of the cargo hooks operation while Ryan and I performed the specific called for functions.

a) BAT switch—on.
b) Cargo release switch—arm. The cargo release light should illuminate.
c) Pilot electrical release switch—Press and hold. The cargo hook should open with slight pressure applied to the hook.
d) Cargo hook—close. Release the pilot electrical release switch.
e) Copilot electrical release switch—Press and hold. The cargo hook should open with slight pressure applied to the hook.
f) Cargo hook—close. Release the copilot electrical release switch.
g) Manual release—press. The cargo hook should open with 20 to 30 pounds pressure applied to the hook.

h) Cargo hook—close.
i) Cargo release switch—off. The cargo release light should go off.
j) Apply approximately twenty to thirty pounds pressure to the hook. The cargo hook should not open.
k) Pilot and copilot electrical release switches—press. The cargo hook should not open. Release the switches.
l) BAT switch—off.

The entire procedure went flawlessly. I was satisfied, and Bill was too. I could tell that Ryan felt a sense of pride with the operation of his hook. It was a measure of the maintenance stewardship he was responsible for maintaining the aircraft. With that, we departed to operations for the paperwork part for the flight. After stopping at the USAF weather station to get our weather for the mission, we headed over to Red Baron's operations to file our flight plan. The weather forecast was clear, blue, and twenty-two. The forecaster did say that, after it warmed up, there would be some vertical air a.k.a. turbulence to deal with, but other than that, the forecaster predicted it to be very nice weather to fly in indeed. After filing the flight plan with operations, we headed back to the aircraft, got strapped in, and started up the aircraft. Bill was kind enough to seat me in the pilot's station on the right side of the helicopter while he chose the copilot's station on the left side. During training, the instructor pilot always sat on the left side, maximizing the exposure of the student to the right side. This was not a training mission. It was a service mission. Bill was simply growing the next generation by placing me in the right seat. I did precisely the same with the LT during our mission when we flew up to Wonju. When things got a bit more difficult on our return flight, however, I elected to put the LT into the left side so that she could better assist as directed. Very normal cockpit protocol.

When Bill and I picked up the aircraft to a hover, Ryan had arranged for another CE to hook the load, so he put on a monkey harness in the back. A monkey harness allows the CE to freely move around the cargo area and still be secured to the aircraft. He needed to lie flat on the floor of the cargo areas floor and peer over the side of the aircraft while his helper hooked up the load. During hookup operations here and at Salem Top, someone other than Ryan had to hook the load. The prone position in the cargo bay gave him the best vantage points to evaluate how the load was doing during all phases of operation. I picked up the aircraft to twenty-five feet and was looking forward to a routine hookup. Bill armed the cargo hook switch during the hover maneuver so that if we needed to punch off the load, I could quickly do so with the switch on the cyclic. Ryan called the load. When we got to within ten feet of the load, I could no longer see the Water Buffalo. Ryan began to call out directions from there.

"Forward ten, hold your altitude," Ryan said. That meant that I needed to move directly forward ten feet and that I was to hold my twenty-five feet altitude. I slowly moved forward. Ryan gave the countdown. "Forward seven, five, three, two, one, hold position," he ordered. At this point, Ryan was in charge of the operation, and I did precisely as I was instructed. We had a ten-foot leader line on the load, so once the load was in the air, we would have fifteen feet or so between the load and us. "Hold the position while the hookup man mounts the load," Ryan directed. I watched the hookup man approach the load then disappear out of my line of sight below me. He was carrying a long pole. The purpose of the pole is to discharge any static electricity charge that the aircraft may have built up during flight *before* he touches the hook with the cargo ring. I had done this a few times when I was a CE and was glad for the experience. Now, as an aviator, I could easily visualize him grounding the aircraft and hooking up the load. This was also an uncertain time for the guy under the aircraft hooking up the load. If I had an engine failure, I could have crushed him below while performing an autorotation. We prebriefed for this. He was instructed that if Ryan held his arm straight out of the bay parallel with the earth and perpendicular to the aircraft, then he was to immediately dismount the load and clear himself to the three o'clock position. I knew he would go to my right so I would autorotate directly forward and perpendicular to the exit of the hookup person while cushioning the aircraft to the ground with the collective. This I did not want to do. I had not had a real engine failure to date, and I did not want to start today. I had, how-ever, autorotated many times in training and was not intimidated by the possibility.

Our hookup man was on top of the load, and Ryan com-manded, "Down ten, seven, five, four, three, two, one...*hold*."

Holding over the load, I could feel the aircraft being struck from below. I knew that was the hookup guy discharging static electricity. Once that was done, he hooked the load and dismounted. I could see him come from under the aircraft and move away from the helicop-ter. Ryan was watching him too, and once Ryan felt that he was a safe distance away, Ryan began to say, "Let's take the slack out of the load. *Up* steady, steady, steady." I instantly felt the lead line tighten, and all of a sudden, the aircraft had an appendage under it. Ryan began to call out the altitude. "Up one, two, three, five, seven... Sir, the load is flying. You have the load."

With that, we taxied a short distance to the runway and began our takeoff. It was exuberating. I felt pretty full of myself. Once we were airborne, Bill identified the cargo release switch and de-armed it. He did not want me to punch off the load inadvertently. Inadvertently touching the cargo release switch on the cyclic while flying cross country to the drop site is all it would take to lose the load.

The mission went like clockwork. We departed Camp Humphreys and flew northeast direct. Bill was on the map. I had been through these valleys before. "Wonju is about thirty or so min-utes ahead, yes?" I asked Bill.

"Yep. See that mountain peak dead ahead?" he asked. "That is Salem Top. Wonju is beyond that as the crow flies."

Not long after that and once we got closer, Bill identified the cargo switch and armed the cargo hook. I acknowledged the armed switch and took care not to touch the cargo release switch on the cyclic. Global positioning system (GPS) did not exist in the eight-ies. We used HHMs. That would be handheld maps. All navigation was time-distance-heading work all while closely following a map. Challenging and intense work indeed. GPS has to be the single most impactful invention introduced to the aviation industry to date.

We arrived at Salem Top around 0900. Bill asked if I wanted him to perform the first approach. He already knew the answer that I was going to give. I was a PIC in grooming, and as a PIC in grooming, I need to either know my limitations or be willing to define my own boundaries. "I would like to give it a go if it is okay. Stay close to the controls, however. Do not let me out fly your safety envelop," I said. Bill appreciated that acknowledgment. Each army aviator has his own safety envelop that is developed with the introduction of experience.

"Don't worry," Bill said. "I will be close but will not crowd you."

We first flew in a 360-degree orbit around the peak. While doing so, Bill radioed Poncho on their discrete FM frequency and told them that we had arrived. I gauged the wind at 270, and it felt like 10 knots or so. It was a steady wind, not gusty. That worked to our favor as we did not need any turbulence.

To my surprise, I saw a couple of guys come out of their hooch, and one was dressed as the Cookie Monster. Cookie Monster was a character from the kid's show, *Sesame Street*. I had watched it several times with my own daughter. It was funny seeing this creature out in the middle of nowhere. "First time encountering the Cookie Monster?" Bill asked.

"Yes," I said. "What's the deal?"

Bill went on to explain that he had flown many missions here, mostly dropping off supplies and mail. One of the airmen sent home for a Cookie Monster suit. Out of appreciation for visitors, when people fly in, they bake cookies and give them to the aircrews as a thank you. The PIC had to pre-coordinate the arrival time if he expected any cookies, however. I was not surprised. I had witnessed the love service members play out over the eleven years that I had been in the army thus far. Civilians could not fully understand this kinship, and I am guessing they would measure this action as stupid, but the kindness was genuine and sincere. Bill told me that he had called from Red Baron's operation earlier this morning. They knew we were coming with water, and I was guessing we were going to get some world-famous cookies from the Cookie Monster himself. I smiled from ear to ear. I loved being a part of the army family.

Okay, I lined up for an approach into the wind. I confirmed the cargo switch was armed, and once I intercepted my approach angle, I lowered my collective, maintaining my approach angle with collective and apparent rate of closure with cyclic. Bill was close to the controls but respectful. The approach came off without a hitch. I had planned to arrive just as we discussed—twenty-five feet above the pad with the load dead center. Ryan took over as he directed me to hold the position. Once he was satisfied that I was where he wanted me, he called out my descent until the load touched down. I felt the external weight of the load leave the aircraft, and Ryan then directed me to punch off the load. The buffalo was on the ground, mind you. I was just punching off the tether.

Free from the load, I nosed the aircraft over and did an airspeed over altitude departure. We flew to an LZ below to pick up another prepositioned Water Buffalo that a support unit had staged there for this mission. Once we had figured out how much water had to be missing from the Buffalo, Bill radioed that information from our operations this morning so that the supporting unit would have the load partially filled and ready for us. Our part of the mission was to deliver the buffaloes to Salem Top. Salem Top would then drain the water from the Buffalo into a temporary water container, I would take away the empty and continue to bring more water up until the temporary water container was filled. The next lift went well. I dropped off the next just as before. Ryan directed me over to the empty Buffalo to get that one to fly back to the staging area. We repeated the hookup process and departed for the staging area. We dropped off the empty Buffalo and picked up another. We made another textbook approach into the pad. Ryan had me place the Buffalo next to the empty one that we had dropped off earlier. We hooked the empty buffalo to the aircraft and departed again for the bottom of the hill. Once we dropped off the empty, we headed over to the forward arming and refueling point (FARP) for some gas. The supporting unit for this mission was getting as much training in as were we. Their requirement was to not only to bring in fuel for our helicopter but supply the water as well. We took all their hard work for granted as we taxied over to the temporary refuel pad that they had set up and waited for the attendant to service the aircraft. Unlike the happy Cookie Monster at Salem Top, this soldier was not very happy at all, and it showed in his body language in the delayed time it took to service the aircraft.

We eventually topped off and headed back over to get another Buffalo. We had the routine down pat by now and was moving through the process effortlessly. In total, we made nine lifts and were hooking up for our final lift of the day. During the other lifts, I could feel the afternoon thermals awaken and get busy, and I remembered the caution of the forecaster. Expect vertical air as the day warms up. I asked Bill about the conditions, and he agreed we needed to be concerned. If we got into any turbulence at all, the load could easily double or triple in weight when it reacts to the vertical air. The sudden up and down movements would trigger the safety mechanism of the cargo hook and simply drop the load on its own. All it took was twenty to thirty unannounced pounds of immediate downward force on the cargo hook, and we would lose the load. That is why turbulence is not a good thing.

Bill agreed that this would be the last lift. He called Poncho on the FM so advising, and the Cookie Monster said he appreciated the water and would meet us with our cookies after we dropped off the last buffalo. Well, we hooked up the load and departed and began our climb. The turbulence was concerning.

"Let's slow our airspeed down by forty knots," Bill said.

"Roger," I replied. I very carefully and slowly put aft pressure on the cyclic all while lowering the collective correspondingly.

Simultaneously, while hearing Ryan scream into his mic, "Loads away," I felt the helicopter rocket upward as if I had pulled five inches of collective.

I laid the aircraft over on its right side and orbited intently over the spot where we lost the load.

"Ryan, have you got a visual on the load?" I asked.

"Watching it now," he said excitedly.

"Did you punch the load off," Bill asked incredulously.

"*No*," I said unequivocally. "Little busy right now," I continued. "Ryan, did you see that explosive water plumb?" I asked.

"Yes, sir. Did you see how close that came to that family's hooch?" Ryan added.

"Yes I did," I said unbelievably. I continued to orbit the site. "Bill, if it is okay with you, I want to land just there beyond the hooch and assess the situation," I stated. We were landing; I didn't care what Bill said. I wanted to make sure that I had not killed someone.

"Of course it is. Let me give you a break, I have the controls," he said.

"You have the controls," I responded.

"I have the controls," he finished out. Bill landed us closer than I would have to the hooch. He brought the engine down to engine idle, and Ryan jumped out. I started to unstrap, but Bill caught my arm, "Stand by WOJG, let's let Ryan do his job." I thought about what he said and knew nowhere in Ryan's job description did it call for this nor in mine not to assist. But I knew he had his reasons. This was now an accident site, and Bill was our safety officer. I respected Bill's request and stayed put. It did not take long for Ryan to assess and return. He was all but laughing when he plugged in.

"*Wow*," he exclaimed, "that Water Buffalo looks like it was hit with a 105. *Kaboom*. Did you see the water plumb when that thing hit, Mr. D? It had to have gone thirty feet in the air. That thing is buried easy six feet into the rice paddy. There is no one home. The hooch is empty. It is undoubtedly their shelter that they stay in while coming from wherever they come from to tend to the rice patty. *Kaboom*, that was awesome…"

"Okay, okay, Ryan. Got it. Strap in." I looked back at him and saw him mouth *kaboom* again with a big smile.

I looked over at Bill, and he said with a smirk, "Identify the cargo switch and de-arm it. I sure don't want to punch off anything flying home." His smile matched Mister Kaboom in the back, so I knew I was not in trouble.

"Well, you have made quite an *impact* on me today, WOJG," he said while enjoying the jab at me.

"*Really*," I said. "It was the turbulence, not me, that triggered the release." I was speaking truths, but it did not matter. I was hazed and cajoled by Bill and Ryan the rest of the way back to Camp Humphreys.

Not to be outdone Ryan popped up on the net and asked, "Hey, what about those cookies? We got some of the water there before *kaboom*. We going back?"

"Really, Ryan," I mumbled…

Bill knew it was not my fault. When we got back to operations, I overheard Bill tell the commander when he debriefed the mission that he was keenly aware of my hand position and finger location on the cyclic. He was acutely aware of the location of all my fingers because he was waiting for a training moment to develop and to tell the new guy not even rest the pinky on that cargo switch while holding the cyclic. The pinky finger has to be purposely used, and apparently I never did, otherwise I would have reaped Bills instruction. Bill went on to brief the commander that turbulence was the reason that we lost the load. It did not matter. All the other officers of the unit better enjoyed Bill's different versions of the story where I had punched off the load rather than the annoying weather phenomenon.

Even Ryan continued with the story when he heard me comment to the LT that we were getting close to departing Poncho's airspace and we needed to get ready for a frequency change. Even while we were in dire straits, Ryan couldn't resist when he piped up and asked, "Hey Mr. D, before we leave Poncho's freq, I wonder if we can get a rain check on those cookies?"

I needed the comic relief of the moment and privately appreciated the ribbing, even though we were in real trouble. "Probably not this trip Ryan," I said. "But we will be back." Who can forget the kaboom boy?

Okay LT it's time to say goodbye to Poncho and frequency change to Osan Approach. From here on out it is going to get a bit busy," I said. "LT please put Osan ATIS up in the no. 3 and monitor it. Make sure my no. 3 switch is up as well. I want a heads up when I contact Osan on the conditions there. LT please put me up no. 2," I continued.

"Poncho this is RB93. How long before I leave your airspace?" I asked,

"Roger, RB93. I show you approaching the edge of my airspace now. You are two zero miles from Osan, contact Osan approach control on 125.4 or 270.35. Safe flight and Merry Christmas," he completed.

I got a bit choked up over the routine dialogue. Had I flown us into a mountainside upon initially upon entering IMC, a whole lot of other people would have been having a totally different conversation. Yet we survived thus far to embrace a routine radio call with just enough personalism to make the exchange pleasant.

I keyed the mic and happily replied, "Hey, Poncho, thanks so very much for the flight follow. My crew and I appreciate your assistance, and on behalf of the crew, we wish you and yours a very Merry Christmas." And just like that, we were finished with Poncho.

CHAPTER 27

ATIS Reports Zero/Zero Conditions

23 December 1982, ROK. Somewhere South of
Wonju. Thirty-Five Minutes into IMC.

I asked the LT to dial in Osan Approach and to monitor the no. 2. I also asked her to dial in Osan ATIS in the no. 3 position so that I could have the numbers for Osan before making the call. We both listened to the no. 3 and heard the following automated recording: "Osan information Alpha. Time 11:37, automatic. Runway 27 in use. All published frequencies are in use. Expect an ILS approach. Surface wind 250 at 10 knots. Snowshowers. Visibility 0+. Ceiling 0+. Temperature +15, dew point +12. Altimeter 29.94. Construction work in progress on the parallel taxiway suspended for snow conditions. Advise on initial contact that you have information Alpha."

The LT immediately picked up the snow conditions from ATIS and began to remark, but I waved her off. We were getting closer by the second, and the pace was picking up. I had no time to spare as I needed an initial contact from Osan.

I keyed the mic and said, "Osan Approach Control, RB93 with you at five thousand feet, squawking 7700 with Information Alpha."

It only took moments for Osan Approach to return my call. They said, "Roger, RB93. Change your squawk to read 3745. I show you two five miles northeast at five thousand feet. State your intentions."

I was electrified. What we have been enduring as something horrible, they sounded pretty routine from their standpoint, and that is precisely what I needed to spur me on. Maybe this will conclude with a no-big-deal approach after all. "Roger, RB93 squawking 3745. RB93 has two gyro failures and request a no-gyro approach to Runway 27, full stop," I said rather confidently. I asked the LT to listen and carefully identify the ILS at Osan. We had already tuned the station, I wanted it confirmed that our navigation radio was correctly identifying the station.

While the LT was intently listening to the Morris code identifier for Osan, Osan responded, "RB93, understand two gyro failures. State your status." I had to steel myself up before answering. For the first time since entering IMC, I had to admit to someone that we were in such peril that we had to announce it. Since Poncho was not an ATC facility working under strict ATC rules, they were helpful, but I did not have to declare an emergency. I could even imagine the Cookie Monster while speaking with Poncho. It was a casual exchange with Poncho that made me feel peaceful. Osan was different. They were the real deal. I felt that there was someone there who was going to be able to talk me safely to the ground. It did feel like my instrument check ride again, but in a good way. No tricks, just real flying. I needed to hold it together a bit longer. This time, the stakes were much higher, and I had to get past it quickly. Even though my transponder said so, I needed to articulate and announce our emergency fully.

"Roger, Osan, RB93 is declaring an emergency." And with that, if there was a secret, it was no more. By declaring an emergency, I instantly owned the airspace. All efforts to bring our arrival to a safe conclusion would be brought to bear. I was fully invested in doing my part. Just before Osan continued, the LT gave me a thumbs up while pointing to the ILS frequency, and I squeezed in the following, "Osan, RB93 appreciates all the assistance." She knew I was busy multitasking the landing details in my head while simultaneously in full conversation with the controller. I just looked at her and nodded my head in acknowledgment.

CHAPTER 28

The First Approach into Osan— Final Controller Issues

23 December 1982, ROK. Somewhere North West of Osan.

Osan began, "RB93, this will be a no-gyro surveillance approach to Runway 27 at Osan. On current heading, leave five thousand feet for 2,000 feet. Latest weather remains same as ATIS information Alpha. Lost communication instructions. If no transmissions are received for 15 seconds on final approach, attempt contact on alternate 127.90 and proceed VFR. If unable, proceed with the ILS 27 Osan. Maintain 2,000 feet until established on the approach procedure."

"Roger, Osan. RB93 out of five thousand feet for two thousand feet," I acknowledged.

Before I could have a conversation with the crew, Osan came alive again on the radio. "RB93, turn right. This is a correction for a thirty-degree intercept into Osan pattern." Osan was beginning to position and align me for the final approach course into Runway 27. Our current en-route heading was approximately forty-five degrees from the runway centerline. The controller wanted to trim that down a bit so that the turn to final would not be so abrupt. The right turn instructions made sense. We were descending out of our en-route altitude and setting up for the approach altitude. I lowered the collective and set a 500-feet-per-minute rate of descent on the VSI. 500 feet is a standard rate of descend and is recommended during IFR operations in a helicopter. The rate may be accelerated if needed, but the pilot must be acutely aware of his situational awareness when leveling out. VFR maneuvers are not recommended in IFR conditions. The descent seemed natural. At this rate, I would be at instrument approach altitude in six minutes.

A few moments later, Osan said, "RB93, you are on the thirty-degree intercept for the approach. Stop turn."

"Roger, RB93 stopping turn," I responded. I took the instruction at the controller's word. I knew I was level, and after referring to my mag compass and turn and slip gauge, I reached over and reset my attitude indicator. I knew there would be at least one more right turn to go before I intercepted the two-seven centerline into Osan. I took as much time as I possibly could to bring my crew up to speed. The instructions between the controller and us would be coming faster as we got closer. I explained to the LT that everything that went into the cockpit had to be recorded on her kneeboard. I would immediately respond to Osan *only* after I got a thumbs-up from her recording duties. I needed strict attention to detail, and no detail was too small to overlook. Check and double-check. I would be concentrating on flying and processing the information coming into the cockpit. I needed the LT on her game to validate my actions and to challenge anything that may seem out of order. The LT said she understood. Things were good. The descent triggered my memory, and I asked the LT to look at the Osan approach plate and tell me the published glide slope (GS) for the approach as well as the threshold crossing height (TCH) for the ILS 27. I was still very focused on flying and cross-checking. We were a few thousand feet from leveling off. She was feeding me a lot of silence. I have heard that length of silence from others, and it usually meant that they did not understand the instructions or had no idea what to do. Time was ticking by, and I needed that information. Satisfied that we were still descending and that the attitude was still okay, I stole a moment from my flying and cross-checking and looked over at her.

"Place the plate on the center console," I said. "Look there, just below the ILS dart," I pointed. "Do you see GS and TCH? There, right there." I waited.

"Yes, I see it just there now," she said.

"Okay," I said. I returned to flying and cross-checking and asked her what the GS and TCH was. With a sense of confidence, she said that the GS was 2.70 and that the TCH was 57. I painfully remembered the many instrument orals that I had had to date, and those are seemingly irrelevant facts that instrument examiners scar fledging aviators with when they would point to the very smallest thing on the plate and ask for its meaning and application. But on this day, I was grateful for those scars. The GS and TCH tells me a lot of information. I knew that if I kept the VSI on the controller's decent rate instructions, then we would be maintaining a 2.70-degree controllable rate of descent. Helpful, as it tells me that my control actions are either too harsh or to light. Information was useful indeed as I will see it play out in real time each time the final controller issues me glide slope altitude changes. If I did my job correctly, then I will be onglide slope when I arrive at the runway threshold at fifty-seven feet. This is information that I can use to make the safest approach possible.

Ryan was doing a great job keeping my windscreen clear. Even his best efforts could not stave off the rate at which the ice was accumulating. The wipers were now bouncing off the ice dams that had been created at each side of the wiper swipe. Frozen to the windscreen, unimpressed by the best efforts of the wipers. We were running out of time for any real visibility through the windscreens. Soon after we entered IMC conditions, I directed all available bleed air to the windscreen defrosters. It is difficult for me to say that that air diversion directed to the windscreen has had much effect. I could say that the humans in the aircraft did not enjoy the warmth that could otherwise have been available if I sent that air to the heater instead. The windscreens took the priority for the heat. The bleed air deflection to the windscreens had been working during the en-route work but was now being overcome by our time spent in these freezing conditions. A buildup of ice during the setup for an approach to landing was difficult to bear. We needed to get on the ground quickly.

Back to flying and cross-checking, flying and cross-checking, flying and cross-checking, and then all of a sudden, we were approaching two thousand feet. I planned my arrival so as not to balloon past the assigned altitude, but I did anyway. I went about 100 feet below but quickly corrected.

"Osan, RB93 level at two thousand feet and correcting," I reported.

"RB93, you are one five miles from the centerline, turn right." Osan's instructions were followed to the letter.

"Roger, RB93 turning right," I responded. I was glad that I had just updated the attitude indicator because, except for the extreme conditions that we were flying in, things looked perfectly normal.

A moment or so later, Osan said, "RB93, stop turn."

"Roger, RB93 stopping turn." To the untrained ear, the call-and-response terminology between pilot and controller may sound foolish, but it represents the very fabric of our communication. The standardized call and responses make for no surprises for anyone, and the seeming tedium actions are music to aviator's ears. The regular exchanges take me back to the reason that I associate standardization to the Barney creature from Sesame Street.

I didn't have much time to myself as the radio crackled to life. "RB93, you are one-zero miles from Osan, perform before-landing check." That was music to my ears. This ordeal was almost over. I asked the LT to get the checklist out and run through the before-landing check. She dutifully got out the checklist and began calling out the actions.

"Before landing," she said. "RPM 6600."

"RPM, 6600," I responded.

"Systems Check," she said.

"Oil temps and pressures normal. Conformation fuel check still running," I answered.

"Crew, passengers, and mission equipment," she completed.

Ryan sang out from the rear, "Everyone's secure."

With that, I called Osan back and reported, "Before-landing check complete."

Osan Approach came back on the radio and said, "RB93, you are eight miles from Osan on a thirty-degree intercept for Osan's 27. Contact final controller on 323.1 or 125.5. Merry Christmas."

"Merry Christmas indeed, sir. Appreciate the assistance," I responded. I had no time to waste. "LT, I need 323.1 in the no. 2 and 125.5 in the no. 3 please." The LT quickly dialed up 323.1 into the no. 2 and without waiting on her to comment or complete the no. 3.

I keyed the mic on the no. 2 and said, "Final controller, RB93 with you at two thousand feet."

"RB93, this is Osan final controller, how do you hear me?"

"Final controller, RB93 has you five by five."

"RB93, do not acknowledge further transmissions.

"You are seven miles from Osan, turn left.

"Your missed approach instructions remain the same as previously issued.

"Stop turn.

"Make all half-standard rate turns.

"On final. Prepare to descend in two miles. Minimum descent altitude is 440 feet.

"On course, begin descent.

"On course, on glideslope."

"On course, slightly below glideslope and correcting."

"Slightly left, of course, turn left. On glideslope.

"*What is that guy talking about!*" screamed MAJ Burns. He did not need to key his mic. I heard him plain as day even through my helmet. But he did key the mic, and I felt like he blew out my eardrums. The guy with the big star on his wings finally said something, which I thought was rich at this stage in the game. He had plenty of time thus far to participate and assist, but his silence was deafening. And now that cockpit was screaming along, and I did not need the distraction.

I threw up my hand in protest and ordered, "Hold on. That guy is the final controller. He must be seeing something that we are not. We are the ones with two failed gyros. Like the instruments, *I must follow his instructions.*" I knew that what he was saying made no sense. He shows me left, of course, and then has me turn left? What sort of crazy instructions was that? I had to do what that guy said. Never in flight school had any of the controllers given conflicting directions, and our flight instructors made it clear that the controller controlled the airspace. The PIC, however, controlled his cockpit. I made a bunch of dumb decisions by getting us into this mess, and now at the finish line, the approach turns to crap? Really! I simply had to reason out what was happening. I think I am going to interrupt the final controller and confirm his instructions. But just as I begin to depress the mic and ask, and if the approach was not challenging enough, the twenty-minute fuel light just came on. Now I really want that freeze button.

I kept flying and cross-checking. I knew that I was not going to run out of gas on the approach. The fuel quantity low caution light, otherwise known as the "twenty-minute fuel caution light," illuminates when approximately 170 pounds are remaining. I asked the LT to cancel out the master caution light on the panel. Did not need that distraction either. How could there be only 170 pounds of fuel left? My last fuel burn rate had us at just over 600 pounds. Well, a quick check shows that the fuel gauge reads right at 220 pounds, so the light is set high. That gives me some wiggle room. Still, have to fly the aircraft. I can see that we are still 200 feet from our decision height. A quick scan out of my side window shows only blowing snow.

There is a voice inflection in the controller's voice now as he says, "Going further left of course now, turn left. Slightly below glideslope and correcting." More than an inflection, I could hear real fear in the controller's voice when he stated, "Going left of course and diverging rapidly now, turn left. On glideslope."

The fear that I last heard in the controller's voice now was palpable terror when he said, "RB93, you are well left of course now and beyond approach limits, initiate missed approach."

A new, very calm voice came on over the radio and said, "RB93, you now have an experienced controller on the scope. Initiate missed approach."

What! No time to think, fly the aircraft, fly the aircraft, fly the aircraft, I kept telling myself. "Final controller, RB93 is executing a missed approach at this time." I thought I would puke. If we were going to break out, we never got close enough to break out. I climbed out on runway heading. Based on the final controller's wacky instructions, I knew that I was on the left side of the runway. I also knew that there was a small hill in otherwise flat terrain just to the south and center of the airdrome. When flying VFR from Humphreys to Osan along the flat terrain, you could easily see the hill from a distance. It rose some 300 feet and was directly abeam and to the south and center of the 27 active. When the final controller had me steer left, I knew I was flying into the proximity of the hill. Since I was in snow conditions, I could not see just how close I had come to that hill; however, maybe even the tower itself. And now we get to do it all over again.

CHAPTER 29

Osan Missed Approach and Another Controller's Shocking Statement

23 December 1982, ROK. Somewhere
in the Osan Traffic Pattern.

Except for the confusing instructions from the final controller, the cockpit mood was professional. More than a few things were going on. If landing safely was not significant enough, now I really needed to understand what was going on with the fuel. We left Wonju with one thousand pounds. We should have burnt no more than six hundred pounds. Since we had apparently burnt eight hundred pounds, we were either leaking fuel or burning excessively. I was pretty sure that we were not leaking fuel. We had to have been burning the fuel excessively. Was it the ice? Was it all the bleed air that was being diverted from the engine to fight off the ice? Was it a combination of the two? My thoughts were interrupted when a voice came on the radio and said, "RB93, as a reminder, you have an experienced controller on the scope. Continue your climb out to two thousand feet. I will call your right crosswind turn at fifteen hundred feet."

Oh my gosh, I thought. Experienced controller?

Again, unhelpful and furious comments from MAJ Burns as he broke in. "What was that…" And I cut him off mid-sentence.

"Listen, we have to fly the aircraft. Clearly, something is amiss down there. Let's let them work that out. We still have to get this aircraft on the ground." My stomach turned over and over. At Fort Rucker, everyone is in training, even ATC. When ATC puts student trainers behind the scopes for their own training, they always announced, "Controller training in progress." I am sure that there was an experienced controller on station ready to step in at any time while giving instruction to the ATC student. But we were not in a training environment. I had declared an emergency. Undoubtedly, they would not have trained during a declared emergency. I had to hope not. I get it that it was the Christmas holidays. Maybe they were shorthanded for the holidays? I'm guessing the ATC crew on station were minimally staffed. They may have thought it was a full-blown blizzard out, and who would be flying in this weather anyway? Right, wrong, or indifferent, I was flying, and I needed their help. I was going to do exactly what the controller said. And I was grateful that the major was respectful enough to let this play out and not further interrupt again with non-helpful comments. Though I knew inside, he was just dying to get into one of the front seats. I would climb to two thousand feet and expect the controller to turn me right at fifteen hundred feet. Since he said it was a crosswind turn, I naturally assumed it would be a ninety-degree turn and that he would direct me in a traffic pattern and set me up for another approach. I didn't want a do-over. I wanted it over. Since the experienced voice did not identify himself, I made the following call, calling him Approach.

"Approach, RB93 is minimum fuel."

"Acknowledged RB93," he said. Begin right crosswind turn."

I looked at the altimeter. We were about to pass one thousand feet. Five hundred early? Because of the fuel status, I reasoned, but I did not want to spend any more time on that now. I just flew the aircraft. I did a standard rate turn and waited for Approach to call my stop turn. Since the RMI was so badly precessing, I was all but done with the RMI. I checked the mag compass and saw that it was approaching ninety degrees from the runway heading and Approach called and said, "RB93 stop turn."

"Roger RB93 stopping turn," I responded. I was still climbing and knew that he would turn me again soon for the downwind leg.

Approach said, "RB93 turn right for the downwind leg. Perform before landing check."

"Approach, RB93 is in a right turn leveling at 1,500 feet," I reported. After taking a quick inventory of my crew, I reported to Approach that the before-landing check had been completed. It was an easy call since nothing had changed since the last time we did the before-landing check. I looked over at the LT, and as if by telepathy, she already knew the question as she gave me a thumbs up.

Ryan echoed in the back, "Good to go, Boss."

"RB93, stop turn."

"RB93, stopping turn," I responded. Since we were in a level flight mode, I took the time to update the attitude indicator again. The LT watched me adjust mine, and as if on cue, she likewise pulled to cage hers. We flew just a few minutes on the downwind leg. It seemed like time stood still, tick tock, tick tock, flying and cross-checking, still flying and cross-checking.

The LT broke into my thoughts when she asked, "Dean, we only have one hundred and fifty pounds of fuel left. What happens if we do not break out during the approach?" I knew the angst that was behind each of the words that the LT had spoken. This was possibly my most adult moment of the entire flight. My dad and twins fate ripped through my mind as I suffered with my answer.

CHAPTER 30

Final Approach into Osan—Full Stop

23 December 1982, ROK. Final Leg
in the Osan Traffic Pattern.

I said, "LT, we are landing this aircraft on this approach. If the runway environment is not in site at decision height, then I will decelerate the aircraft from ninety knots to sixty knots. I will flare the aircraft and keep the nose up in the air as we continue to the earth. If all goes well, we will impact the earth and slide the aircraft onto the runway. The controller will talk us all the way to the earth. I know it sounds scary, but we only have enough fuel for this last approach. There is nowhere else to go. We are totally committed to this approach." I am not sure what I expected, but I did not expect silence. I knew my world was a bit upside down right now. I could only imagine how her world was. Ryan, ever prompt, reached up and turned on the wipers again. I told him just to leave them on. I didn't need the *whoosh, bump, bump* noise as the wipers did their best to clear the accumulated ice on the windscreen, but there it was, *whoosh, bump, bump* while I continued to do my very best to concentrate with flying and cross-checking, flying and cross-checking.

Just before the next radio call, I realized that I had not frequency changed. I was still on the final controller's frequency. I guess they were gauging my workload and were working with me on that frequency. "RB93, this will be a no-gyro approach to Runway 27. Turn right and join the base leg. Begin descent. To facilitate your fuel conditions, expect an early turn from base to final. Missed approach instructions remain unchanged." Okay, things were falling into place. I appreciated the calmness in the controller's voice. It gave me the confidence I needed. I knew we were taking this to the ground one way or another.

"RB93, do not acknowledge further transmissions. This is the final controller." I was happy to hear that it was the experienced calm guy on the radio. He must have shifted from his own station to that of the final controller's station so that he could work me on the final controller's scope. I was guessing that he was the supervisor.

"You are seven miles from Osan. Turn right."

"Stop turn. You are now on final approach for the 27 runway into Osan."

"Make all half-standard rate turns. Continue descent."

"Minimum descent altitude is four hundred forty feet."

"On course, on glideslope."

"On course, slightly below glideslope, and correcting."

"On course, on glideslope."

"Slightly right of course, turn left. On glideslope.

"Slightly right of course and correcting nicely. Slightly below glideslope and correcting."

"On course now, and coming up on glideslope nicely."

"On course, on glideslope."

"On course, on glideslope."

"On course, on glideslope."

"On course, on glideslope" was music to my ears. I could see that I was approaching my decision height, and I had to embrace my decision quickly to place the helicopter into a landing attitude. I could only pray that, after the impact, we would remain upright. If I slow the aircraft down enough that when we hit, it should be nothing more than a run-on landing. We were still in full whiteout snow conditions. Could I miss the runway centerline? Visibility was still limited to the windscreen, and there was ice beyond that. Before

I heard the next bit of instructions from the final controller, I heard the LT exclaim, "I see railroad tracks."

I broke from my instrument cross-check concentration and looked over at her and, just as excitedly, exclaimed, "*Are you sure you saw railroad tracks?*" I was almost giddy. I knew she could not see a thing through the windscreen to the front of the aircraft. I snuck a look, and I couldn't see anything.

"No, out of my side window," she said. "It was just a flash, but I know for sure that I saw railroad tracks." The controller never skipped a beat and had no idea of the drama being played out in the cockpit. He just continued to drone on wonderfully.

"On course, on glideslope."

"Approaching decision height."

I calculated what the LT had reported in my head. The railroad tracks that she saw were real tracks just off the end of the active. There was a transition that helicopter pilots often took as a shortcut, whether northbound or southbound. We called it railroad transition. Whether flying from the south to the north or north to the south, all one had to do was come up Osan Tower and ask for railroad transition. If there were no opposing traffic coming into land, at the discretion of the controller, and while following the railroad tracks, we would be cleared to cross the extended active at two hundred feet or below. I personally have done that very transition many times. I was very familiar with it. That was terrific news from the LT. I could see in my mind's eye that we were exactly where we were supposed to be to execute this approach into Osan.

"On course, on glideslope, at decision height. Do you have the runway in sight?" the controller asked. I did not have the runway environment in sight. I did know that the TCH was fifty-seven feet, however. I decided to go below Decision Height and continued with the approach. I was still in full-on snow and had no visibility. To slow the aircraft and prepare it for an impact, I began to rotate the fuselage with a combination of cyclic and collective movement. Basically, I was starting a VFR maneuver called a Nap of the Earth (NOE) decel only at a higher altitude and airspeed and while blind. I was positioning the aircraft for the best impact. The LT was not silent any longer.

With some vigor, she reminded me that we were below Decision Height and that we were decelerating. I was glad for her input. That told me that she was paying attention to what I was doing, and I needed all the help I could get. I did brief what I had intended. It must have only briefed well because she was all voice now. She was not verbal at all when I briefed my intentions. Living that briefing out is a bit scarier I'm guessing. We were going to smite the earth soon, I was thinking, and all this will be over. This was our best shot at survival. We were out of gas, and there was nothing else I could do but keep flying the aircraft I told myself. Keep flying the aircraft all the way to the ground...

"On course, below decision height." His instructions got faster now. We were flying down that ILS dart, and the closer we got to the earth, the more sensitive the transmitters became. Funny, I had the LT prepare and tune in the ILS into our navaids so that I could follow the approach down on the CDI while the controller talked me down. I was so busy updating the attitude indicator via the mag compass and cross-checking and applying the controller's instructions and playing out the approach options in my head that I barely remember even looking at the CDI if at all.

"Slightly right, of course. Slightly below glideslope."

"Slightly right of course, and correcting. Slightly below glideslope and holding." Still, there was no breakout. I saw nothing. The earth was just feet from me by this point, and I knew we were going to hit. I was just praying to stay upright. I slowed the rate of descent to one hundred feet per minute and waited. I waited. I waited. Still no visibility. It really was a zero/zero approach. We were not going to break out before hitting the runway. We were seconds from crashing. All I knew to do was to keep flying the aircraft.

"Beyond safety boundaries, initiate missed approach," was the last thing that I heard from the final controller.

CHAPTER 31

On Second Final at Osan and We See a Bright Light

23 December 1982, ROK. Another Final Leg in the Osan Traffic Pattern.

Final controllers are trained to talk the aircraft all the way to the ground, and in the background, he was doing just that. He had no idea what was going on in the cockpit. There was an explosion of activity. I was expecting to smite the runway at any moment. Instead, through my chin bubble, I saw the brightest light ever. It was like looking at the sun. Because of the snow, I could only see the lights glow. I could not see the definition of the light itself, only the glow, and it was the brightest ever. I immediately dumped the collective and pulled back on the cyclic into my gut. Doing so dropped the tail and the nose rose upward. I momentarily lost the lights glow but then reacquired them when the aircraft began to settle. Sensing that the aircraft was falling, I centered the cyclic and pulled up on the collective. There may have been some violence implied as I very radically displaced the flight controls in an attempt to come to a hover over those lights.

"Right off course and below glideslope," the final controller continued. I barked at the LT to put my no. 2 selector off his fre-

184

quency. The final controller would have continued to instruct me all the way to the crash site, hoping to assist all the way to the end. I was still IFR and incredibly still in zero/zero conditions, but I had a glimmer of hope if I could just wrestle the helicopter to a hover over the light. While I was working the flight controls to arrest the aircraft over the lights, I heard the final controller's voice stop. The LT was successful in taking my no. 2 selector off station so that I could concentrate. I sensed that we were entering into an unusual attitude which any flight instructor would agree that all the motoring of the flight controls would induce, but I was determined to bring the helicopter to a hover over the light. Then, without warning, the light was gone! I suspected that I had some forward movement in play when I first attempted to acquire to the light, so I did what no sane person would do, I tried to back up. Seconds later, I reacquired the light, and that light turned into many lights out of my right door. Once I had a reference, I was no longer lost in the snowstorm. I was able to hover over the lights, and once the aircraft was stable, I lowered the collective to lower the aircraft to get a better look. The glow from the many lights changed their definition from a glow to an interpretation of the many lights. If not for the brightness of the lights, I was close enough to read the wattage. I was euphoric! I could have cried. I composed myself as I knew there was still some flying left to do. It was a wonderful feeling knowing that we had come through what we had all while not crashing. I composed myself and asked the LT to put me back up the final controller selector no. 2 position.

The final controller was still issuing conflicting instructions when I broke in, "Final controller, this is RB93. We have acquired the lights at the end of the runway and are hovering over them. I am ready to change to tower frequency but would like to thank you so very much for your assistance. God Bless you, sir, and Merry Christmas."

"Roger RB93, understand you are hovering over the high-intensity runway lights (HIRL)?"

I could hear the disbelief in his voice. Frankly, I was in shock myself. I was expecting to impact the earth, yet here we are, hovering over these lights.

"RB93 frequency change approved. Contact Osan Tower on 122.10 or 308.80. Merry Christmas."

I looked over at the LT and smiling from ear to ear asked her to put me up 308.80 in the no. 2. She gladly did so, and I squeezed the mic and said, "Osan Tower, RB93, good afternoon. RB93 hovering over the HIRL lights and requests taxi assistance to parking."

"RB93, surface winds variable at 8, altimeter 29.93. Hover taxi forward to taxiway hotel. No need to contact ground at hotel. Remain this frequency." I began to move slowly forward and quickly realized that I was hovering out into snow abyss. I stopped and reacquired the lights and called tower and asked, "Osan Tower. Please send out a follow-me-truck. I am unable to depart the lights without assistance."

Again, a bit of surprise from the controller when I referred to the lights. He replied, "RB93, remain in place while I send out the follow-me-truck. Once the follow-me-truck is acquired, you are cleared to follow the directions of the truck."

"Roger, RB93 standing by," I replied. I was trying hard to maintain my professional exposure. All I wanted to do was land and put this flight to bed. The snow showers seemed to be subsiding. Instead of a mass of snow falling from the sky, I now saw less. It was a welcomed change. Remaining still over the lights was helping the windscreens too. Since we were no longer adding the chill factor of forward airspeed to the equation, the heat directed onto the windscreens seemed to be having some effect as demonstrated by the wipers ability to move the ice jam from the windscreen. There was still a glaze of ice on the windscreen. But with each swipe of the wipers, it was getting better and better. We needed all the help we could get.

The radio came to life as the tower reported, "RB93. The follow-me-truck is approaching you with some difficulty. There is a lot of snow that they are working through but should be there shortly. What is your fuel status?" they asked.

"Roger, RB93 has under a hundred pounds. I guesstimate that we will flame out in ten minutes at this power setting."

I needed to assure the crew that our situation was much better now than that radio call sounded like. I explained to the crew that, as scary as a pending flameout seemed, I was not unusually intimidated by that possibility. Falling out of the sky at the whim of the aircraft, I explained, was a non-option. Like a water autorotation, I knew that if I had to, I would fly forward of the lights and intentionally execute a planned hovering autorotation rather than allow the aircraft to flame out and crash into the lights below. The problem with that was I was about twenty-five feet and still had visual acuity problems. After what we had just flown through, a hovering autorotation was much more palatable than flying into a mountainside. Still unsettled, the crew agreed that an intentional hovering autorotation was the better option when compared to an unannounced flameout. Hopefully, the follow-me-truck would solve that problem for us, and there would be no need to execute that plan. I liked it, however, that we were still thinking, and that we had a plan was priceless. In command of the aircraft and the conditions that we found ourselves in was a welcomed change indeed.

It was the LT that saw the lights of the follow-me-truck first. While driving toward us, we could make out the glow of the headlights with the yellow flashing lights on the top of the cab. I was choked up when I called tower and said, "Osan Tower, RB93 has the follow-me-truck in site. Please ask them to flash their high beams so that we are sure."

The follow-me-truck must have been monitoring the transmission because I could see the high beams flash. I barely could make out the yellow lights on the top of the truck. Then all of a sudden, his headlights were no longer visible. I can only guess that once he flashed his lights, he turned around in preparation to escort us out.

"Osan Tower, can you ask the follow-me-truck to come closer? I can see that they have reversed course and am having difficulty maintaining visual acuity." Again, the follow-me-trucks headlights became visible, and I could see that he was moving closer.

The tower reported, "RB93, the follow-me-truck, for the snow conditions, cannot come any closer."

"Roger. RB93 understands. Instruct them to turn around and slowly lead me to taxiway hotel. Because of the ice on my windscreens, I will turn the aircraft ninety degrees and hover sideways to maintain visual acuity." I knew that turning the aircraft and hovering sideways would help me see better. The windscreen was clearing but not yet clear. My side window was clear enough. I turned the helicopter ninety degrees and put the follow-me-truck out my window, and we began to move away from the security of the lights. As we left the lights, I could easily see that it was getting a bit darker, but the brightness of the snow was enough to illuminate the area from total darkness. It was only early afternoon, and on any other day, the sun would have been bright and beautiful. This was a monster snowstorm. We were still in cloud at five thousand feet, and my -1 told me that the ceiling went all the way to ten thousand feet. That is a deep natural mass working to block the sun, so it was no wonder that the illumination from the snow was as good as it got.

We both moved together slowly. With some trial and error, I found the sweet spot to my altitude and speed. If I were too low, I would white out from blowing snow from the rotor system. If I were too high, then I would lose the truck and have to return to IMC flight conditions. So I remained high enough to stay clear of the rotor wash and low enough to maintain visual acuity with the follow-me-truck. I noticed the power needed to remain at this altitude was surprisingly high. Typically, a Huey hovers at thirty-two pounds of torque. Were we hovering at forty-six pounds of torque. I was too busy to ponder the excessive amount of power needed to hover our aircraft that was all but out of gas. At this point in the flight, I just wanted to conclude the flight safety. I knew we were over the active now. We began to see a series of red lights that were originating from the crash rescue crews that were dispatched. They were staged along the active. I counted two fire trucks, two ambulances, and other smaller vehicles that I have to guess is the military police. It was nice to know that we were not in as many pieces as they were expecting. Hitting the earth at one hundred feet per minute in VFR conditions is something we train for and is, frankly, no big deal, skidded helicopter or no. Do that maneuver blind, however, when you are not really sure if you are over the runway centerline, and it becomes another story altogether.

Except for the final controller's instructions, I had no idea where I was. The closer I got to the earth, the greater the difficulty in doing a run-on landing. Praise God we were just hovering along. I was very grateful for everyone who came out to assist. At some point in the hover, I peddle-turned the aircraft back ninety degrees to the right so that if the helicopter did flame out at least, I was headed in the correct direction to facilitate a successful hovering autorotation.

The tower called and said, "RB93, you are approaching hotel taxiway on your left side."

"Roger, RB93 requests that you notify me the moment I clear the active." I followed the tracks from the follow-me-truck onto the taxiway. "Osan Tower, am I clear of your active?" I asked.

"RB93, my radar shows that you will be clear in another twenty feet," the tower replied.

"Roger. I do not wish to shut down your runway, but as soon as I am clear allowing for heavy aircraft to continue to work the airstrip, RB93 intends to precautionary land (PL) on the taxiway," I reported. The moments that ticked by after that call seemed likes hours to me.

"RB93, you are cleared of the active and cleared to present position PL," the tower graciously stated.

"Roger, RB93 is declaring a presentation position PL for fuel." And with that radio call, I slowly lowered the collective. The first thing that disappeared to the rotor wash snow was the lights on the follow-me-truck. We were in total whiteout conditions again. I knew the earth was down there, and I knew that I had about three knots forward airspeed working for me. I felt the left rear skid strike the taxiway first. That was quickly followed by the right side. I fought my instinct to dump the collective. With the heels of the skids firmly on the ground, I knew we were almost done. I continued to slowly and deliberately lower the collective. The aircraft settled squarely onto the front portion of the skids as well. With the helicopter firmly on the ground, I lowered the collective and centered the cyclic. If not for the grace of God, that landing would have been significantly different. The final movements of the flight controls were a relief. It was over. We survived.

CHAPTER 32

Safely Down at Osan

23 December 1982, ROK.

Per protocol, the crash rescue followed us during our hover taxi from the active onto the taxiway. There is not an aircrew anywhere that does not appreciate the work of these great Americans. As soon as I rolled the throttle to engine idle, I saw them charge the aircraft. They wanted to make sure that we were all right. That is when the tears welled up in me. I knew that there was no crash rescue team for my dad and twin. Given the impact of their crash, Dad and Dan would not have known anyway. But I knew, and as I looked into the eyes of the firefighter, I was humbled. He opened my door, and I was awash with the cold. There was a lot of noise. He stood upon the skids, slapped my right shoulder, and shouted over the noise, "Nice approach, Chief. You okay?" He knew I was unable to respond. Must have been the tears on my cheeks. Knowing that my crew and I were okay, he just smiled, nodded, slapped my shoulder again, and shook his head. He shouted back over the noise, "Nice, nice approach. Merry Christmas." And with that, he closed the door and headed away. I gulped in a bunch of cold air a few times while still looking where he had stood. Doing so allowed me to compose myself a bit.

I reached up and wiped the tears from my eyes and turned to the LT and said, "Okay, LT, let's get the checklist out and shut this thing down." While she was doing so, I keyed the mic and asked for a vehicle for my codes onboard. Let no emergency interfere with flag officer protocol.

The two flag officers left the aircraft while we were still going through the shutdown. They were quickly picked up by the USAF. There were no goodbyes when they left. It was cold, I surmised, and they just wanted to move on. MAJ Burns also disappeared along with them. I did salute them as they departed in case they may have looked back. They didn't. I didn't know their destination; I only knew that I had done my job. I picked them up, took them to their meeting, and returned them safely home.

The LT got out the checklist and began the call and response process for engine shutdown. The routine was a wonderful feeling. I continued to either flip switches or acknowledge switches as she called one item after another. The turbine engine requires a two-minute cool down before I can roll the throttle off. We had been sitting there more than ten minutes when she got to the part in the checklist that requires me to roll the engine off. I hesitated. Before I rolled the throttle off, I dialed in Red Baron Operations and checked in with operations. I was stunned that they knew how much trouble I had been in. I guess Osan called them. I am not really sure how they knew, but I could tell that there was a lot of high-fiving going on. It did not take long for the hazing to begin over the radio, and I smiled when I said I had to get back to real work.

I needed to secure the aircraft and, with that, signed off. After the radio call, I gladly rolled off the throttle off and watched the engines exhaust gas temperature (EGT) gauge decline until it stopped and began to rise only slightly, indicating the presence of radiant heat within the engine. A standard rise due to the drop in N1 speed that provides cooling air for the engine as it diminishes to zero rotation. A vital check indeed so that the person monitoring the controls can confirm that there is no onboard residual fire in the engine. Satisfied that there was no onboard fire, I directed my attention to closing out the book while the LT was securing her stuff. I heard the back door open and, as quickly, close, not before flooding the cabin with arctic air. Ryan had undoubtedly jumped out to secure the rotor system that was slowly winding itself to a stop.

I was logging the flight time on the -12 when Ryan opened my door and said, "Mr. D, you have got to see this." He was quite animated. I didn't want to get out of the cockpit. My warm spot, thanks to Ryan, however, had been replaced with the icy coolness of the season, so I unstrapped and grabbed my flight jacket and jumped out. Quietly, without letting Ryan know, as soon as I jumped out and stood on the ground, I began to shake. I couldn't seem to stop. I was flooded with gratitude to stand out in the cold on a flight line. I was really shaking physically. Fortunately, the cold masked that. I was not shivering from the cold, although it was freezing. I was emotionally drained and was trying to shake it off, I guess.

I closed my eyes, thanked God for his many blessings, gave myself a good shake, and asked Ryan, "What could be that important?" Ryan just stepped back and pointed to the airframe and fuselage. Oh my gosh, I thought. It looked as if the fire department had sprayed down the helicopter only to have the water freeze.

The frozen water all over the aircraft was aerodynamically compacted into every nook and cranny. Seeing the helicopter like this was a bit scary. No surface was without some layer of ice. Main rotor blades and the rotating controls as well. Most telling was the area around the engine. Where the side engine barriers were supposed to be instead were small openings that resembled portals. One could easily imagine the air being sucked into the engine, and with the passing of each water droplet, some were left on the side where they eventually froze over, creating the portal. That portal of air is what kept the engine from flaming out.

Ryan quickly apologized for the flak that he gave me when I directed him to take off the side barriers before departing Wonju. "I had no idea how important that direction was going to be," he said.

"Me either, Ryan. This afternoon, the angels were flying with us. I was prompted to have you remove those barriers by the direction of the Holy Spirit. I am not smart enough to get that right all by myself. We should have never flown. By the looks of the ice on the aircraft, we were blessed to have made it alive. If the barriers were still on the aircraft, we would have flamed out a long time ago. Let's get this aircraft secured and go home."

I jumped back into the cockpit to finish out the logbook. With the -12 complete, I turned my attention to the -13 and made this simple entry. "Flt no. 2: PL at Osan for low fuel."

The LT had jumped out and was chatting with Ryan while I was finishing the logbook. I quickly joined them, and all of us were picked up by USAF transportation. The USAF is very attentive to its flight crews. I knew this from other VFR missions that I had flown into Osan. Aircrews were tended to. The army could have learned a thing or two. In the army, not so much, but the USAF would spoil you for sure.

Nonetheless, just in time, airfield transportation arrived. MAJ Burns jumped out and was very excited. "Crew of RB93, let's go," he proclaimed. "I am taking you guys to the officers club. Drinks are on me."

CHAPTER 33

Osan Officers Club: Drinks for All and All for Drinks

23 December 1982, ROK.

The major was thrilled. We arrived at the officers club, and he ushered us quickly to a table. I didn't drink a whole lot, but I did drink. I was not used to drinking at 1400 in the afternoon, however.

"Beers all the way around," he shouted to the barkeep. You could tell he was really up. He was going on about the flight and the professionalism that I had displayed. He apologized for the role he played in rushing us into the air at Wonju. He knew I was just a WOJG with a butter bar for a copilot. If a major said go, he realized we, as new guys, would take that as a go. I was not going to let him bear any responsibility for my decision to fly. I reminded him that the conduct of the flight rests with the decisions made by the PIC. I was the PIC after all, and though the -1 made the weather look marginally legal, I should have never left.

"We should have RON'ed," I said.

All of a sudden, the major got really intense when he said, "Listen WOJG," the MAJ began. "This is what army aviation is all about. I won't argue that your decisions would have been better served with more experience, but this is exactly how you gain experience," he went on.

If you live through it, I thought to myself.

"Look," he continued. "Let's break down the flight."

All of a sudden, I felt like I was about to be professionally ripped. Is this what it is like when you survive an emergency? I wondered for a moment if this was the beginning of a kangaroo court or the ramblings of a guy who was already working on his second beer?

"Okay, we all agree the better decision was not to fly, granted," he began. "LT, you showed incredible courage not to wrestle the controls from your PIC. Even I thought he was flipping out at first, but you held your cool. I was familiar with the Wonju Valley, however, and quickly realized that we were IMC and that Mr. D was modifying the IMC emergency procedure to fit the geography of the area. You, not knowing that, I don't know if I could have displayed your coolness at that time."

I was glad that he recognized the actions of the LT. Her fighting me for the controls would have killed us.

"I thought the whole Poncho exchange went beautifully," he went on. "Everyone knows we are not supposed to bug those guys, but the conditions were ripe for some assistance." He finished his second, maybe third beer. I could tell that he too was coming down from his own high and this was his way of doing so. I hoped not too many more beers, however. He put his finger up in the air, indicating another round. I was still nursing my first, and Ryan and the LT were not far behind me. Beers came anyway.

"When you told Poncho that you had two gyro failures, I almost flipped. I did not want to bother you. I knew you were busy working things out. I opened the logbook in the back and read of the two circle red x's. One for the attitude indicator and the other for the RMI. My heart skipped a beat wondering if you were going to pull this flight off partial panel, in ice, in cloud!"

All of us just sat there in a moment of silence, grasping what Major Burns just said out loud. Saying it out loud was a little different than enduring the real circumstances.

The LT said, "I never saw that coming. You did an exceptional job, Dean, working those difficulties."

"Exceptional job indeed," said the major. "Anyone would have first gone to the turn and slip. You did as well but quickly found the mag compass to be your best friend. Combine that with the information of the VSI, and you found your sweet spot. Why not just look over at the standby attitude indicator in front of the LT?" he asked.

"I did not want to disturb my head movement discipline any more than necessary. I tried to keep my head still so that my inner ear would not interfere with what my eyes were seeing. Updating the attitude indicator and RMI while flying along was just easier for me," I explained,

"Well, it looked like a lot of work, but it worked for you," he said. He took another long slug of his beer and continued. "The hand-off from Poncho to Osan was pretty seamless. I thought you guys worked well setting up for the ILS and asking for the no gyro, but during the first approach, what the hell was with the controller? He said you were left, off course, and then turned you left? What kind of instructions are those?" he asked.

"I don't know, sir, and I apologize for putting you in your place. I was a hostage to their game plan and had to trust that he was seeing something that I was not seeing."

"No apology needed. You were right. You had to follow his instruction. My only negative critique—I would have challenged him sooner, that's all. But you have a set of gonads to have followed his instruction and for making the missed approach. I know that was a difficult decision," he concluded.

"I have to say that I don't know how you did not pull those red tabs on the LT seat and take her spot," I joked.

He surprised me when he said, "I thought about it."

Ryan got in on the conversation when he asked, "MAJ Burns, did you see that ice cycle of an aircraft that we left parked on the taxiway?"

"I did see the ice, and by the power needed to hover, I suspect there was a lot of it," he said. He went on to ask, "Mr. D, you remember what the hover torque was when you hovered away from the lights?"

"Forty-something," I said.

"It wasn't forty-something. It was forty-six pounds of torque. I was looking right at it. Strike you as odd?" he asked.

"It did. I was a bit busy when I saw that and quickly dismissed it as the power needed to Out of Ground Effect (OGE) hover," I said.

"Me too," he agreed at first. "But while you were doing all that work, I contemplated that a lot. You were OGE for sure, but you were OGE in an aircraft empty of fuel. The weight of the PAXs and crew was nominal. You took off with one thousand pounds of fuel. By your own calculations, you did not burn the normal six hundred pounds per hour but were on the other side of eight hundred pounds per hour. That strike you as funny?"

"Of course it did," I said. "But I was a hostage and could do nothing about it."

"What about an altitude change," he asked. "Maybe you could have flown out of the ice."

"Like flying in the first place, that decision rests with me. That is a lesson, as well as others, that I will carry with me throughout my career."

"Fair enough," he said. He went to wonder aloud, "How much ice do you think was on the aircraft?"

I shrugged. "LT, care to stagger a guess?" Now I really did feel like it was an oral or at least a formal debriefing.

"Let's do some beer math," he said. "You left with one thousand pounds of fuel from Wonju. Flew for under an hour en route. You were burning fuel and weight at the same time. The thousand pounds of JP-4, at 6.5 pounds per gallon computes out to be…" I saw the effects of the beer as he was scribbling on the napkin. "Six hundred fifty pounds. We should have been six hundred fifty pounds lighter. Instead, we hovered at forty-six pounds of torque at arrival to Osan. The rule of thumb for cargo is one pound of torque equals two hundred pounds. The difference between thirty-two pounds of torque and forty-six pounds of torque is…"

"Fourteen pounds," the LT chimed in. She continued by saying, "I get it. Fourteen pounds works out to be twenty-eight."

"That's right, LT," said the major. "That twenty-eight means you had twenty-eight hundred pounds of ice on the aircraft that was all but empty of fuel after applying the rule of thumb," he concluded.

There was a pregnant pause, maybe two, when he continued, "Think about another altitude next time, Chief."

It was a sobering statement. I do not rejoice in my bad decisions. I accept them and try and grow from them. This flight has taught me so very much about IMC and IFR, not to mention what I personally can endure. I thought to myself that even though it almost killed us, it was a great flight.

"This, Mr. D, is army aviation at its finest," he said. "You screwed up, but you addressed each challenge well. Your actions are in keeping with the finest traditions of army aviation. Well done." You could tell he was a real live officer (RLO). I have heard that kind of pep talk before. He finished his last beer and winked at me and told me as he was standing up and taking my hand, "Mr. D, when I departed with the flag officers, I stopped and called your commander and told him that, despite the IMC/IFR, the mission was a total success and flown by a real professional. Your commander asked me to put my IP hat on and debrief your flight. This was not a check ride, but I am honored to have witnessed what I witnessed today. *Hoorah*," he concluded and was on his way. He stopped a few feet from the table and turned around and said, "You guys sit right there for another thirty minutes or so. My driver will drop me off at my hooch and will be back to carry you guys back to Humphreys. *Hoorah*." I don't know how he stayed upright as he summarily departed. I felt better, I think. I could tell the LT was carrying a heavy load. She was way too quiet as we kept sipping our beers. As if her head was someplace else…

CHAPTER 34

The Long Cold Drive Back to Camp Humphreys

23 December 1982, ROK.

The driver showed up about forty-five minutes later and drove us the hour or so through the snow back to Humphreys. The wipers were working hard to keep up with the falling snow. Like the aircraft's wipers, they were just barely effective, and like the aircraft too, the defrost was in full blast. Unlike the aircraft, the vehicle was sort of airtight, and with the four of us exhaling, I had to wonder if the poor visibility out of the windows was not partly from uncleared moisture on the inside. My window in the back had lots of moisture at any rate. I was not the PIC and was glad to sit back and relax during the drive. No back seat driving from me. I sat in the back with Ryan. The LT sat in the front with the driver. Unlike Ryan, the LT was very quiet. Ryan was very chatty. I could tell that he was still excited about the flight. He was somewhat entertaining as he was recounting his view of the flight from his seat and what he saw, where I thought that Major Burns was totally disengaged, Ryan told me that the major was giving him a play by play interpretation. He said the major did not want to interrupt my concentration or flow. Ryan told me that the major had assured him before the second revolution, after entering IMC, that he had determined that I had modified the

IMC emergency procedure for the terrain. He first pointed out the torque gauge and said with all that power and fifteen degrees on the attitude indicator that he knew it was a deliberate climb. He said that the major thought that I went one thousand feet too high before leveling out. The Poncho call also surprised him. We were not supposed to call them, but after he realized the gyros were bad, he was okay with it. I guess the majority of the flight after that was okay because Ryan did not mention any backseat comments referred by the major until we were making the first approach. Ryan said he was so excited that he thought he was coming over the seats. When you shut him up...*wow*. Ryan said he thought his eyes were going to pop out of his head. I was beginning to feel a bit like another critique of the flight, and I almost waved Ryan off, but I knew he too was coming down from the adrenalin rush and that he just needed to process the whole thing. I did perk up when he gave me the intel on the PAXs. Ryan said that the two flag officers were just chatting away, going over their meeting, and neither had any idea that we were in any sort of peril... until we were landing.

"When you manhandled the helicopter over the lights that seemed to get their attention rightly enough. Until then, everything was smooth feeling. With the different changes in the aircraft's attitude, one could tell that you were wrestling with the aircraft. It was the abrupt arrival to a hover that got their attention."

I apologized for the rough handling of the aircraft over the lights. I could understand why PAXs in the rear, not knowing what was really happening upfront, would become very interested at that time. I tried to aerodynamically explain to Ryan how I was trading off all that forward and downward energy that the aircraft was experiencing on the approach and transition that energy to nothing either forward or downward by beginning with an NOE decel and following that up with a stabilized hover. Challenging to do VFR, but blind? Very difficult. Ryan said he got it; it was just entertaining watching the flag officers react.

"Since you had their attention, the Korean admiral was closest to me, and he was speaking broken English when he asked what was going on."

Ryan said that his sign language was more effective than his broken Korean, but when we were hovering in, and I began to pass crash rescue, the Koreans eyes got huge, and he pointed out to each red light and then pointed to himself. Ryan said that he nodded his head in agreement that the crash rescue was here for us. That seemed to stun the Korean, and he got reticent while he waited out the rest of the hover to the taxiway. Ryan laughed out loud.

Ryan said, "You had to see it for yourself, Mr. D, to really appreciate it." Then Ryan asked, "Why did you PL on the taxiway and not go all the way to parking?"

I was quiet for a minute thinking about that question. I was reliving the emotions of the moment. I could not tell him that I was an emotional mess and that I was expending all the energy I could to hold things together. I could not tell him that I had been challenged to my very core. I could not tell him that my dad and twin were not as lucky as we had been and how surprised I was that, all these many years later, their passing became something I had to process again while fighting for my own life. I had no words for his question other than, "Just seemed like the right thing to do."

He smiled and nodded his head. "Yes, it certainly was the right thing to do. Thank you, Mr. D, for bringing us home," Ryan concluded.

I blinked a few times while I nodded in agreement and then looked away outside. I could not let him see the emotion that I was fighting back. I also was glad to be alive. My crew and PAXs were alive and well too and had a story to tell.

We were getting closer to Camp Humphreys. Things were beginning to look familiar. I could see that we were on the outskirts of Pyeongtaek. Pyeongtaek was the more substantial town outside of Camp Humphreys. It was almost 1600 hours by now, and you could see that the shops were beginning to transition to closing. There weren't many people out. The Korean people were a hearty people, but it was still cold. The holidays were everywhere too. Christmas decorations seemed just as tired as we were, but again, they showed out as best they could. The drive through the town was the same everywhere. I closed my eyes for a moment, maybe a few moments. I was thinking about the LT. She was very quiet and had not said one word the entire ride home. Was that odd? Ryan talked my ear off the better part of the trip, and still, the LT was silent.

I opened my eyes and realized that I may have dozed off for some time. Pyeongtaek was well behind us now, and we were halfway through villa outside the Humphreys gate. Anjeong-Ri was a small villa that seemed to service Humphreys. The surrounding area was very rural. By contrast, the villa had lots of bars and small shops. Steam and smoke were rising from everywhere. Many homes and buildings were heated with ondol. Ondol was the preferred way that Koreans heated their homes. It was said to be efficient, but also deadly. Round ondol black briquettes the size of coffee cans with holes in the middle for airflow were placed into furnaces that would burn all night. Ondol smoke was routed through flews under the floor to heat the house. As long as there were no leaks, it worked well. The carbon monoxide smoke, however, if leaked into the house, would kill you. There were enough reported deaths that commanders and first sergeants had engineers go through the village of Anjeong-Ri just outside Camp Humphreys and check for excessive carbon monoxide, all to educate the soldiers. The worst places were placed off-limits. Like Pyeongtaek, the Christmas decorations were tired and well used, but I was glad for them and appreciated the efforts of the Koreans to display them.

CHAPTER 35

Arrival to Camp Humphreys

23 December 1982, ROK.

We arrived at the front gate just before 1630 hours. Knowing that we would be asked for identification by the military police (MP) at the gate, we all automatically passed our identifications to the driver. Right on cue, we were met at the gate by an SP4 who was as bundled up as he could get. The driver rolled down his window, and the driver gave him all our identifications. He looked over them and us and was made satisfied and, after saluting, raised the barrier and waved us through. Camp Humphreys mostly consisted of an airfield with hangars, support buildings, and the like. The buildings that surrounded the airfield were old and well-used buildings indeed. Some cinder block buildings, mostly Quonset huts. Quonset huts were a building constructed with corrugated metal and closed off at each end. They were closely related to wind tunnels for aircraft. These Quonset huts, however, were smaller, and because they were closed off at each end, they made adequate billeting. They usually housed four men. Each man had a room in each corner of the building partitioned by non-loadbearing walls, and the center section was the common area hosting the kitchen and a gathering area. A single latrine was included in the design of the floorplan, servicing all those who were housed there. Some loved living in the Quonset hut housing. I did not live in a Quonset hut, but I visited them often when visiting with friends.

Cinder block buildings dominated the housing needs of the soldiers. The Quonset huts used for housing seemed to be an after-thought undoubtedly realized with each surge of soldier assignment. At the southwest side of the airfield, several three-story cinder block buildings housed soldiers and accommodated some administrative functions. There was a chapel as well as a small commissary. A post exchange (PX) too. The PX was as small, maybe even tiny, as the commissary had mostly essential items. The PX carried a few inventory items for purchase, but those items were more like trinkets than real inventory. Each Wednesday, the commissary was restocked, so naturally, Thursday was the best shopping day. By the following Monday, the shelves would be all but bare, and the cycle would continue week after week throughout the tour. There was a small movie theater too. They boasted that every third day a new movie would be delivered to the Hump. I often went if only to break up the monotony. There were very few first-run movies. Most of the film that they presented in the theater I had seen before. Also, the Armed Forces Korea Network (AFKN) was our only television station. Since there were so many soldiers, the programmer's felt that mostly sports would be liked and best appreciated. I didn't particularly care for TV sports, so I did not watch much AFKN. All in all, it was a bleak existence, long on function and short on life's niceties. It was a great relief for me to simply fly away in my helicopter and either explore Korea from the air or do some sort of training flight off Humphreys. I felt terrible for those who did their entire tour there on the ground.

The driver interrupted my thoughts when we pulled into the parking lot for Red Baron Operations building. Another Quonset hut. This one is quite large as it housed all the administration functions for the unit, including the commander's office. We thanked the driver and opened the doors to be greeted by the arctic cold. Wow, was it cold! The three of us moved quickly inside where we were met by most of the aviators assigned to the unit who were not on Christmas leave. The hazing began in earnest. It was all in good fun. They were all genuinely happy that our story had a happy ending. I learned that our operations had been on the radio with Osan's operations, which gave them all a play by play of the landing into Osan. Oh, the yells and laughter I endured as they poked fun at us, mostly me.

"Nice first landing attempt," one shouted.

Another. "How about that fuel management there, Chief. How did that work out for you?"

And another read aloud from the -10 where it talked about flights into icing was prohibited.

CW3 Roger Wills, the units instrument examiner who had turned my last instrument check ride attempt into a training ride, followed that last remark with a firm handshake. His left hand simultaneously grasped my forearm as we shook, looking me straight in the eye as a measure of respect, said with a grin, "Chief, if you could have squeezed in a non-precision approach and some holding, I would be signing off your instrument evaluation right about now."

Most hazing is just good fun. This remark, however, was different. He and I both knew that I allowed my check-itis to cause me to choke, performing lousy in the simulator during our last flight. I knew without a doubt, however, that I had won the respect of the IFE, and for a WOJG to do so…well, that was something.

"Doudna," I heard someone shout down the hall. "A minute of your time please?" asked the commander. Major Barter was the current commander. He had changed commands with the previous commander while I was on mid-tour leave. He and I did not enjoy the same facetime as I and the former commander. This guy was a good commander but did not allow himself the pleasure of getting to know the officers under his command in the same manner as the previous commander. He was a bit intimidating. Very business-like. I entered his office and was prepared to salute when he waved me off and directed me to take a seat. He had the same large desk, and the same two comfortable chairs in front of his desk remained unchanged from my last visit with the previous commander. I took the chair that he had pointed to and he took the other.

"Well, you have had quite a day," he remarked. "Major Burns tells me that he was on that flight. He is a friend of mine and is currently serving as attaché to the two-star. I asked him to put his IP hat on and debrief the flight," the commander said matter-of-factly. "While you and your crew were being recovered back to the Hump," he continued "Major Burns called and said the debriefing went well. I could tell that there was alcohol involved. You must have scared him. He said it was a *hoo-ah* flight. Pretty high praise from Major Burns, I can assure you."

I was stunned. I didn't know what to say or do, and I think the commander sensed that too.

"Listen," he said. "This is not an ass chewing. I am proud of how you handled the flight. Looks like it was full of lessons for you. Glad it all worked out okay. Any questions?" he asked.

"Am I grounded, sir?" I asked.

"Hell no. Somebody has to get that aircraft you left at Osan. You departed the Hump today with one of my helicopters. I fully expect you to fetch it home as soon as the weather allows. Now get out of here. I have real work to do."

I smiled and said, "Yes, sir," saluted, and smartly departed." I returned to the thinning crowd in the hall only to be further hazed by my fellow aviators. I finally broke away and headed out the front door for my hooch.

CHAPTER 36

Headed to My Hooch

23 December 1982, ROK.

I strolled to my hooch. It was usually a fifteen-minute fast walk from the hangar to the hooch, but today, I was just trodding along, lost in thought. I needed some mental downtime to think about anything but the flight. I wanted to wrap myself with my family. I wanted to escape. It took forty-five minutes to get to the hooch today. It was almost Christmas Eve, so there were only the occasional persons out and about. It was too cold to be social. My mind wasn't up for it, I guess. I was well bundled up, and I was lost in thought about my family. Coming that close to losing them was sobering.

I lived in a cinderblock building. The luck of the draw, I guess. We called it a six-pack. There was a long hallway down the middle and three bedrooms on either side of the entrance. At the end of the hall was a common latrine. The building was functional. I only slept there. The rest of my time was spent at work. It was easy to do; there really wasn't much else to do anyway. I was ten months into my tour. The tour was twelve months, so I was a short-timer. I went home late for mid-tour and conspired to bring my wife back. It was, of course, all illegal. There was a lot of officer's wives living in officer barracks. It was the worst kept secret on the compound. Everyone turned their head, even the commander. As long as we maintained a low profile, he didn't care. Before I brought Diana over, I knocked on each hooch-mate's door and said I was planning on bringing my wife to Korea, and I wanted to know if they had any issues with that. It was their home too, and bringing a woman into the hooch that was not a woman of the evening took some coordination. All five of my hooch-mates were a bit casual with the ladies, and I reminded them before bringing Diana over that they would have to be on their best behavior. They understood. True to their word, there was never an issue with any of my hooch-mates. I welcomed the cold and the walk. I wanted the time to remember just how beautiful our lives were together. I could have died, and that was not lost on me. I thought about a lot of things really. Bringing Diana over was something of a story of its own.

I went home late in my tour to get her. Rather than taking my mid-tour leave at the sixth-month mark, I took my mid-tour leave eight months into my assignment. The unit's missions interfered with my leaving until then. As it turned out, it was a blessing in disguise. I wanted nothing more than to spend time with the family. Seems odd saying that when I chose to separate myself from the family. A civilian will have difficulty processing that oxymoron, but another service member totally understands. Being in the army has always been a pull and tug as all service members balance professional requirements with family requirements. I chose to come to the ROK on purpose. I needed to create a career path built upon lessons learned in the ROK. For the married service member, it takes a good woman to tolerate that. Diana may not have understood the logic of my decision, but she trusted me when I told her that this was the best move for our career, and I loved her for her sacrifice. Our daughter likewise sacrificed. She was robbed of seeing her dad during the unaccompanied tour. To heighten that sacrifice, when I arrived home at mid-tour, my bride and I talked with Jenny about the remaining months of my tour.

"Jenny," I began. "You know I have to return to Korea for the last four months of my tour. What do you think if I took Mom with me?" Jenny was ten and my best friend in the whole wide world. Blond like her mom and petite, She has striking blue eyes, and she trusted every word out of my mouth. Her little hands were swallowed against mine, and I loved picking her up and hugging and kissing her. She was the best thing that I had ever done. I told her that she could come to Korea too, *but* if she did, "Mom would have to homeschool you." Diana had never done that before, and we were weeks from returning to the ROK. Coordinating and signing up for such an endeavor had its own challenges. I continued to explain that "if Mom did not get the homeschooling correct, and if you did not pass your final exams in school when we returned, there was a real chance that you would have to stay back and repeat the same grade." That was a lot of information for a ten-year-old to process. Military children, I believe, mature either faster or different from a like-aged young person that may stay in the same house for their lifetime. I continued to counsel Jenny that if she chose to say in the States, then she could stay with Grandpa or with Terry and Vickie. Terry and Vickie were lifelong friends and were more family than anything else. I told the daughter to spend the weekend thinking on it but that I needed a decision soon so that we could either arrange for transportation to the ROK or arrange for a four-month-long sleepover with Grandpa or Terry and Vickie.

I could tell over the next few days that she was processing the information. She asked some excellent questions. Some concerning staying back a year, some concerning just how Mom was going to work homeschooling into an overseas profile. I was most interested in the lack of conversation about where she would stay if she did not go the ROK with us. I spoke with Diana about it, and we both thought that the lack of questions about where she was to stay while we were gone went to her desire to go to Korea.

The next few days uncomfortably passed. Then Jenny put her best adult face on and told us that she thought it best if she stayed in the States. Wow, was I impressed. That took a lot of courage. A vast subject for one so young. We had some family discussions about her decision, but at the end of the day, we honored her choice. From an adult's perspective, it really was the best decision. Maybe the better decision was not to take Diana to the ROK in the first place. History will have to be the best judge of that question. For the two of us, the draw of the adventure was too much to pass up. We knew that she would be in reliable hands with Grandpa, so that was reassuring. Funny thing is that she chose to stay with Terry and Vickie instead of Grandpa. She really suffered trying to find a way to tell us that she wanted to stay with Terry and Vickie. We were surprised since we pretty much assumed that she would stay with Grandpa. Terry and Vickie were closer to our age, I'm guessing. They also have a son a few years younger than Jenny. Once Diana and I stepped back from the decision matrix, I could see why she decided to stay with them. I could not have been prouder.

We contacted Terry and Vickie. Terry was a military guy too, and both of them were gracious enough to say yes to our request. We quickly got started planning our return to the ROK. We only had $350 between us. Pretty limited funds for international travel. I was on an unaccompanied tour, so I was pretty sure that it was illegal for Diana to fly on a military hop to Korea. Pretty sure, not totally sure, however. So to make totally sure, I contacted McCord AFB. It was super convenient as Terry and Vickie lived but a few miles from McCord AFB. The call became a visit. I couldn't believe what they told me on the phone, so I dove to the terminal and asked in person. I spoke with the airman who was assigned to work the information desk and explained as clearly as I could that I was on an unaccompanied tour to Korea and wanted to be put on a hop back to Korea and additionally wanted to take my wife as well. He acted like he did not hear the unaccompanied part of my opening. He got out the book and asked when we wanted to fly out. He said there were flights on Mondays, Wednesdays, and Fridays. Again, I reminded him that I was unaccompanied.

"No matter," he said. "Just tell me the day, and you are in."

We were giddy. I selected a Friday flight so that we could stay as long as possible with Jenny before departing.

That Friday, the morning of our departure, came early. Everything comes early in the military. We were scheduled for a 0630 departure. Back that up for an hour arrival before departure, and then another two hours for the wakeup and drive time to McCord AFB put our day beginning at 0330. Nobody is happy at 0330 in the morning. Add that to family separation, and the mood was challenging, to say the least. We said our goodbyes and got hugs and kisses that had to last for months. Terry and Vickie dutifully drove us to McCord. Arrival to McCord AFB was equally emotional. There was a lot of activity afoot getting the C-141 ready for departure. Yes, I said C-141! Oh my gosh, who flies a 141 all that distance?

The military does, that's who. Like all flights, this was a service mission and training mission combined. The C-141 is a cargo airplane. It is a military workhorse. We were stuffed to the gills with cargo. There were only six seats open for PAXs. Yes, those seats were the cargo netting type seating that all soldiers are familiar and accustomed to. The seats were killer after only a few hours. The military is long on function and short on comfort. There is no insulation in the aircraft. It was pressurized, however, allowing us to operate at commercial altitudes. Diana often asked why she could see the aircraft's structure, all the wires and tubing. I teased her that it was the best way to check for leaks while flying. Funny, there is a lot of truth in that statement. I was glad that she thought I was just teasing, however. I did keep a lookout for leaks. We aerial refueled twice for training. The crew was kind enough to invite the PAXs, one at a time, up to the cockpit to witness the aerial refueling. Diana did not want to go forward to see. I was all but pushing her out of her seat as I unbuckled her seatbelt and shoulder harness, telling her when she would ever get another opportunity to see that. She went forward and was glad to get back as she excitedly reported that we were dangerously close to another aircraft. At that moment, I just thought about how lovely her long blond hair was.

Commercially, the flight is about thirteen hours or so. In the C-141, we spent the better part of sixteen hours. Multiple crew members rotated through the cockpit to get the flight done. Sixteen hours and two inflight refuelings later, and we landed at Kadena AFB, Japan, tired and cranky. The flight was scheduled to RON in Japan for a crew rest period. I smiled to myself. In the army, we crew rest too, but in this case, we would have flown on. There were two crews on board to relieve each other after all. But I was not arguing. I was ready to stretch out on a bunk somewhere. I, along with all the

PAXs, was stiff, and our bodies were humming from the constant vibration of the aircraft. A RON sounded pretty good to me.

Once the plane was secured, the ground crew approached the aircraft with a forklift. The aircraft's cargo had to come off for some reason. All of our bags were on the first pallet to come off. We were told to claim our bags and meet the airman at the service desk for our bunking assignment. Diana was the first to the pallet and was busy fetching our bags. I began to help Diana with our bags when things went downhill very quickly.

"Mr. Doudna," an airman called out.

"Here," I responded.

"Come with me please," he said as he lead me past the counter.

As he was leading me, I tried to sound authoritative as I asked, "Is there something wrong, airman?"

My question stopped him from taking me back into the bowls of the operations area when he stopped mid-stride and turned and said, "I see that you are on an unaccompanied tour. Can you explain how your wife got on the aircraft?"

"Yes, of course, I can," I said. "I approached the subject with the McCord personnel. I told them numerous times that I was on an unaccompanied tour, and even with me pressing the point, they were unconcerned and allowed her on the flight."

He was outraged and began to tell me how he was going to put us both on a flight back to the States, where I would face charges. At hearing that, I was more than upset. I began to flex every ounce of military might that my W01 bar could bring to bear as I began to articulate that there had clearly been a misunderstanding. Returning us was a non-option, I went on. He insisted that he was going to repatriate us with the United States as he disappeared into the bowels of the operations office to get his operations officer. I quickly retreated, grabbed Diana and the luggage, and like Butch Cassidy and the Sundance Kid, we moved as promptly as possible out of the terminal, jumped into a cab, and escaped. I think the airman was unable to find his leadership as the escape was much too easy. There apparently was no follow-up. I kept waiting for the military police to catch us. I am not even sure that they were notified as nothing came of them. I, on the other hand, was terrified. My career as an officer would have been ground to a halt had there been any sort of follow-up.

The driver took us to post billeting. It was an unremarkable building. We entered tired and confused and asked if they could house us for the evening. They could not have been more helpful.

"Of course we can," said a very nice woman behind the counter. "Just need to see your military identification and form of payment."

I was relieved. I showed her my identification. Back in the day, we traveled with a checkbook. Not even sure that we had a charge card. We would settle up in the morning at checkout.

Fatigue and fear hit me almost at the same time. I don't remember lying down on the bed. I slept like the dead, I was so tired. Diana has always been able to function on less sleep. When I awoke, I asked if she had slept. She said that she did sleep some, but most of her sleep had been interrupted by an idea. She got on the phone while I was asleep and managed to book us two seats flying out of Narita Airport, Japan, for Seoul Airport, Korea. All we had to do was pay for them. The problem was that the two tickets took most of our $350 that we had set aside until the end of the month. We also had to get from Kadena AFB to Narita Airport. Kadena was in the southwestern portion of the country. Narita was in the northeastern part of the country. Through happenchance, she discovered on the phone that there is a train that runs the route. We would later realize that there was nothing happenchance about this journey. God was watching out for us in spite of ourselves. We were told to expect a three hour or so commute. We just needed to get to the train station. I couldn't believe the trouble we were having with this return journey to the ROK. If we could have stayed on the hop, we would be landing in Osan Korea in a few hours.

We explained our traveling dilemma to the clerk when we were checking out. She said that that journey was no problem. Everyone flying commercially from Kadena takes the train to Toyoko and then the bus to Narita. No big deal for them, I guess. They were culturally acclimated. We had only been in Japan a matter of hours and were about to embark on a cross-country train and bus ride to catch a plane at the other end of the country. What could possibly go wrong?

When we settled the bill, we asked if they would cash a check for us so that we could purchase the plane tickets. Unbeknownst to them, it was all the money we had until next payday. The clerk, because I was an officer, was able to extend the limit from $150 to $250. I asked he very nicely if she could consider cashing the check for $350. She said she would have to get her supervisors' approval for the additional $100. We said a prayer. She was gone for a long time. Neither one of us were very good at being Sundance or Butch. We were very nervous. The clerk finally came back with a smile.

"Here is your $350 less the night's stay. Our manager typically does not do that. You were in luck." I just felt blessed.

The clerk was helpful enough to write down the instructions on how to get from Kadena to Narita. We were to take a cab to the train station; at the train station, buy a train ticket from Kadena to the Tokyo Central Station; at the Tokyo Central Station, buy the plane from Narita to Korea; and then board a bus from Tokyo to Narita. It was hard for me to keep up. We were taking a train to Tokyo. Then once there, and after buying a plane ticket in Tokyo, which is in the center of the country by the way, we would purchase the ticket and then board a bus northbound for the airport. Tokyo was in the middle of the country. Who does that? Sounded pretty hokey to me. We had no time to digest it. All I wanted to do was get in a cab and off base. I kept waiting for the military police to snatch us up at any time. They did not.

The cab picked us up at our RON quarters. The clerk was kind enough to say something in Japanese to the driver, and he spirited us right off base. "Drive very fast" must have been the words she spoke, because he sure did. Using the United States as a measure, the car's steering wheel is on the wrong side of the car, and we were driving on the wrong side of the road. I sat upfront with the driver. I found myself hitting the brakes on my side with each close encounter. He was an excellent driver, fast and focused. He spoke no English. When we arrived, we were deposited beside a kiosk with a very long line. He got out, took the bags out of the car, and pointed at the kiosk.

He helped me get the correct amount of Japanese money out of my wallet to pay for his services and was off before I could say much else.

Diana and I just stood there looking at each other. Time was ticking. so we smiled, grabbed a bag, and headed toward the kiosk. The Japanese people had little tolerance for our inability to understand their system. We observed patrons use the kiosk, and after we could no longer tolerate the suspense, got in line to try and operate the kiosk. While we were watching others in front of us, we began to understand that the kiosk dispensed tokens for the train. There still remained many unanswered questions: which train, how many tokens for that train, where did the train go, and how much did it cost was even a mystery to us. We bravely stood in line, waiting our turn. When we did get to the kiosk, we found no words in English. I had no idea which button to push nor did I know what to do with this machine to get a token out. A frustrated man behind me couldn't stand my incompetence any longer. He reached around me, and before I could watch all that he had done, he put money in the machine, and he quickly took his token, or tokens, from the device and departed.

Feeling like we may get trampled, we stepped out of line and just stood there looking like we needed help. Not long afterward, a British woman who spoke Japanese came up through the crowds of people and asked, "You look like you need help."

I was almost in tears with gratitude. I began to tell her our story, and she shushed me, telling me, "No time for that. This is rush hour. Where are you going?"

"Tokyo," I squeezed in.

She took money from me, put it in the machine, and out came tokens for Diana and me. She gave me my change, purchased her own, and she and her entourage were off in a flash.

"Wait," I called out. Diana and I were doing everything in our power to drag our bags through the sea of people that were working their way to the train as we tried to catch her.

She stopped for a moment and said, "We are going to be on the same train. Let's go. I am getting off before Tokyo. You need to be close and act quickly. Stay close. Wait."

We worked our way to the train station platform and waited. There was no time for a conversation. Very shortly, our train pulled up. Like a coach issuing an instruction to her team, she shouted above the noise, "When they open that door, push, push, push. Expect to be squeezed and packed into the train!"

I had spent some time in the Orient (Vietnam and Korea) and never expected to experience what happened next. Just as she said, those doors opened, and there was no rule of the road at play; everyone exited the train car and everyone entered the train car at the same time as if they were Vikings colliding in headlong battle.

"Push, Push, Push..." I heard her say. I am not sure how we got in, but we did.

The British woman's name is lost to time now. She was personable, delightful, and I could easily see that she was a wonderful Godly woman. It turned out that she was a missionary, and the love of God was all over her. She was traveling with a group of four others on a mission trip to somewhere. On the train, we had a little time to catch her up with our predicament. She just laughed and said, "God will work it all out for you. I don't really believe you will end up in jail. Sounds like a simple mistake."

Strangely, I believed her. I gave her the clerk's directions and asked her to read them and correct them if necessary. I was delighted that she confirmed the instructions that we had been given. The whole Tokyo thing was throwing me for a loop. "No fear," she interrupted my thoughts. "Actually don't worry about taking a bus from the Central Station in Tokyo to Narita. Compared to the States, it may seem odd, but it is the way they do things here."

With that, she took out a piece of paper and wrote four Japanese characters. I had no idea what she wrote. She looked at me and smiled at my confusion. "Look," she said. "These characters will appear at your stop. It will not say Tokyo or anything else in English. Compare these Japanese characters to the sign. When you see it, get off quickly. My team and I are getting off at the next stop. God bless on your journey. Go in peace." With that, the train came to a stop, and just as when we boarded, a flow of people came out of the car, taking our English-speaking rescuer and her team with them.

The train left the station as quickly as it had entered. We were traveling with a whole new group of people who didn't pay us any mind. We moved silently. Thinking back to when the missionary was with us, come to think of it, we were the only ones speaking. There was silence, interrupted only by the clang of the train cars rattling down the tracks toward Tokyo. At each stop, fewer people came on and more got off. It only took a few stops, and the train cars were empty enough to expose seats. Diana and I took one that gave us the best vantage point to compare the words written on the paper with the train stop stations. An elderly man was watching us. He remained expressionless as he watched us hold up the paper to each sign that passed.

We must have humored him. Before long, his stop was approaching as he got up and readied himself at the door. He turned and looked at me and held up one hand and slowly exposed one finger after another. One, I counted. Two. Three, then four fingers. He smiled and departed the train at his station. Diana looked at me and said, "I'll bet our stop is the fourth stop."

Sure enough, we anxiously watched the signs at each stop, and four stops later, the letters matched the station's signs. We realized we had to move quickly. We grabbed our bags and began to exit. There were only a few people to contend with that were getting on. As the door closed, it scrapped the bag I was dragging, reminding me that we had taken too long to exit. No damage to the bag but glad to be off the train. Since it seemed to be a rush-hour crowd, I didn't understand why the crowd thinned the closer we got to Tokyo. No real time to ponder that. We had to get to the Tokyo Central Station to buy a plane ticket to the ROK and then travel on by bus to Narita to fly out. It had already been an action-packed day, and the travels ahead promised more.

We found the cab pickup station and caught a cab. I have no idea how we were able to communicate our intentions. Actually, I did communicate our plans. I just do not know if the driver understood English. We wanted to go to Central Station. The cab driver spoke no English. What could go wrong, I pondered as we departed for the journey. It had to have been the Holy Spirit that helped that man understand us. The countryside was beautiful. It was October when we were traveling, and it was easy to see that the foliage throughout the landscape that we were able to see anyway was in full transition. The colors were breathtaking. The wonderment of the journey was a natural tonic for the weariness that both Diana and I felt. It was still very fresh in my mind how much Uniform Code of Military Justice (UCMJ) trouble I could yet be in. That haunted me and would have to wait until we got to the ROK to work that out. Not long later, the driver pulled up in front of this massive building. In English, it said "Tokyo Central Station." I was ecstatic and very grateful for the driver. He could sense all of our emotions. Again, I was moved to choking back a tear. My throat began to swell, and he could see and sense my appreciation. I dug around in my wallet to pull out money for the fare. Not fully understanding the currency, I gave him a few bills. I was hoping that he would take his fare and give me the change back. He smiled and just handed me back the money, smiled and, without a word, turned and got into his cab and departed. I felt that choking feeling again and could feel my eyes water a bit. Diana asked me something about the fare. I could not speak and used securing our baggage as an excuse to ignore her for a moment or two while I collected myself. Satisfied with the luggage, I answered her and said, "The fare was just right." She surprised me by not pressing me. And just like that, we collected our bags and headed up the stairs to the station.

It reminded me of the New York Central Station. I had never actually seen the train station in New York but had seen plenty of movies where shots were taken in it. Like the New York Station, Tokyo's Central Station was cavernous. Everything seemed to be made of marble and other polished stones. Not sure what the theme of the decorative carvings was, but everything seemed to be in proper order. It was charming and intimidating all at the same time. We seemed to be standing the middle of the structure and had a clear view of the many, many counters that were handling customers. Like a script, a man approached us and said the same thing that the missionary had told us earlier, "You look like you need some help?"

I was elated, and without hesitation, I responded, "Yes, we need some assistance. We need to buy two airline tickets to Korea and then catch a bus to Narita. Can you help us?" From his accent, I believe the gentleman was from Australia or possibly New Zealand. He began to explain what we needed to do but realized that he was going to be late for his own departure if he dallied too long. He quickly said to us what we needed to do.

He then proclaimed, "I have to go, but I am not going to leave you stranded. I am going to ask my porter to guide you to the ticket booth and stay long enough to ensure that you get on the correct bus to catch your plane." I felt myself choking again, and like the cab driver, he could sense that we really needed the help. I was grateful that he was determined to get us where we needed to be. I reached into my back pocket for my wallet. I wanted to give him something. Seeing me, he waved me off and said, "None of that. This is a blessing. Now go quickly, my porter is already moving your wife's bags to the ticket window. Go in peace..." And with that, he was gone. I turned and saw that the porter was well on his way and not waiting a moment for us, so with great haste, we caught up with him.

The line to purchase airline tickets was manageable. No one was pushy or in a hurry. When we got to the ticket counter, the young Japanese attendant spoke perfect English. She was pleasant and explained the process. I suspect she had done so before. It sounded very practiced.

"Purchasing tickets in the middle of the country and then traveling to the other end of the country in a bus to catch a plane may seem odd for our western patrons, but we find it most accommodating," she explained. She went on to explain how and where to catch the bus. Our porter was quietly waiting determined to escort us to the bus. After we had purchased the tickets, the three of us departed for the short walk to the bus pickup area. Still unsure whether he was Australian or New Zealand, his brogue was understandable. We expressed our gratitude as we departed, and like his employer, he withdrew by saying, "Go in peace." And with that, he quickly disappeared into the Central Station, making his way back to his employer.

I did feel at peace boarding the bus headed to Narita. Diana and I quietly took our seats and just enjoyed each other's company and the tranquility of the moment. Watching Japan whip by out of the windows was entertainment enough. I will say of the country, I found it to be clean. The population is very compacted, yet I viewed order and hospitality out of our window. Diana asked the occasional question as we traveled northward along the highway, and I did the best that I could to share what I had learned of the Orient from my time in Vietnam and Korea. The only commonality with those other countries was the Orient. The countries and peoples of Vietnam and Korea were vastly different from what we were experiencing and seeing in Japan. This was Diana's first time in the Orient, so I did my best to let her form her own opinion as I offered only answers to her questions in the most general of terms. It did not take long for the humming sound and gentle sway of the bus to liberate me from my fatigue and stress. I drifted off into a nap and woke up when the bus pulled into the airport. As I woke, I stretched and was glad to embrace Diana as I said to her, "Well, looks like the final leg of our adventure is upon us," or so I thought.

Getting on the plane in Narita was as routine as it could have been but for the layover. We had to wait some five hours to board the flight. I suppose we could have taken a later bus from Central Station, but all I wanted to do was to get to our gate and make the departure. We were early enough for sure. We spent our time discovering all there was to window-shop for at the airport. We didn't have much in the way of expendable dollars left. I believe we had a modest meal, but most of that afternoon is lost to time now. I clearly remember getting on the on-time plane. We pushed back from the gate precisely as advertised, and in no time, we were in the air. Thus far, since the morning departure from the Kadena, we had been traveling upward of fourteen hours. We were tired and ready for the journey to end. During the flight, I again explained our housing arrangements in the six-pack to Diana. I explained that we would have building mates, not roommates, and all would share the latrine at the end of the hall. For all her modesty, she seemed to tolerate all that I had said. We were, after all, beyond the point of return now. I had explained the circumstances while still in the United States, but now quickly approaching Korea, the reality of our decision had much more critical relevancy, particularly since at that very moment, the plane touched down in Korea. It is a very short flight from Japan to Korea. We were here. Pennies in our pocket but in Korea. The local time was two in the morning. This was the redeye flight out of Japan and just right for our budget.

We pulled into the gate and, in no time at all, found ourselves deplaned and headed for the baggage pickup and customs. Diana was not just holding my hand, but it felt more like she was holding on for fear of falling off a cliff. I asked if she was okay, and she said, "Tired but okay." By her grip, I sensed she was not okay at all. Home was thousands of miles away, and I was her only lifeline. Based on the travel to Korea thus far, she had good reason to be apprehensive. We got our bags and headed for customs. A few questions later, and we breezed right through. We departed the secure area of the airport into the unsecured area. As we were passing through the large opaque doors from customs to the general area, you could see family members waiting on their loved ones and drivers holding signs with names of those they were charged to pick up. We passed them. I was looking for the USO desk. The service members detailed for duty at the USO desk offered free bus rides to the inner parts of the country where the military bases are located. I did not know which direction, either right or left, to go to find the desk. Rather than drag Diana and the baggage all about, I asked her to stay put and await my return while I went in search of the USO. With much argument, she did not want to stay there alone. I reassured her that, even though we were in Korea, she was safe in the airport. I would not be gone long. What I did not realize was there was a Korean businessman who observed us from afar. I departed and soon found the USO desk. There was a sign on it that read, "Back at 0800." I was deflated. I returned to Diana and tried to be upbeat when I said to her that we would have to wait another five hours for the USO to open.

"How long after that for the bus, and how long is the bus ride?" she asked.

"I don't know what the departure time is for the bus bound for Humphreys, but I do know that it is about an hour and a half to the Hump," I responded.

She too was more than deflated. She was road tired and cranky. The fun of the adventure was quickly vanishing. The Korean businessman who had observed us approached us and, as the English speaking missionary and the Australian had asked, "You look like you need some help."

Again, I felt my throat constrain, and I immediately felt at ease. Diana, however, not so much. The Korean businessman continued and said, "My driver and I have come to the airport to pick up a business associate. Outside of the customs exit, I had my driver hold a sign with his name on. But apparently, he missed his flight. The doors have now closed, and no one else is clearing customs. How may I help you?"

I began to explain that we had taken the red-eye out of Japan and just needed to wait 'til 0800 for the USO desk to open so that we could get a bus ride to Camp Humphreys. Not long into our conversation, I realized that Diana was gripping my hand so tightly that it was now aching. He and I continued our small talk. He said he also had been a soldier. He asked if I had been to Vietnam, and I said that I had. Well, he drilled down a bit more, and he told me the name of the fire base that he had been assigned to. I did not recognize the name of his, but I told him that I had spent my tour on Fire Base Bearcat and rotated in and out of Fire Base Mase.

He became animated. He said, "You were right up the road from me, and your Cobra Gunships had saved us many, many times."

I had heard many stories over the years about the punch that the Blue Max brought to the fight. I knew well that we had indeed saved many all while destroying the enemy. I was very proud to be a Blue Max alumni. We shook hands, embraced, and then he declared that he could not leave us stranded in the airport. I explained that we were fine. The USO would take care of us at 0800 but appreciated his concern. Diana was gripping my hand so tightly that it was beyond aching. I was becoming distracted by the pain. I looked at her as if to reassure her and continued with our newfound friend.

"I insist," he said. "You will come to my house, and my driver will take you to Camp Humphreys tomorrow after you have rested." Before I could say another word, he directed his driver to gather our bags and take them to the car. Diana has never been a ball nor chain to me but, at this point, was figuratively acting like one. The two men walked ahead, and Diana protested in the strongest terms.

"Do you know that guy? No, you don't. I am not getting in the car and going anywhere," she protested. I believe if she could have gotten back on the plane to the United States, she would have. It was clear that she was scared. I comforted her, hugged her, and assured her that it would be okay. She took a new grip on my hand and squeezed even harder. When we got to the car, I realized that I had not introduced ourselves. I did so, and likewise, he introduced himself and his driver. His name was Mr. Kim. I do not recall the driver's name. The driver was skilled at not being noticed. He did to the letter what Mr. Kim told him to do. He did wear a bus driver's hat and a dark suit with driver's gloves. Mr. Kim was dressed impeccably in a tailored suit.

We all got into the sedan, and the driver remained inconspicuous while negotiating the Seoul traffic. It was a thirty-minute drive from the airport to Seoul. Mr. Kim and I chatted about our Vietnam experiences as if we were long lost friends. He also told us of his business. He was in fashion. The name of his business, A Touch of Class. I was trying not to be stereotypical. During my tour thus far in Korea, I only knew of the countryside and small villas. Most of the farmers in the outlying parts of the country lived in grass-thatched hooches that were floor heated with ondol charcoal. The outside of the buildings was devoid of color and was cement gray. In the villas around the military bases, there were business people, but on the very bottom rung of the business latter. There was a lot in "fashion." Most had sewing machines and made their own inventory and sold it to the passersby's. Embroidering hats were also popular. Most of the shopkeepers slept with their families in their showrooms by night. It was a very sparse and meager existence, to say the least. Kim was also a popular and common name, not unlike Smith or Jones. The merchants that I am used to, however, did not live in Seoul, have drivers, nor picked up business associates in airports. I was trying the best I could not be small-minded, and wasn't I pleasantly surprised when the driver pulled up to a condominium. The building had to be thirty to forty stories tall. It sat amongst other like buildings. Because of the time, there was no one out and about. The driver dropped us off at the front door, and there were persons at the front door who took charge of our bags. I knew Mr. Kim had not told his wife of our coming. Mr. Kim confirmed this when he said, "My wife will be surprised with the two of you. She is expecting my business associate, so the guest room is already prepared. There will just be another, that's all." I understood the nonverbal communications that he was having with his wife in his head. I have to wonder how much his hand would have been squeezed had she been with us.

We rode the elevator to the twentieth floor and went directly to his door. His wife met us at the door and immediately assessed what was going on without saying a word. I had to think about that squeeze again. She was as beautiful inside as she was outside. She graciously asked us in and followed to a tee the brief instructions that Mr. Kim had given her in Korean. Diana and I followed their lead. We were offered a very light meal—more snacks, really. It was just enough and much appreciated. Mr. Kim, rather proudly, gave us a tour of the condo. Each room he showed us was furnished with western furniture. There was something in the way that Mr. Kim remarked how much he appreciated the comfort that western furniture offered. When we got to the guest bedroom, he apologized that the room remained traditional Korean. He said that when his Korean in-laws visited, they were much more comfortable with Korean furnishings. I assured him that the room was great, and we were blessed indeed to be housed in such luxury. The bedroom had a small wardrobe for a closet and a yo. Yo is a Korean bed comprising of a mat placed on the floor for sleeping. The floor was heated. I hoped that the floor was not heated with ondol. A shower later, and Diana and I were in sleep-full bliss.

We were woken up later by the sounds of children watching cartoons. We showered and were invited to join the family watching cartoons while Mrs. Kim fixed breakfast. It was funny watching western cartoons dubbed to the Korean language. The Kims were a beautiful family, and I was very relaxed as I teased the two younger girls to what would happen next with the cartoons. Mrs. Kim called everyone to breakfast. It was a traditional bacon and eggs meal. Not sure if that was for us or if they always ate bacon and eggs. What was not conventional, however, was that Mrs. Kim ate at another table. I wasn't sure what to make of that. Mr. Kim sensed my uncomfortableness and remarked, "It is customary for the wife to eat as you see her." I made nothing more of it.

We were ready to go but did not want to be impolite as to ask for the exit plan. After breakfast, we took our coffee in the living room while the kids continued to enjoy the cartoons. It could have been a Saturday morning anywhere in the United States. Mr. Kim then said, "I have spoken with my wife and have decided to make a day out of it. We will have the nanny to watch the children, and I will drive all of us to Camp Humphreys. We will make a family day of it. It will be a nice drive. My wife does not get out much, and she will enjoy it. I would like to stop by the shop before we depart, however. It will only be a small delay and then we will be on our way."

Of course, Diana and I were all in. I did remind Mr. Kim that a ride to Yongsan (H201) where we could catch a bus from there would be fine. He would hear nothing of that, and it was settled. He gathered up the family, turned the kids over to the nanny, and we were off. Diana's introduction to Korea was significantly different than mine. My introduction—military bases long on function and short on luxury. Diana's introduction—penthouses, drivers, nannies, and luxury. I could only imagine how that would square the moment she sees where we would live. I did not want to pop any bubbles and was enjoying, if only for a moment or two, the opulence of this life.

He took us to his "shop." It was a massive warehouse four stories high. He did not leave us in the car as he ran into the shop. He parked near the door, and we all went in. We entered an elevator and went up to his office. The office was as functional as it was personal. There was a large desk with a glass top on it. Under the glass top was pictures of the very kids that we had interacted with this very morning, so I knew that he was who he said he was. He filed something in the side drawer of his desk, then got a document out of the center desk drawer, and reviewed it and his calendar. Then he asked Diana if she would like to see his spring lineup. This was a real treat. We were already in the fall season, and he was working on the upcoming spring season. He left the office only to come back with clothes racks on wheels and showed Diana the prints and dresses. That is when Diana noticed the label, Touch of Class. It was a real treat to get the preview of the spring lineup for sure. Diana reported that the work was exquisite. Diana, a seamstress herself, recognized the quality of the work. Diana did not sew for the profession of it. She made a lot of her own clothes as well as those of our daughter. A soldier's salary does not go very far, and making clothes was a talent that went a long way in our financially strapped family.

Tour and business complete at the shop, we got into the car and headed south for the hour-and-a-half ride to Camp Humphreys. Mr. Kim and I sat in the front, and Diana and Mrs. Kim in the back seat. Mr. Kim and I continued our conversation about Vietnam. He was no longer in the military, but I could tell that he enjoyed talking about his service. He had more than a few exciting stories to be sure. The time passed quickly, and before we knew it, we were pulling up to the front gate of the compound. Military police (MP) man the gates, and when Mr. Kim pulled up, an MP approached the driver's side window. Mr. Kim rolled down the window and gave him the ID card that I had passed to him as we were pulling up to the gate. The MP looked at the ID card, saluted me, and asked what my intentions were. That surprised me. I told the MP that the Kims were my guests and that they were going to accompany me onto the base. The MP made it clear that the Kims did not have a pass and that, without a pass, they would not be allowed on base. Mr. Kim's military training kicked in, and he asked the MP if there was a bus that would come around and collect his friends and take them to their quarters. I answered for the MP and told Mr. Kim that there was indeed a post-shuttle that ran every thirty minutes. I apologized for the inhospitality being displayed by the U.S. Army, but rules were rules. He understood. He dropped us off outside the gate, we said our goodbyes, and before he and his wife departed for the return trip to Seoul, Mr. Kim and I embraced and he said, just like the other angels that helped us along our way, "Go in peace." One of my greatest regrets of this incredible journey from the United States to the ROK was that we lost track of the Kims. We entered the base and caught the shuttle bus for our quarters. If Diana was disappointed, she never said. What she did say was enough.

"Home at last," the good military wife declared as we entered the common hallway of the six-pack building leading to my room.

My long stroll from the airfield was coming quickly to a close. I looked up and saw the six-pack building. Diana was waiting for me to get home. She commonly heard my hooch-mates opening and closing their doors, walking either to the latrine or out of the building. Robust foot traffic was pretty standard. This day, however, was different. All of them did not go near the hooch for fear of running into Diana. They all knew I was out flying in weather that I should not have been in, and fun-loving hazing aside, all were quite worried. They had no words for Diana, so they just stayed away. Diana knew I was flying this mission up north, but it was an early morning departure, and I promised that I would be home by 1400 hours or so. It was now bumping 1800 hours, and I had just opened the door to the long hallway. I entered the building and started down that hallway. My room was the second on the right. I saw that the door was open. Odd, I thought. We were supposed to maintain a low profile and wondered why our door was open.

Diana heard me enter the building and bounded out of the room and met me in the hallway and gave me a long kiss and a hug. I was so happy to see her that I just held on and almost made Diana feel uncomfortable. "Okay, you are squeezing the air out of me," she said.

I released a little pressure and said, "Take another breath. I am not ready to let go yet." So we just held each other in the hallway until it began to get awkward again.

"Okay, what's wrong, and why are you so late?" she asked. We had been married eleven years to date, and I knew there was no getting around telling her everything.

"Okay, it's been a long day," I said. "Let's get around and head to the officers club for some chow. I will tell you all about it."

As we were walking back to the room hand in hand, I asked, "So why is the door open?"

"I wanted to ask one of the guys where you were and why so long, but the place has been a ghost town. First time I had seen it that empty since I have been here," she said.

"Okay, I get it. I think the guys were avoiding you. Something horrible happened during the flight, and they did not know how the flight was going to end. I think they were giving you some space and wondering which one of them was going to tell you about the accident...that didn't happen by the by," I concluded.

She looked at me as she was closing the door to our room. With all the courage she could muster, she said steadily, "tell me everything."

And so I began. I told Diana that it was all my fault that we should not have been in those conditions. Still, we were, and it became my responsibility to get us out. I told her that I was pretty sure that I was being prompted by the Holy Spirit to overcome obstacles. My altering of the IMC emergency procedure would have come with sharp criticism in the schoolhouse environment, I told her, yet it was precisely what needed to be done to get us to altitude safely. And of all the times to reach in my past, the crash that killed my dad and twin, not to forget the two PAXs on their plane, haunted me throughout the flight. I could not imagine what it must have been like for all four of those on Dad's plane during their final moments. I was determined that I would not repeat that ending and would successfully conclude the flight. I told her of the crazy approach into Osan, and if it had not been for the HEIL lights at the end of the runway, I would have to have gone through with setting up the aircraft for a calculated impact/run-on landing...blind. I felt myself shaking, and Diana did too. I was grateful that these past eleven years of army marriage had toughened her up to the scary flights that I had been on thus far. The army does not fly commercially; instead, we fly as we fight. If the conditions are less than favorable, then we need to know that we can safely operate in those sorts of circumstances. It was totally unplanned, but the flight steeled up my metal. I needed her support. I did not need her to tell me that, for the sake of the family, my flying days were over. She didn't. She hugged me and said calmly, "Let's go get some chow." I loved her for that.

CHAPTER 37

Back to Osan to Recover the Aircraft

24 December 1982, ROK.

It was Christmas Eve, and the unit looked like it. There was barely anyone about. Folks were sleeping in, off, or on leave. Operations were only staffed by a skeleton crew. The duty officer for the day was manning the phones and otherwise bored. The commander was insistent that his helicopter be recovered when the weather allowed. It was cold outside, but it was clear blue and twenty-two. Just the sort of beautiful weather you would expect after a big storm. I looked at the mission board to see who would be flying Ryan, the LT, and me over to Osan. I was glad that one of the aviators assigned to the ferry aircraft was another WOJG. There was a lot of us in the unit to choose from, and holiday or no, any reason to fly was a reason good enough. The PIC for the ferry aircraft was a CW4?

We did not see many of them. Even Stan, our SIP, and Roger, our IFE, were CW3s. I had not met the CW4 yet. He had only been in-country a month or so but was already a PIC. I whispered to the other WOJG, "It took me seven months to make PIC. That guy must be something. Only a month in the unit and already a PIC?" My naivety was raging. I would later learn throughout my career that, of course, persons of his experience should be considered as soon as possible for a PIC position. He was oozing experience. Making PIC was not about seniority in line; it was about maturity, judgment, and experience. I made MTP in my fourth month, three months before making PIC. I made MTP so early because I oozed maintenance experience. I came to the unit with eleven years of helicopter maintenance as well as combat experience in Vietnam; of course, the commander recognized that breadth of exposure. The CW4 had a greater breadth of experience and presented a much deeper and diverse skill set. Upon reflection, I realized how much I yet needed to grow and mature, and I was a bit embarrassed for myself. Maybe I wasn't all that and a bag of chips too.

I looked forward to getting to Osan and getting my aircraft back home. I watched from afar and did not want to interrupt what the flight crew was doing. I observed, knowing full well that they were reviewing their -1 and filing their flight plan. I was seated in one of the overstuffed chairs along the wall in operations. Ryan was in another. I just suspected the LT was running late, and then in walked CW3 Roger Wills, our instrument examiner.

"Hey, Roger," I said.

"Hey yourself," he replied. "Beautiful day to fly, huh?" he commented.

"Yep, sure is. Way better than yesterday. You flying today?" I asked. "We are waiting for our ferry flight crew to finish up filing, and we are hitching a ride to Osan to retrieve my aircraft," I said.

Ryan quickly corrected, "My aircraft that is." CEs own the aircraft. It is an undisputed truth in army aviation. I was a CE for many years, and as a CE, I am not sure I would have allowed a WOJG to forget that either.

"I stand corrected. We are fetching back Ryan's aircraft. The same one he allowed me to leave at Osan," I said with a smile. "Did you see the LT out there on your way in?" I asked Roger.

"No, it's you and me today. The LT will not be flying." Rogers words fell flat. I didn't know what to say or do. I tried not to overthink it.

"Okay, I said. Which of us will be the PIC?" I asked.

"You will be. I am just a sandbag. Let's enjoy this beautiful weather," Roger said. I was glad for that. I didn't need anything other than a good flight after the ordeal yesterday.

Our ferry flight crew finished up the paperwork and walked over to introduce themselves. "Guessing you guys are our PAXs that we are flying over to Osan to fetch the PL'ed aircraft?" asked the CW4.

"We are." Roger stood up and introduced us. "You know who I am. That is our CE, Ryan, and this is Mr. Doudna," Roger said. "Dean is our PIC for the recovery," Roger added.

CW4's are an exotic breed. There are not a lot of them out there. The very first CW4 that I had ever met was our maintenance officer when I was assigned to Redstone Arsenal after my tour in Vietnam. CW4 Willey was highly respected, and we hung on every word he spoke. I was a specialist five (SP5) at the time. I witnessed the army's warrant officer change in rank from the previous gold and silver bar to the current bar of today. Back in the day, RLOs had trouble distinguishing the warrant officer ranks. All warrant officer bars used to be gold and textured and have either gold or silver squares on them.

W1 rank had one gold square in the middle of a gold textured bar. The gold square was not textured but polished to stand out against the gold texture. The W2 rank had another gold square and was not textured and polished to stand out. Both golden squares were centered on the gold textured bar. To distinguish the W3 and W4 grades, those golden squares became silver. One silver square for the W3 and two silver squares for the W4 on the gold textured bar. I rarely saw W3s and infrequently saw—only heard of—W4s. I have to admit the previous grades were tough to distinguish. Somewhere around 1973 or 1974, the army dropped the gold textured bars with polished squares for warrant officers and converted to a silver bar, not unlike the 1st LT bar. This bar, however, had several black squares evenly spaced. One black square for W1 all the way to four squares for W4 on a silver bar. Each black square indicates a grade. Meeting this CW4, with his big four black squares on a silver bar on his hat, reminded me of the day that CW4 Willey came into the maintenance office when I was assigned to Redstone Arsenal after Vietnam. When he came in, he was debuting the new army's rank for a CW4. He found immediately that someone in the sheet metal shop had made an oversized CW4 bar out of sheet metal and had fixed it to a hat that always seemed to be on his desk. That oversized bar made out of sheet metal measured two inches by four inches. The four black squares were perfectly aligned. Our NCOIC gathered us for the unveiling, and when Mr. Willey stepped into the office, he immediately knew something was awry. He always had a very business-like appearance that bordered on gruff.

"What?" he asked. That was all that he said. He went to his desk and found the hat and the fashioned W4 bar. Mr. Willey taught me a lot about leadership that day. I thought he was going to kill us all. Instead, he took off the hat that he came in with, picked up that hat that was on his desk, and put it squarely on top of his head and barked at us, "And don't you ever forget it. I am the big dawg, and this is how big dawgs are identified. Never forget that," he concluded. Then I saw something never before seen. I saw a smile from ear to ear, followed quickly by, "Get out and get some work done." He wore that hat with the big bar on it the rest of the day and then retired the hat and bar to his desk, where it remained through the day that I had rotated out of Redstone. A keepsake, I am sure…

Seeing the CW4 bar on this gentleman's hat had me smiling as I mentally recounted that story in my head. I put my hand out and shook his hand. CW4 Robert Bell was a very nice fellow. Gracious and kind, I could quickly tell. With Rogers's introductions complete, we began walking down the hallway to the other end of the building for the flight line. The commander's office door was opened, and he was at his desk. He heard us herding down the hall. "Mr. D, a moment," the commander called out."

I stopped and backed up to the door. "Yes, sir?" I asked.

"When you complete your mission, come find me," he said.

"Roger, sir. Anything you need now?" I asked.

"After the mission. Go, don't miss your ride," he said. He didn't seem upset. Maybe loose ends, I pondered.

The crew flying us over had already pre-flighted the aircraft, so when we all arrived at the aircraft, my crew and I just made ourselves comfortable in the back while they ran through their before starting engines checks. Their CE spun his finger in the air and shouted clear, and we knew that it was time to put our helmets on. Everything about the flight over to Osan was extremely routine and unremarkable. Osan is due north of Camp Humphreys. A fifteen-minute flight or so direct. I had spent the first ten years of my career in the backseat of helicopters, so I was right at home. When communicating with Osan Tower, Robert asked for a landing directly to hotel taxiway. Even though a helicopter can fly in any direction, even helicopters regularly follow traffic patterns, but there was no one out flying, and the controller cleared us for a direct approach into hotel taxiway. The crew landed just in front of our aircraft and summarily dumped us off. No fanfare. They were just doing a simple ferry mission. We exited the aircraft, I turned to thank the crew with a thumbs up, and they returned the same and departed.

Roger, Ryan, and I got a good look at the aircraft. Just like yesterday afternoon, the helicopter was in total ice. Roger was awe-struck. "I have never seen anything like this...ever," he said. It was very imposing and impressive.

Ryan got Rogers's attention and said to Roger, "Look at the intakes, sir."

"Wow." Roger was genuinely surprised. "I can't believe you guys survived the flight. Seriously, never mind the part of the -10 that says that you were not supposed to fly in icing. Look at those intakes. I'm guessing that hole is no bigger than eight inches. How much weight did that major IP calculate you gained?" Roger asked.

I began to answer but was interrupted by Ryan's activity on the top of the aircraft. "Easy Ryan," I said. "I know you are trying to expedite the ice removal, but you cannot keep hitting the ice without the possibility of creating damage to the structure of the aircraft below the ice. Let's try carefully prying without beating what we can pry off. The sun is going to be our friend," I continued.

The ice was thin in some places and super thick elsewhere. It took about three hours to clear the ice. The sun did prove to be our best friend. Once the metal began to heat up a bit, the ice then began to release itself enough for us to pry the ice from the aircraft's surfaces carefully. Some gentle prying and, ta-da, the aircraft was de-iced. The aircraft got a meticulous pre-flight, and it was not long before we were ready to depart. Roger and I walked over to Flight Operations to file and put fuel on request. Ryan waited by the aircraft and took care of the refuel while Roger and I filed the flight plan. When Mr. Bell got the weather for the ferry flight this morning, he was kind enough to add us to his -1, so the weather portion of our filing was complete. The operations officer took our flight plan, gave it the once over, and accepted it. He wished us a Merry Christmas and safe flight. He did remark, however, as we were leaving that he was so glad not to have been on that aircraft. The duty logs showed from yesterday that there was an all-hands-on-deck crash rescue response waiting for it on the active. Lucky crew for sure. He had no idea that I was the PIC of the aircraft. He was right; there was a lot of fire rescue yesterday afternoon. I could still hear the conversation of the fireman as he opened my door in my head. It was chilling. I was also very grateful to those professionals.

We found Ryan lying stretched out on the seat that ran along the transmission bulkhead. I had taken that position waiting on my pilots many times, wondering where those guys go and what they do. Being an aviator now, I better understand that the pilots just don't disappear. There is a lot of paperwork to do in order to take off.

I gave Ryan a bad time as I called out, "Hey, soldier, let's go flying."

"Today?" he replied with a smile.

I loved my job. It was hard to believe that I was being paid to fly. Ryan, you could tell, loved job his too. He got straight up and grabbed the tiedown and swung the blades ninety degrees.

"Your turn," Ryan said with a smile.

Roger and I strapped in. Roger reminded me again that he was just a sandbag. I was not intimidated in the slightest. I briefed him on our crew duties and the fifteen-minute flight back to the Hump. I was very comfortable in the right seat. It was not long before I was ready to start the aircraft and hollered clear. Ryan returned the command with "Clear." This protocol was standard practice so that the pilot knew that the tiedown was off the rotor system before starting the engine. Hearing Ryan's "clear," and watching him spin his hand in the air, I started the engine. The T53 roared to life, and it did not take long for the rotor to spin up to RPM. Roger called out all the before starting and starting checks out of the checklist.

"Easy-peasy," Roger commented.

Ryan jumped in and strapped in and slapped me a couple of times on the left shoulder, indicating that he was ready to go. Roger picked up the logbook and began to work the health indicator test (HIT) check on the engine before we departed. I asked Roger to pass the logbook to Ryan. Roger looked a bit off-center, and then I remarked, "Let's develop the CE. I sat in his seat for years and was not included in those sorts of things. During my watch, I wanted to totally immerse the CE in as many duties as he can tolerate."

"I like it," Roger said. "I do believe I will follow that lead."

And with that, Ryan was handed the book, and I called out the OAT to him. "Find the associated N1 on that chart there," I told Ryan.

Ryan responded, "I need 70.2 percent N1 for these conditions."

I pulled up on the collective and held the N1 at 70.2 percent. A few moments later, I read the EGT to him. "Tell me the difference in the baseline EGT?" I asked Ryan.

"Four degrees," he responded.

"And the standard?" I asked.

"Plus or minus twenty gets a write up in the -13. Plus or minus thirty will ground the aircraft," he said.

"I like it," Roger said again.

We continued with the few remaining items that needed to be checked. Once all was completed, I called for the before take-off. Roger called out each item, I counterchecked, and just like that, we were ready to call ground for hover taxi instructions. Without prompting, Roger dialed up ATIS and recorded the airdrome information on his clipboard.

"Information Bravo is current," Roger reported.

Next, he dialed up operations so that we could update our weather. -1's are issued with an hour and a half weather void time connected with them. If the crew departs within that time frame, they are legal. If outside the hour-and-a-half window, then the crew has to get an update.

"You're up no. 1 for the weather update," Roger said. Meaning that he had dialed up the frequency in the FM radio and rotated my

C-1611 selector. I keyed the mic and asked for a weather update. The forecaster updated our weather and gave us a new void time. He told us what we already knew; it was still clear blue and twenty-two. It was a beautiful day, but now, we were legal to fly in the beautiful weather.

"You're up no. 3 for ground. Bravo still current," he said.

"Roger," I said. "Osan ground, RB93 good morning. RB93 requesting hover taxi instructions to the 27 active for a VFR release to the south."

"RB93, contact tower, Merry Christmas," Ground responded. I looked over at Roger and gave him that questioned look.

He understood and said, "VFR present position departure, I am guessing," as he shrugged. Roger was already ahead of me. He tuned tower into the no. 2 position and said, "You're up, no. 2. Osan tower, RB93 good morning. RB93 requesting presentation position to the south."

"RB93 surface winds light and variable, altimeter 29.94 cleared for departure to the south. Merry Christmas. Come back and see us soon," the controller said.

Since I was still pretty new in the front seat, I wondered if other military locations were so personable. I acknowledged him and began to pull pitch. Once the aircraft was light on the skids, I rocked the tail rotor pedals, ensuring the skids were not frozen to the ground. With that done, the toes came off the ground first, and then the right rear skid followed by the left rear heel. I gently picked up the aircraft to a three-foot hover. I momentarily hesitated to perform a hover power check. Checking the actual hover power against predicated hover power is a requirement before takeoff. I was startled to see that, with a full bag of gas and no PAXs, the hover power was thirty pounds even. I took just a moment to consider the difference against yesterday's evening's hover power of forty-six pounds in a helicopter with only a sip of fuel in it. Roger sensed the hesitation and asked if anything was wrong. I told him no, I was just remembering the torque from yesterday's flight as opposed to the torque now.

"That ice is scary stuff," he commented.

And with that, I pulled pitched and climbed out for a southerly heading back to the Hump.

CHAPTER 38

No-Notice Instrument Check Ride

24 December 1982, ROK.

The flight with Roger back to the Hump was friendly. It was nice flying with someone who was ahead of my requests. I asked Roger if he wouldn't mind if we did a VOR or ADF upon landing to the Hump.

"You read my mind," Roger said.

"Great, put up Osan Departure in the no. 3, and I will pick up a clearance," I said.

He did so quickly. I was still on the no. 2 with Osan Tower. I keyed the mic and requested a frequency change to departure. Osan Tower acknowledged the frequency change and again wished us a Merry Christmas. Once clear of Osan's tower frequency, I keyed the no. 3 position. Roger was ahead of me and pointed to the no. 3, indicating that I was up. It was great flying with someone who got it. Osan is only about fifteen miles as the crow flies north of the Hump, and we were about halfway now. Things were ticking right along.

"Osan Departure, RB93, good afternoon. RB93 seven miles north of Camp Humphreys, requesting the VOR A full stop into Humphreys, negative ATIS," I requested. Roger quickly said to me that he had information Quebec at the Hump. Before Osan

Departure could respond to my request, I keyed the mic and said that I had information Quebec for Humphreys.

"RB93 squawk, 7321," requested Osan.

"7321 for RB93," I responded.

Roger was already dialing up the transponder to 7321. The 7321 request is a code that aviators tune into their transponders so that ATC can readily identify a targeted aircraft on their radar scope. Moments later, Osan Departure responded back, "RB93, radar contact. Climb to 2,000 feet, proceed direct the Pyonteck VOR. Cross the Pyonteck VOR at 2,000 feet, cleared for the VOR A approach. Contact Desadairo Tower on the descent from the VOR A on 123.75 or 237.50." I read back the clearance, Osan acknowledged and also wished us a Merry Christmas. Roger had the VOR A plate out and passed it to me. I, in turn, passed the controls to Roger and began to study the plate. The approach was very straightforward. I could see that the no. 2 needle was pointing right at the VOR. We would cross the VOR at two thousand feet and begin a descent to no lower than 1,200 feet, where we would transition to land visually. The no. 2 needle began to wobble around, indicating that we were close. I laid the plate down on the center console so that I could brief Roger on the approach.

"Roger, we will be executing the VOR A into Humphreys. The inbound course is 010 degrees. We should break out by 1,200 feet. If not, we will do the published missed. There is no time inbound. Questions?" I asked. "Got it. You have the controls."

"I have the controls.

"You have the controls," he concluded. Just in time, as the no. 2 needle flipped around, indicating that we had passed the station. I began to descend down to 1,200 feet. Roger pointed over to me and said, "You have the controls, I have the radios." Roger then keyed the mic and said, "Desadairo Tower, RB93 out of 2,000 for the VOR A with information Quebec. Request published missed."

"RB93, you are cleared for the option."

I looked over at Roger and said, "Missed?"

He said, "I have not seen the missed on the VOR A approach yet. Humor me."

"Okay," I said. "No time now. I am approaching 1,200 feet. Climbing right or left back to the VOR?" I asked Roger. I had the controls, and he had the plate. It is a normal cockpit protocol for the person on the controls to ask the person on the plate to call out the requirements of the approach. This is different, as Fort Rucker taught the flight students that they must do plate duties as well as flight duties. Single-pilot functions, even for an experienced guy, is busy let alone for a student. Once arriving in a unit, that training habit was quickly broken. When Roger was ARL progressing me when I was first assigned to the unit, he made it very clear that there were two pilots in the cockpit and to use all tools to your benefit.

Roger continued with the instructions. "Climbing right turn will get you a direct entry into standard holding on the VOR." Roger continued to handle the radios and reported the missed as I executed the missed. The no. 2 needle took me straight to it, and at 2,000 feet, the needle fell, and I entered holding. Roger told tower that we would take one spin and then break off for a visual to Alpha Pad. The holding was a piece of cake. I saw the no. 2 needle 90 degrees showing me abeam, and I continued with my turn. When the tail of the no. 2 was at the forty-five tick mark and sixty seconds tapped out, I began my turn.

"I've seen enough. I have the controls. Relax WOJG. I want to fly it to Alpha Pad. I never get to fly," Roger said. I passed the controls to Roger and just sat back. Not for too long, however. I wanted to return the favor to Roger. I picked up the plate and found the ground frequency and tuned it in. Over Alpha Pad and upon clearing the pad, I put Roger up ground and pointed to the no. 2.

He keyed the mic and said, "Desadairo Ground, RB93 hover taxi to Red Baron ramp."

And just like that, ground finished out the clearance and also wished us a Merry Christmas. While Roger was hover-taxiing in, I got out the checklist and readied myself for the shutdown checks. Roger landed, and as a crew, we began the shutdown requirements called for in the checklist. Roger reached over and slapped my left arm with his right hand. "Nice job," he said.

"Thanks," I responded.

"Clearly, you get it," Roger began. "This was a commander-directed, no-notice after-incident check ride."

"So that is why the LT did not join us for the recovery," I said.

"I will let the commander cover that with you. I was asked, per AR 95-1, to give you a no-notice instrument check ride. Let's face it, you sucked a few weeks ago in the simulator. You, my friend, have the worst case of check-itis that I have ever seen. You need to fix that. Clearly, when the chips are down, you perform to standard, and I would even say above standard after what you demonstrated with your ice flight yesterday. Your weather was marginally flyable. Major Burns has already briefed us on your actions. Next time, if your gut tells you not to fly, don't fly. That aside, you completed your precision approach yesterday. I respect that. What I just saw you do...in a few minutes, you transitioned well into a posture to perform a non-precision and holding as well. Precision approach, non-precision and holding, along with your radio work and cockpit management, will earn you a satisfactory from me." He smiled when he finished the debriefing with these two final comments. "Stop saying roger so much on the radio. Oh, before I forget, how is the fuel check going?"

"Oh, I had totally forgotten to start one upon departure from Osan. It was a fifteen-minute flight, and I got busy quick."

"Got to harass you, WOJG," Roger said with a smile. "I will fly with you anywhere, anytime," Roger said.

Ryan piped up and said, "Hey, me too, Mr. D."

"I'm out. You and Ryan can finish up securing the aircraft. I need to brief the commander before he sees you." He knew his statement of needing to see the commander would bother me, so just before he unplugged his helmet, Roger said, "You are not in trouble, WOJG." And with that, he unplugged, grabbed his stuff, and headed toward operations and the commander's office.

"You in trouble, Mr. D?" Ryan asked.

"Not sure," I answered. "The commander said he wanted to see me after the flight. I am guessing that he needed Rogers's information before speaking with me." With that, I continued to watch the EGT gauge decrease after the engine shut down all while filling out the aircraft logbook. While I was in the zone with the book, the blades came to a stop. They rested directly over the aircraft. I looked at Ryan and said, "Really…"

CHAPTER 39

The Final Information for the IMC Flight

24 December 1982, ROK.

I thanked Ryan for all his professionalism and headed to operations. I stopped off at the hangar first to drop off my flight gear in my locker. There was nobody in the hangar. Of course not, it was Christmas Eve. I needed to get back to my hooch and my bride. Had to stop and see the commander first; however. I was hoping that he was still there. I strolled slowly to his office and thought about all the things that had happened over the past few days. I was grateful to be alive. I softly spoke to God, thanking him for his deliverance. I knew that it wasn't a very fancy thank you, but I was pretty sure that God understood. I was just finishing my pondering when I got to the operations building. I opened the door and headed down the long hallway. I thought how many times I personally had polished hallway floors over my career. This floor was as shiny as any in flight school. When I got to the commander's door, it was open, and he was at his desk.

"Come in, Mr. Doudna, and close the door," he said. I felt a knot developing in my stomach. "Sit there." I did so, and just as before, he took the other seat. "Tough flight yesterday," he began. "As a commander, I am the guy who signs your PIC orders, and that is something I do not do lightly. Major Burns tells me that you did not recklessly depart into extreme weather, but he felt you made an honest mistake. Major Burns went on to speak very highly of some complex decisions that you were forced to make. I asked Roger to give you a no-notice instrument ride, and he tells me that you did well and that he would fly with you anywhere at any time. Mr. Doudna, do you know the difference between a PIC and a copilot?"

I began to wiggle in my chair for a moment, pondering if he was going to reduce me back to a copilot. I was unsure of the answer he wanted, so I just said, "Sir, I would rather benefit from your experience rather than stagger a guess at an answer to that question," I said.

"Mr. Doudna, the difference between a PIC and a copilot is simply this—maturity and judgment. All of us who wear wings have demonstrated the ability to motor skill an aircraft. But what comes next? Everyone graduates from flight school as a copilot. It is up to the individual to grow into the next step. You demonstrated, as reported by Major Burns, a better-than-satisfactory level of maturity and judgment by addressing each bad decision you made to a safe conclusion. You endangered your crew and PAXs, but you completed the mission and grew as an aviator as well. You did not break down under extreme conditions. You sucked it up and continued to fly your aircraft. The following flight day, you did very well on a no-notice instrument check ride. Roger tells me you have check-itis. Get over it. I have no intention of pulling your PIC orders, but as your commander, I want to make sure that you learned every lesson your flight produced."

"Sir, yes, sir," I responded. "I fully understand the errors that I made and will not repeat them. I will use those as life lessons as I embrace my flying career."

"Good," he said. "About a flying career," he added. "Do you know why 2LT Boyle did not accompany you today to recover your aircraft?"

"No, sir. I have to guess it is so that the seat would have been open for Roger to give me a ride," I responded.

"Yes and no. Yes, I did want Roger to give you an instrument check ride. No, 2LT Boyle asked for a branch transfer last night. She said that if this is what army aviation is all about, she wanted no part of it."

"She turned in her wings?" I asked, shocked.

"Yes, she did. You bear some responsibility for that. You may have recovered well from you bad decisions during your ice flight, but you scared the hell out of her. She told me that, when you laid the aircraft over and spun up to altitude, she did not wrestle you for the controls because she was too scared to. She could verbally tell you what to do but did not possess the courage to act upon it."

I was stunned. I may have eleven years invested into army aviation to this point, but I have never heard of anyone who had turned in their wings.

"As you ponder those lessons learned during that flight, remember that. If not you, then someone else would have been that guy to scare her. You happen to be that guy in this case." We both let that sink in. It was a very sobering statement. "One last thing," he continued. "About those lights?"

"Lights?" I responded.

"The HEIL lights. You said that you came to a hover over them on the second approach. Major Burns confirms that they were as bright as day. Since you declared an emergency, the tower is required by procedures to send over a report. The tower chief tells me that he has some controller training issues to deal with in his report. Guessing that was the guy who was acting as the final controller on the first approach. He went on to say that the lights were out of service? There was a notice to airmen (NOTAM) saying so." He handed me the report as well as the NOTAM.

I felt my chest tighten. I could feel my eyes filling with tears, and when the first teardrop fell, I looked up at him as I said, "Sir, I swear those lights were bright as day."

"Given the NOTAM, apparently the United States Air Force does not believe so. I believe in miracles too," he said. "I have just never seen one before firsthand. Sit there as long as you need to and collect yourself. When you are ready, go give your beautiful wife a hug for me. I am sure she will be interested in the rest of this story…"

END

ACRONYMS

1. Republic of South Korea (ROK)
2. Wonju (KNW)
3. Inadvertent Metrological Conditions (IMC)
4. Pilot in Command (PIC)
5. Pre-mission Planning Card (PPC)
6. Initial Entry Rotary Wing (IERW)
7. Warrant Officer Candidate (WOC)
8. Training Advising and Counseling (TAC)
9. Warrant Officer (W01)
10. Military Occupation Skill (MOS)
11. Instructor Pilot (IP)
12. Centennial United States (CONUS)
13. Knots Indicated Airspeed (KIAS)
14. Second Infantry Division (2ID)
15. Demilitarized Zone (DMZ)
16. Permanent Change of Station (PCS)
17. Passengers (PAX)
18. end of mission (EOM)
19. Camp Humphreys (KSG)
20. Crew Chief (CE)
21. Foreign Object Damage (FOD)
22. Second Lieutenant (2LT) aka "Butter Bar"
23. Osan Air Force Base (KSO)
24. Estimated Time of Arrival (ETA)
25. Estimated Time of Departure (ETD)
26. Remain Overnight (RON)
27. Visual Flight Rules (VFR)

28. Special VFR (SVFR)
29. Instrument Flight Rules (IFR)
30. Standard Operating Procedures (SOP)
31. Radio Magnetic Indicator (RMI)
32. Revolutions Per Minute (RPM)
33. Health Indicator Test (HIT)
34. Aviator Readiness Level (ARL)
35. Airframe and Powerplant (A&P)
36. National Transportation Safety Board (NTSB)
37. Density Altitude (DA)
38. Pressure Altitude (PA)
39. Instrument Flight Examiner (IFE)
40. Initial Approach Fix (IAF)
41. Non-Directional Beacon (NDB)
42. Instrument Take Off (ITO)
43. Locater Otter Marker (LOM)
44. Course Deviation Indictor (CDI)
45. Decision Height (DH)
46. Wire Strike Protection System (WSPS)
47. Precautionary Land (PL)
48. Ground Control Intercept (GCI)
49. Global Positioning System (GPS)
50. Hand Held Maps (HHM)
51. Forward Arming and Refueling Point (FARP)
52. Glide Slope (GS)
53. Threshold Crossing Height (TCH)
54. Nap of the Earth (NOE)
55. High Intensity Runway Lights (HIRL)
56. Add Exhaust Gas Temperature (EGT)
57. Out of Ground Effect (OGE)
58. Real Live Officer (RLO)
59. Post Exchange (PX)
60. Armed Forces Korea Network (AFKN)
61. Specialist Five (SP5)
62. Health Indicator Test (HIT)
63. Aircrew Training Manual (ATM)

About the Auhor

I struggled with the impacts of this flight for the rest of my forty-seven-year flying career. The greatest struggle was the realization that I caused my copilot to resign her flying career. There were real people on that flight that were counting on me to do the right thing. My peers, as well as superiors, encouraged me to farm the experience and to learn from them. They were right, of course. Army aviators fly as they train regardless of the environment. Superbly trained for this event, the event happened too soon for my experience base at the time.

I was most surprised at how I had repressed the single-engine-airplane accident that killed my father, twin, and his passengers. At fourteen, that loss is difficult to adjust to and—no fault of my mom—my mothers' schizophrenia did not balance the books well as I was growing up.

I did successfully farm the lessons learned from this flight. I retired a CW5 Master Aviator. Standardization Instructor Test Pilot, as well as governed the Fort Rucker flight community while performing the Government Flight Representative duties for Fort Ruckers 650 helicopters during the remaining eleven years of my career.

Retired two years now and finally brought closure to this event by writing the words down. I was most surprised by the post-traumatic stress disorder that I experience from the safety of my keyboard while recounting the story. Once I began to put the words down, great healing came over me.

Most important is the role God played in this event. Had he not fortified me that day, there would have been another story that would have been told of that day. It is my sincerest hopes that the reader sees the deity of Christ in this story.